W9-BNO-306

John F. Kennedy

THE PRESIDENTIAL PORTFOLIO

John F. Kennedy

THE PRESIDENTIAL PORTFOLIO

HISTORY AS TOLD THROUGH THE COLLECTION OF THE JOHN F. KENNEDY LIBRARY AND MUSEUM

Charles Kenney

INTRODUCTION BY Michael Beschloss

PublicAffairs NEW YORK

Published in the United States by PublicAffairs™, a member of the Perseus Books Group.

Printed in the United States of America.

For information, address PublicAffairs, 250 W. 57th Street, Suite 1321, New York, NY 10107.

Book design by Edwin Schlossberg Incorporated, Jenny Dossin, and Joan Greenfield.

LIBRARY OF CONGRESS CATALOGING-IN-PUBLICATION DATA

Kenney, Charles.

John F. Kennedy : the presidential portfolio : history as told through the collection of the John F. Kennedy Library and Museum / Charles Kenney; with an introduction by Michael Beschloss.—1st ed.

p. cm.

ISBN 1-891620-36-3

1. United States—Politics and government—1961–1963.

2. Kennedy, John F. (John Fitzgerald), 1917–1963.

3. United States—Politics and government—1961–1963—Sources.

I. John F. Kennedy Library and Museum.

II. Title.

E841.K467 2000

973.922—dc21

00-057581

First Edition

10 9 8 7 6 5 4 3 2 1

CONTENTS

Introduction by Michael Beschloss *vii*

Overture *xi*

"Carry on" 1

The Closest Election in U.S. History 37

Perilous World 61

Civil Rights 91

The Power of Symbols 109

Jacqueline Bouvier Kennedy 121

Robert F. Kennedy 145

The Cuban Missile Crisis 161

"A great change is at hand" 191

Nuclear Test Ban 207

Dallas 219

The John F. Kennedy Library and Museum 232

Acknowledgments and Source Notes 234

Photo Credits 237

Index 238

INTRODUCTION by Michael Beschloss

When Americans look back on past presidents, they usually remember less the leaders' flaws than those facets of their lives that changed history and inspire us.

There is no better example of this than John Fitzgerald Kennedy. Despite decades of skeptical histories, investigative biographies, and tabloid journalism, JFK remains one of our most popular presidents—even among Americans too young to remember him.

This book will show you why. The first in a series of volumes on America's Presidential Libraries, it takes you not only into the public exhibits and archives but also the back rooms and vaults of the John Fitzgerald Kennedy Library and Museum.

Read Charles Kenney's judicious text, look at the hundreds of vivid illustrations, listen to the supplementary compact disc of seldom-heard recordings of JFK behind the scenes, and you will have the experience of roaming through the Library and Museum in search of one of the most fascinating and elusive personalities in American history.

Look at the president's letters to his family, top-secret national security memos, his wartime medical records, the artifacts of his daily life, and you will begin to understand what it was like to be John Kennedy and why Americans are still mesmerized by him so long after his death.

It all begins with the fact that when JFK became president, he was the youngest man ever to be elected, the first Catholic, the first Irish-American. As his friend Theodore White wrote, Kennedy "unlatched the door," and through the door marched Catholics, African-Americans, Jews, women, and many others who before 1960 would never have dreamt that they could rise to the top in our national life.

The same was true of young people. Before 1960, for example, it was rare to find a corporate mogul under the age of fifty-five. But with a forty-three-year-old president on the television screen day after day, it no longer seemed so radical to throw the dice on someone who in an earlier age would have been ruled out as "unseasoned."

During the 1960 campaign, Kennedy's chief rival, Lyndon Johnson, warned that the presidency required someone "with a little gray in his hair." JFK privately lamented that he was not in his mid-fifties because it would have been so much easier. He would have loved to have lived to see the day that twenty- and thirty-year-olds run Hollywood studios and Internet companies.

But go back to his childhood. As one of his siblings joked, JFK's biography might well have been called "John Kennedy: A Medical History." Kennedy suffered from stomach disorders, an unstable back (later injured and reinjured), malaria, and Addison's Disease, which before the 1940s was fatal.

His brother Robert wrote that Jack spent half of his days on this earth in intense physical pain. Just as Franklin Roosevelt spent huge amounts of time and energy trying to keep his paralysis from interfering with his daily life, it took fortitude and ingenuity for Kennedy to simply make it through a workday as president—and ensure that Americans never knew how much he was really suffering.

One of the most famous scenes of the Kennedy presidency is in the summer of 1963. As JFK walks off of an aircraft, his jubilant two-year-old son John, Jr., in white shorts, races to greet him. The image is so appealing that you almost don't notice what is wrong with this picture. What is wrong is that unlike almost every other father, when the president leans over to kiss his son, he does not lift him into his arms. The reason was that he couldn't. Kennedy's back was so fragile that, in private, he wistfully told his friend Ben Bradlee that John would pick him up before he picked up John.

Many mornings during his presidency, before donning one of his handmade suits, Kennedy was forced to lace onto his torso an evil-looking steel and canvas corset that looked almost like an antique torture device. This held him bolt upright and gave him the almost-too-perfect posture that Americans admired.

Kennedy was also an authentic hero of World War II. His proud and ambitious father made sure that his adventures on the PT–109 were written up, widely circulated—and even showcased in a motion picture starring Cliff Robertson.

JFK's legendary display of self-sacrifice and maturity in the South Pacific went a long way to silence voters' worries that this might simply be a rich, spoiled brat propelled by his father's money. More than half a century after VJ–Day, as we rediscover the glories of the generation that fought World War II, Kennedy's heroism seems almost contemporary.

Like few of his White House predecessors, save the Founders, Lincoln, the two Roosevelts, and Wilson, JFK was absorbed by books and ideas. He made it possible for later American leaders to talk about literature without incurring the ridicule once heaped on two-time Democratic nominee Adlai Stevenson as an "egghead."

Kennedy famously published a bestseller at twenty-three and won a Pulitzer Prize for *Profiles in Courage.* Few would argue that he was an intellectual, if being an intellectual means debating ideas merely for their own sake. But throughout his presidency, Kennedy was animated by what he read.

During the Cuban Missile Crisis, Barbara Tuchman's *The Guns of August* helped him to be hypervigilant that no accident or miscalculation usher in world War III. In the fall of 1963, Michael Harrington's *The Other America* helped him to see the crying need for some kind of war on poverty.

Compare the pictures in this book of President Kennedy to similar images of Presidents Truman or Eisenhower. You'll notice that JFK's predecessors dressed and carried themselves with almost nineteenth-century formality. But Kennedy looks like a man you could easily imagine seeing on television in our own time. Part of the reason is that he was so much younger than his predecessors. But a larger reason is that JFK created a political style that has shaped the way our leaders have looked and sounded ever since.

Jacqueline Kennedy, while growing up, disdained politicians as "corny old men shouting on the Fourth of July." In contrast, her husband, vain about his looks in any case, knew how much the new phenomenon of television would elevate the leader who could connect through his looks and public manner.

Kennedy's efforts to remain slender, well-groomed, and carefully styled don't seem extraordinary nowadays. After all, when Gerald Ford suddenly became president in 1974, almost the first thing his handlers told him to do was to lose twenty pounds, grow his hair longer, and find a new tailor. But you wouldn't imagine a Truman or Ike soliciting or taking similar advice. After the 1960 election, Jacqueline privately wrote that she wanted Jack to be as well-dressed as if he were "president of France."

He always wore his hair longer than any other national figure of his time (although by 1960 he asked his barber to cut it more closely to make him look older and keep it from falling onto his forehead). Worried that he would inherit his father's baldness, Kennedy had regular scalp massages—and accused his bald national security adviser, McGeorge Bundy, of failing to "plan" his hair very well. For several days before important public appearances, he would shun rich desserts so that his cheeks would not look too fat on television.

JFK avoided public gestures that the corny old men of an earlier age—including his own Boston grandfathers—relied on. During the 1960 campaign, he once drew a sketch of a politician raising his arms high in the air and said that if that was required to be president, he would never be president.

The same dislike of ostentation went for press conferences. The first president to gamble on having them televised live, he was economical, direct, and spontaneously witty—even once being subtly risqué. Asked about a provision in his civil rights bill that would exclude small establishments like "Mrs. Murphy's boardinghouse," he broke up the audience by retorting that it would depend whether Mrs. Murphy's boardinghouse had a "substantial impact on interstate commerce."

Before Kennedy, politicians who joked too much were often accused of lack of seriousness. Since Kennedy, a politician who does not have (or pretend to have) a sense of humor does not go far in America.

None of these things would have the impact they do today if Kennedy had not led the nation through one of the most turbulent times in its history. As you will see in this book, at the most terrifying moment of the half-century of Cold War, JFK's leadership in the Cuban Missile Crisis managed to keep much of the northern hemisphere from being incinerated.

In June 1963, although criticized for delay, Kennedy became his own profile in courage by sending what was for that time a revolutionary civil rights bill to Congress, demanding an end to segregation in places of public accommodation. Within five months, he knew how great his sacrifice had been. By the day he left for Texas, his public approval ratings had plummeted due to civil rights and he was in serious danger of losing several Southern states that had provided his narrow margin of victory in 1960.

In this volume you will read about and look at other evidence of Kennedy's enduring legacy. The Peace Corps was the embodiment of JFK's idealism about youth, national service, and aiding less developed countries. On the accompanying CD, you will hear him talking to his brother-in-law, Sargent Shriver, director of the Peace Corps, about how to make sure that the Central Intelligence Agency does not poison its mission by slipping CIA agents into its ranks.

And you will read about Kennedy's audacious plan to land a man on the moon by 1970. The moon program was conceived hastily after JFK's embarrassment by the failure of a U.S.-backed plan to use Cuban exiles to overthrow Fidel Castro's government from the Bay of Pigs. It was criticized by leaders like Dwight Eisenhower for unbalancing the existing space program in order to throw money behind a single "stunt." But it is entirely possible that generations hundreds of years in the future might look at the moon landing as the most important human accomplishment of the twentieth century.

These events of state are interspersed in this book with images of the romantic, elegant, and irreverent young First Lady who fastidiously restored the White House and made it safe for later presidents to exalt the best in American culture—and a presidential daughter and son, Caroline and John, who brought the old mansion to life as it had not been since Theodore Roosevelt's children raced through the East Room.

This volume finally shows how the Kennedy years abruptly ended with a thunderclap in Dallas on November 22, 1963. About her husband, Jacqueline Kennedy scrawled, "So now he is a legend when he would prefer to have been a man."

Decades later, suspicions about John Kennedy's murder (polls find that 80 percent of Americans blame a conspiracy) are fired by a burning sense of how different America might be today had he lived. Even Americans born long afterwards wonder whether JFK could have averted the Vietnam catastrophe, stemmed racial conflict, kept Americans believing in our government and our system.

As they do, they will always ponder the images, documents, artifacts, and sounds of John Kennedy's life. As the historian Michael Kazin has written, those images fuel yearnings for a good and vigorous ruler who can make the old dreams live again: "There he is, our JFK, looking back at us from book jackets, movie posters and Web sites: the upswept hair, the decisive gesture, the buoyant grin. He will always be glancing toward a future that never arrives."

OVERTURE

On the frigid day he is to become the thirty-fifth president of the United States, John Kennedy glides through one event after another, from morning mass to a meeting with President Eisenhower, from the inaugural ceremony itself to a Pennsylvania Avenue parade. All the while, Kennedy smiles broadly, exchanging pleasantries and quips with members of the House and Senate, his cabinet appointees, the chief justice, scores of dignitaries. He addresses the American people in what is destined to become one of the most memorable speeches of his presidency.

It is a glorious day of celebration, yet for all the stylish splendor, for all the youthful vigor and promise, Kennedy knows that out there beyond the Secret Service perimeter, beyond the adoring crowds, beyond the parties and the celebrations, there are harsh realities. These realities do not await Kennedy so much as they confront him, menace him. Some are domestic, including the profound issue of race. But others, more immediately troubling to Kennedy, are international. For even as the young president smiles through the ceremonies, what he sees beyond the moment is the truly perilous nature of the world. Most troubling of all is the ascendance of the Soviet Union.

Though it has been three and a half years since the launch of *Sputnik,* the pioneering Russian satellite, that painful memory is fresh in the American consciousness. The country still feels that blow to American prestige in the world and, worse, to the nation's sense of itself. Humiliation mixes with a fear that American primacy in science and technology is a thing of the past, that the nation's students are falling behind. Fresh in the American mind is the memory of the downed American U-2 spy plane 1,300 miles inside Russia. Fresh in the mind is the attempted U.S. satellite launch at Cape Canaveral where the launcher lifts, explodes, and crashes ignominiously on its own launchpad.

Kennedy is informed that the Soviet economy is growing at an astonishing rate of 6 to 10 percent a year while the U.S. economy grows at 2 to 3 percent. He receives CIA projections that by the year 2000 the Soviet GNP will be triple that of the United States. The Russians are emboldened. They proclaim themselves "the greatest power on earth." Communists are threatening in South Vietnam, Cambodia, Thailand, and Burma. The Russians are helping to build a nuclear reactor in India. Colonialism is rapidly fading. In 1960 alone, nineteen new nations join the UN. Many of these former European colonies in Africa and Asia are allied with the Soviets.

Eisenhower provides Kennedy with a report from the National Security Council indicating locations where the United States might be drawn into war at some level: Laos, Korea, Formosa, Iran, Berlin. Each day more refugees flee East Germany for West Berlin. There are disturbing signs the Communists will try to seize Berlin and even talk of using nuclear weapons there.

The threats are far and near. Ninety miles off the U.S. coast, the Communists have taken over in Cuba. Castro seeks to export his revolution throughout Latin America.

Hatless and coatless in the crystalline air of the capital, Kennedy promises that we will "bear any burden" for liberty. He soon proclaims that this is the "hour of maximum danger."

He does not yet know how prescient his words will be. In a few months, the Soviets will test massive nuclear weapons. Kennedy will come to believe that the odds of a world war are one in five. He will solicit an estimate of American casualties in the event of a nuclear exchange with the Soviets. In such an event, he will be told, some 70 million Americans would die.

John F. Kennedy

THE PRESIDENTIAL PORTFOLIO

Dear Mr. Ross:
month ago - I just wanted
to write and let you know

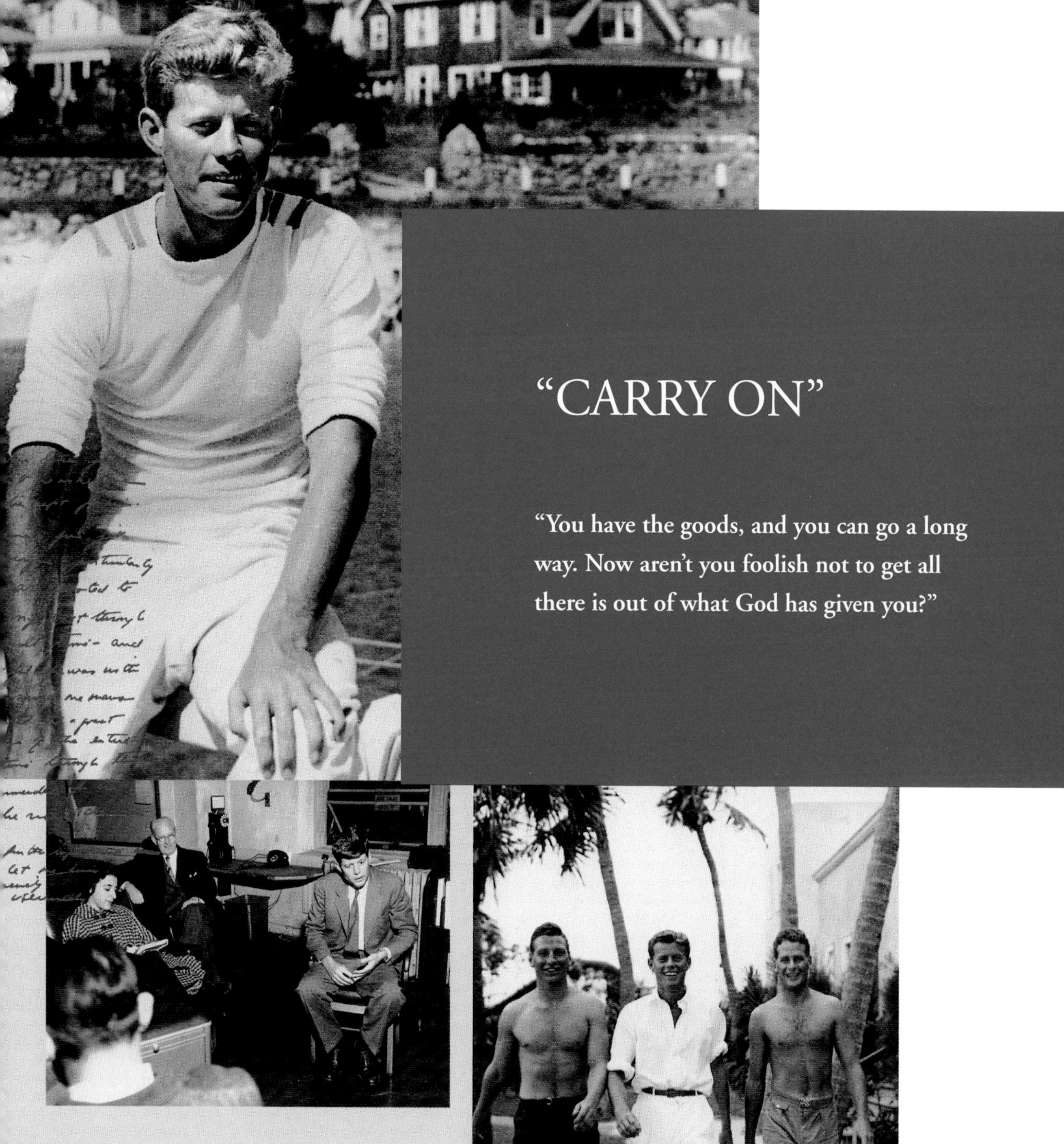

"CARRY ON"

"You have the goods, and you can go a long way. Now aren't you foolish not to get all there is out of what God has given you?"

The fragments of history tell pieces of the story. The well-worn index card bears the careful script of Rose Kennedy, faithfully recording the illnesses of her sickly son. The reflective letter from the Choate School headmaster acknowledges young Jack Kennedy's academic deficiencies even as it illuminates the heart of the young man's appeal and potential for success. The newspaper article from Fleet Street records the demeanor of Jack Kennedy as an overseas emissary from his father, the ambassador to Britain. The Harvard academic transcript reveals the intellectual indifference of a young man who suffered a D in history. Yet only a year later the eight-page, single-spaced rumination Jack wrote to his father on politics and diplomacy illustrates the same young man's deep interest in the issues of the day. The photograph on the glossy cover of the Junior Chamber of Commerce magazine depicting the nation's ten outstanding young men for 1946—with Jack Kennedy at its center—

John Fitzgerald Kennedy
Born Brookline Mass. (83 Beals Street) May 29. 1917
Has had whooping cough · measles - chicken pox
Had scarlet fever. February 20. 1920
At City Hospital Boston · with Dr. Hill · Dr. Reardon
took care of ear.
Has had mumps
German measles 1928
Schick test 1928
Bronchitis occasionally

One of Rose Kennedy's index cards

shows that at age twenty-nine he had already become a figure of national recognition.

Separately, these fragments tell their own stories. Taken together, however, documents, photographs, and artifacts such as these recount a fuller, richer story—the story of John Fitzgerald Kennedy's life and presidency. These items are found on a point in Dorchester Bay, an inlet within Boston Harbor. Perched on the point is the John Fitzgerald Kennedy Library, a white concrete and glass structure facing out to the water and the world beyond, embracing the sea.

Rose Kennedy's index card is but one of the millions of pages of documents collected here, along with 289,000 photographs, thousands of books, reels of film, audiotape, and oral histories. Yet this card reveals an essential truth about John Kennedy—that from the beginning he was plagued by illness. Three months shy of his third birthday, young Jack came down with scarlet fever, a disease that was often fatal. "There were various possibilities that were awful to think about," recalled his mother in one of the books housed in the library collection. "Yet there was no place in Brookline where Jack could be taken—the hospital wouldn't admit patients with contagious diseases—and our family wasn't eligible for use of the Boston hospitals because we didn't live in the city."

In the urgency of the moment, Rose Kennedy's father, John "Honey Fitz"

Nantasket, 1921

Rose Kennedy with Eunice, Kathleen, Jack, Joe Jr., and Rosemary (seated on the grass)

Fitzgerald, the former mayor of Boston, procured a bed in a Boston city hospital infectious disease ward. The child was rushed to the ward so gravely ill that his father went immediately to church and fell to his knees in prayer.

Jack, 1925

In time, the crisis passed and Jack returned to health. Yet even as he grew, Jack remained frail. At age six he was of average height but very thin. "He had a rather narrow face and his ears stuck out a little bit and his hair wouldn't stay put," his mother wrote, "and all that added . . . to an elfin quality in his appearance. But he was a very active, very lively elf, full of energy when he wasn't ill and full of charm and imagination. . . . He was a funny little boy, and he said things in such an original, vivid way."

When he sought a raise in his weekly allowance, young Jack did so with wit and humor in a note to his father that is contained within the library collection.

It was during times of illness that Jack Kennedy turned to books. "The fact that he was so often sick in bed or convalescing in the house and needed entertainment only encouraged what I think was already a strong natural bent," according to his mother. "He gobbled books."

And as he did so, it became clear that he had been blessed with an ample measure of intelligence. While still in grade school at the Riverdale Country Day School in New York, Jack won the school prize for best composition. The plan was for him to follow in the footsteps of his brother Joe, two years his senior, at Choate, a prestigious boys' prep school in Wallingford, Connecticut. Like his father, Joe was smart, determined, and hard-charging.

When Jack applied to Choate, however, administrators

told his parents that he needed a year's preparation at another boarding school. This worked well from Rose Kennedy's perspective. She was attracted to the idea of Jack's going to a Catholic school and Jack was duly sent off to the Canterbury School, a Roman Catholic institution in New Milford, Connecticut. It proved to be a difficult year. His Canterbury report card from November 1930 is preserved at the library. It shows Jack's excellence in but one subject—he achieved a 95 in math—and a woeful score of 55 in Latin. At Easter break he was struck with appendicitis and required surgery. His recuperation took some time, and he lost the rest of the year at Canterbury. Rose Kennedy was often

A Plea for a raise
By Jack Kennedy
Dedicated to my
Mr. J. P. Kennedy

Chapter I

My recent allowance is 40¢. This I used for areoplanes and other playthings of childhood but now I am a scout and I put away my childish things. Before I would spend 20¢ of my 40¢ allowance and In five minutes I would have empty pockets and nothing to gain and 20¢ to lose. When I a a scout I have to buy canteens, haversacks, blankets searchlidgs poncho things that will last for years and I can always use it while I cant use a cholcolote marshmellow sunday with vanilla ice cream and so I put in my plea for a raise of thirty cents for me to buy scout things and pay my own way more around.

Finis

John Fitzgerald Francis Kennedy

Jack's "A Plea for a raise"

"anxious about his physical health in those years; and so was his father. Yet by that time, I suppose, both of us were accustomed to the idea that every now and then he would be laid up by some disease or accident." The family hired a tutor to work with him, and he was accepted for admission to Choate in the fall of 1931.

Jack, circa 1933

Jack's health continued to be a problem throughout his years at Choate. When he fell ill with the flu, Jack was given cod-liver oil. Every winter, it seemed, Jack was confined to the school's infirmary with one malady or another. Most of the time his symptoms were described as flulike, but in January of his junior year he became so sick that school officials were alarmed. He was taken to a hospital in nearby New Haven, and his friend Lem Billings said the belief was that he had leukemia and was near death. In the end the doctors were uncertain what the affliction was, and he was sent to the Mayo Clinic during the summer for more intensive study. But even then there was no definitive diagnosis. His health improved senior year but was still poor enough so that he was not permitted to participate in athletics.

As troubling as Jack's susceptibility to illness was his unwillingness to apply himself in school. "What concerned us . . . was his lack of diligence in his studies," his mother said. "Choate had a highly 'structured' set of rules, traditions, and expectations into which a boy was supposed to fit. . . . Joe Jr. had no trouble at all operating within this system; it suited his temperament. But Jack couldn't or wouldn't conform. He did pretty much what he wanted, rather than what the school wanted of him."

Jack's stubborn rebelliousness touched a nerve at the school. Addressing the student body, the Choate headmaster would often use the word "mucker" to describe the worst of the boys—those with negative attitudes, boys who were slackers, who failed to do their best. Jack was greatly amused by this and, along with some friends, founded a secret society at the school called the Muckers Club. The members would gather in Jack's room above the dining hall after dinner and huddle around his record player. Word spread that Muckers Club members were considering placing a pile of horse manure inside the dance hall at the school's big spring festival. Upon hearing this, headmaster George St. John was enraged.

Kennedy, John

RIVERDALE COUNTRY SCHOOL

Upper School Scholarship Report

Form IA for period ending [illegible], 19[illegible]

SUBJECTS:

Chemistry	
Civics	
Drawing	
English	C 3
French	D 3
General Science	
Geography	A 1
German	
Greek	
History	
Latin	
Manual Training	
Mathematics	B+2
Music	
Penmanship	B 2
Physiology	
Physics	
Average	C+

Absence 2 Demerits

Creditable, Jack 75 [illegible] Head Master.

Now for Honors

(over)

CANTERBURY SCHOOL

NEW MILFORD, CONNECTICUT

Record of John Kennedy, Form II

From November 1 to December 6, 1930.

Any average from 90% to 100% is accounted "Very Good"; from 80% to 90% "Good"; from 70% to 80% "Fair"; from 60% to 70% "Poor"; and below 60% "Unsatisfactory".

SUBJECT	DAILY WORK	EFFORT AND APPLICATION	FORM AVERAGE
English II	86	Good	71.69
Latin II	55	Poor	64.35
History II	77	Good	67.00
Mathematics II	95	Good	61.69
Science II	72	Good	66.62
Religion II	75	Fair	78.46
AVERAGE: 77.00			

This report is not quite so good as the last one. The damage was done chiefly by "Poor" effort in Latin, in which Jack got a mark of 55. He can do better than this. In fact, his average should be well in the 80's.

N.H.

Report cards from Riverdale. . . *and Canterbury*

He summoned the thirteen members of the club to his office and sharply criticized each one. During the course of the dressing-down, the headmaster told the boys they were expelled from school. Hours later, however, he had given the club members a second chance and they were not to be expelled after all. But Jack was a ringleader and his father was summoned to school for an urgent conference with Mr. St. John. After the visit, there was regular correspondence between the headmaster and the Kennedy parents. But try as the adults did, there seemed no motivating Jack.

Muckers Club members: Ralph Horton, Lem Billings, Butch Schriber, and Jack

For all the trials he caused his parents and school administrators, the adults recognized something special about the boy. Part of it was his undeniable charm. "The outstanding talent Jack had demonstrated in school . . . was a talent for making friends and enjoying friendships," recalled his mother. "During vacations and special weekends when he came home he invariably had at least one, usually two, three, four, or more school friends with him. We never knew whom to expect or how many."

Young Jack Kennedy exuded a quality then that would define him for the rest of his life. He was an insouciant individual who hated pomposity and pretension. He was anything but stuffy and old world. He was casual, completely relaxed with himself, and perhaps above all, supremely self-confident. Still, he was self-deprecating and facetious, frequently cutting and sarcastic. Perhaps his most appealing characteristic was his irreverent sense of humor. His sister Kathleen once described him as "the funniest boy alive. He had the Irish maid in fits the whole time. Every time he'd talk to her he'd put on a tremendous Irish brogue." Beyond charm, there was a sense of kindness Jack demonstrated perhaps most poignantly in his treatment of his sister Rosemary, who was just a year and a half younger and suffered from mental retardation. Eunice Kennedy, one of Jack's sisters, remembered how "Jack would take her to a dance at the club, and would dance with her and kid with her and would make sure a few of his close pals cut in, so she felt popular."

Many of Jack's letters home from Choate have been preserved, but none is more telling of his feeling of connectedness to his family than a brief note scrawled late one night before exams, only days after the birth of Edward M. Kennedy: "Can I be godfather to the baby?"

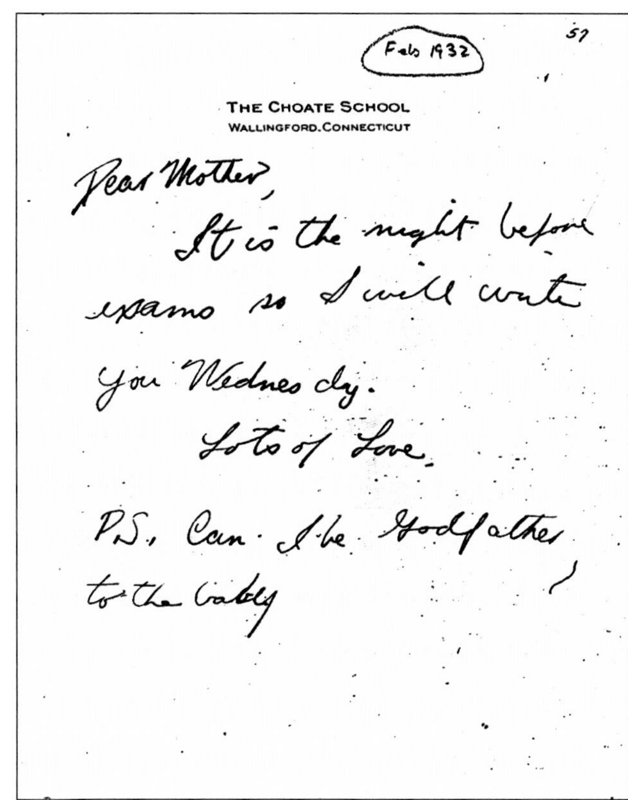
Feb 1932
57
THE CHOATE SCHOOL
WALLINGFORD, CONNECTICUT

Dear Mother,
It is the night before exams so I will write you Wednesday.
Lots of Love.
P.S. Can I be Godfather to the baby?

Jack's letter home requesting to be named Godfather to Teddy Kennedy. He was.

The Kennedy Library holds tens of thousands of pieces of correspondence, but few are as insightful as a letter written by the Choate headmaster, the very man who was so angry about the Muckers Club. When Jack was a junior, George St. John wrote to Joseph P. Kennedy:

> The fact of the matter is that I cannot feel seriously uneasy or worried about Jack. The longer I live and work with him and the more I talk with him, the more confidence I have in him. I would be willing to bet anything that within two years you will be as proud of Jack as you now are of Joe.
>
> Jack has a clever, individualist mind. It is a harder mind to put in harness than Joe's—harder for Jack himself to put in harness. . . . We have to allow, my dear Mr. Kennedy, with boys like Jack, for a period of adjustment. All that natural cleverness Jack has to learn how to use in his life and work, even to cover it up at times, to subordinate it. . . . I never yet saw a clever, witty boy who at some stage in his early development was not considered fresh. . . . The final product is often more interesting and effective than the boy with a more conventional mind who has been to us parents and teachers much less trouble.

Jack's father also saw his son's potential. Joseph Kennedy Sr. wrote to his son during his junior year: "Now, Jack, I don't want to give the impression that I am a nagger. For goodness knows that is the worst thing a parent can be. After long experience in sizing up people, I definitely know you have the goods, and you can go a long way. Now aren't you foolish not to get all there is out of what God has given you?"

It was not only his father and the headmaster who saw something in Jack; his classmates saw it as well. For the Choate seniors in that year of graduation did not choose the class president or the top-ranked student for their most coveted honor. They instead chose Jack Kennedy—ranked an undistinguished sixty-fourth out of a class of 112—as the boy in their class considered "most likely to succeed."

In the summer of 1935, Jack Kennedy sailed for England, but he had been there for only a month when he was struck with hepatitis. Returning to the United States with his parents, he soon felt well enough to go to college. His choice was Princeton, where some of his closest prep school friends were headed. This idea greatly displeased his father. Harvard had been the choice of both Joe Sr. and Joe Jr., and the hope was that Jack would follow suit. Even after father and son discussed the matter, however, Jack did not relent. Though there had already been several weeks of classes at Princeton, Jack was admitted. Less then two months later, however, his hepatitis recurred and Jack was forced to leave school. "We sent him out west to recuperate," recalled his mother. "Most of the rest of that school year of 1935–36 he spent in Arizona, since the sunny and dry climate there was said to be good for health and especially good for asthma, because he had that also."

Lem Billings, Bobby Kennedy, and Jack

He had been so sick so often, Rose recounted, that "someone in the family—probably Bobby . . . said, 'If a mosquito bit Jack Kennedy, the mosquito would die.'" In spite of his health problems, his mother observed, Jack "went along for many years thinking to himself—or at least trying to make others think—that he was a strong, robust, quite healthy person who just happened to be sick a good deal of the time."

In the fall of 1936, Jack finally followed the path of his father and brother by enrolling at Harvard. He gamely tried out for freshman football, and despite his skeletonlike build at the time, he made the squad, although he was a third stringer. He was to get little playing time as either a freshman or a sophomore, when he was on the junior varsity team. Worse, his back was battered, the beginning of a back problem that would steadily worsen and plague him throughout his adult life. He found other athletic outlets where he was more successful. He was a strong member of an outstanding freshman swim team, and he played some rugby and golf. A highlight of his athletic career at Harvard

Front row: Patricia, Robert, Rose, Jack, Teddy, Joe Sr., Jean. Back row: Joe Jr., Kathleen, Rosemary, Eunice

Name: Kennedy, John Fitzgerald — Received S.B. degree cum laude — Class of 1940

Candidate for S.B. — Admitted from The Choate School, Wallingford, Conn. 1935 — Winthrop House

Status: 6-25-40 Bill not paid; 7-9-40 Bill paid

1936-37 Freshman	Grades	1937-38 Sophomore	Grades	1938-39 Junior	Grades	1939-40 Junior	Grades
English A Not Required		English F¹	C	Economics 61a¹	C	Economics 11b²	✓
	C	Fine Arts 1e	C	English A-1¹	B	" 62b²	✓
Economics	B	Government 1	C	Government 7a¹	B	Government 3a¹	B
History	C	History 32a¹	D	" 9a¹	B	" 4	B
French	C	" 32b²	C	" 18¹	B	" 2²	B
		Government 30²	B	History 55¹	B	" 8a¹	B
				2-7-39 Leave of abs.		" 10a¹	✓
						" 28¹	B

Phys. Training: Satisfactory

Date and place of birth: May 29, 1917, Brookline, Mass.
Father: Joseph Patrick Kennedy
Mother: Rose (Fitzgerald) Kennedy
Street: 294 Pondfield Rd.
City: Bronxville
State: N.Y.
Send reports to: Father: 30 Rockefeller Plaza, N.Y.C.; Mother: American Embassy, London

Voted by the Administrative Board: 2-7-39-97 Granted leave of absence for the second half year in order to go to England.

Degree Summary: General Examinations PASSED — History, Gov't and Economics — May 1940 — Recommendation of division: cum laude (Government) — Recommended for S.B. degree with the Class of 1940 cum laude (Government) — Received degree as recommended at June 20, 1940 — Concentration: Government

Report from Harvard

came when he and his brother Joe led the college sailing team to victory in an intercollegiate competition during Jack's sophomore year.

His academic records, preserved by the Kennedy Library, tell the story of a young man with little interest in aspiring to academic excellence. The record of his years at Harvard shows not a single A in any subject. He had a C average as both a freshman and sophomore and made a D in history during his sophomore year. Only when he reached junior year did the Cs climb up and become Bs. Whoever prepared the report included a note for the second half of his junior year at Harvard that presaged Jack Kennedy's intellectual turnaround. The note says, at the bottom of the grade listing, "Granted leave of absence for the second half year in order to go to England."

In 1938 President Franklin Roosevelt sent Joseph Kennedy to England to serve in one of the most prestigious ambassadorial assignments in the world—U.S. ambassador to Great Britain. Kennedy's appointment was a defining moment, imbuing the family with a level of prestige it had never before enjoyed. A photograph shows the family in formal attire on the evening they entertained the king and queen at dinner. The photograph illustrates the family's grandeur and success, yet more telling is the pose of young Jack, whose relaxed smile suggests a comfort in such surroundings borne of an abiding self-confidence.

The time in England was an ideal opportunity for Jack to work and travel in Europe, and so it was that in the second half of his junior year he embarked on a six-and-a-half-

The Kennedys in England, May 4, 1939, prior to dining with the King and Queen

month European adventure that would expose him to the simmering world conflict and engender in him a passion for international affairs that would stay with him for the rest of his life. With his father serving as ambassador in London, Jack was given an insider's view of frantic efforts by the British to both avoid and prepare for war. In London he dined with the queen and Princess Elizabeth. He traveled with his father to Rome for the 1939 installation of Cardinal Pacelli as Pope Pius XII. (Jack had met the new pope on a previous trip to Italy.)

Jack, Joe Sr., and Joe Jr., Liverpool, July 2, 1938

In the spring Jack spent a month working in the U.S. embassy in Paris before traveling to Poland, where he saw what he described as the process of "Nazification." At this, one of the most critical junctures of twentieth-century history, Jack Kennedy bore witness to the tensions that would soon lead to world war. During an earlier European summer trip with a college friend, he had traveled for the fun of it. On this trip, however, he followed his intellectual curiosity, his desire to know and understand world affairs. He carried with him a letter of introduction from one of the most influential men in the world, U.S. secretary of state Cordell Hull.

In Moscow he was struck by what he saw. "I didn't have a high opinion of them before I went—of the system—and much less after being there," he later said. "There was massive inefficiency and life was grim and dour and windswept and dusty. It's a very depressing country."

As he traveled, he sent dispatches back to his father on the political situation in Poland, Russia, Romania, Turkey, and the Middle East. One of the most striking is a single-spaced, typewritten letter that Jack wrote from Jerusalem in the early summer of 1939 as the British Parliament debated the partition of Palestine. He crisply sums up Palestinian history even as the pragmatism that would mark his foreign policy later showed through: "In considering the whole question now, it is useless to discuss which has the 'fairer' claim. The important thing is to try to work out a solution that will work."

He traveled through Beirut, Damascus, and Athens, all the while talking with people, soliciting their assessments of how events would play out. Back in London, he worked for his father at the embassy helping to draft ambassadorial correspondence and reports. He was in contact with his tutor at Harvard, who was impressed with Jack's letters concerning the increasingly ominous situation in Europe. It was then that he settled on his thesis topic—Britain's lack of preparedness for war—and he once again set out on a European trip for a final, firsthand look at the political scene.

In Germany storm troopers saw the British plates on Jack's car and showered the vehicle with bricks. He recognized the Nazi propaganda for what it was, writing to his father that "the German people are being whipped into a fierce hatred of the British." At the U.S. embassy in Berlin, Jack was briefed and given a secret message for his father: There would be war within a week. (It turned out to be two weeks.) He was witnessing a level of international tension—"Europe on the eve," as he put it—the world on the brink of war, that would not be repeated until his own administration. It was an extraordinary opportunity to observe one of the defining moments of history in the twentieth century, an opportunity to see the type of tyranny that he would spend precious years of his life combating. The

Jack in Europe

curiosity that emerged during this trip would in many ways foreshadow the politician and world leader he was to become.

Jack joined his father in the House of Commons as Prime Minister Neville Chamberlain sought a declaration of war on Germany. Only days later the British ship *Athenia,* bound for Canada with 1,400 passengers, among them 300 Americans, was torpedoed by a German U-boat and sunk. It was the first civilian ship torpedoed in the war, and it claimed the lives of more than 100 people, including twenty-eight Americans.

Ambassador Kennedy wanted a report on the status of the survivors, who had been brought to Glasgow. He wanted the survivors interviewed and comforted, and he wanted it done with skill and sensitivity. For this mission, he chose his twenty-two-year-old son.

"Joe sent Jack up there to interview the Americans—most of whom had survived—and to file a report to the embassy on the circumstances of the sinking," remembered Rose Kennedy, "and also to do for them whatever was possible to do, within the powers and resources of the embassy. . . . Joe trusted him to do a proper job." Jack visited the survivors in hospitals and hotels and expressed concern for their well-being on behalf of the government of the United States. The London *Evening News* reported that "his boyish charm and natural kindliness persuaded those who he had come to comfort that America was indeed keeping a benevolent and watchful eye on them."

Returning to London, he made recommendations to his father, who then put him in charge of the survivors' repatriation. Finally, he flew back to New York on September 20. The *Boston Globe* reported he was "the general favorite with all on the [airplane], not because he was Ambassador Kennedy's son but because he was himself, bright and helpful and interesting."

Jack returned for his last year at Harvard and immediately immersed himself in work on his senior thesis, an attempt to "analyze Britain's failure to re-arm in the face of a re-arming Germany." It was modeled in part on Winston Churchill's book *While England Slept.* His father sent the thesis to Arthur Krock, a family friend and chief of the *New York Times* bureau in Washington. Soon thereafter the thesis was revised and published as a book, *Why England Slept,* to laudatory reviews and impressive sales. The only sour note surrounding publication came with the wondering aloud in some quarters about whether Krock had actually rewritten or coauthored the book.

The thesis enabled Jack Kennedy to graduate from Harvard cum laude in 1940. He was uncertain what to do after college and initially decided to go to law school at Yale. He changed his mind, however, and in the early fall of 1940 went to Stanford, where he intended to enroll in a course at the business school. While he was in California, an intense national debate raged over whether the United States would enter the war in support of the British. Ambassador Kennedy had been a supporter of Prime Minister Chamberlain's, and he had said during this period that it was unlikely that the United States could come to Britain's aid. Kennedy reflected the isolationist views of a majority of Americans. He believed that only the appeasement of Adolf Hitler could avoid a war that Germany was certain to win. Ambassador Kennedy took this position even as Winston Churchill was bravely standing against Nazi tyranny and declaring that Hitler could be defeated. Both Churchill and Roosevelt held Kennedy in contempt for his views.

The press as well sharply criticized the ambassador, and in the fall of 1940 Kennedy asked his son what he might say to defend himself. In December Jack sent his father an eight-page, single-spaced letter with a suggested approach. The letter shows a bit of naivete on young Kennedy's part, but it also reveals a keen interest not only in defending his father but also in the issues of war and peace. Early in the letter he writes, "Dad: You might work in here some of your own ideas of Munich and background of it. That is, what you thought;

The Book of the Day

Which Explains Why England Failed to Rearm in Face of a Rearming Germany.

In 1938 Winston Churchill re-published, under the title of "While England Slept," the ...

Lucid Account of British Policy

WHY ENGLAND SLEPT. By John F. Kennedy. 252 pp. New York: Wilfred Funk, Inc. $2.00.

Reviewed by HARRY L. COLES, JR.

ABOUT TWO YEARS ago Winston Churchill published a book ... While England ... Kennedy writes ... Why England ... question in ... more than an ... whatever may ... foreign affairs ... fact that ... United States ... economic ... these institutions ... by the ... certainly any ... may have ... the totalitarian ... us.

Democracy and War Plans

Why England Slept, by John F. Kennedy. New York: Wilfred Funk. $2.

THIS SOBER, reliable, straightforward analysis of Great Britain's slowness in rearming to meet the Nazi menace derives additional weight from the fact that the author is the son of the United States Ambassador to Great Britain. He may therefore be presumed to have enjoyed unusual opportunities for first-hand information on the course of international affairs. Its timeli... view of America's ... with problems ... is ...

... war was at its doors until it was almost too late.

While Baldwin and Chamberlain were at fault in failing to give a stronger lead to the national effort and sometimes in issuing soothing statements which were calculated to lull public opinion as to the seriousness of the danger, they had to reckon with the existence of a str... all th... ...ifist current in ...al parties and ... of domestic ...political and ...d not have ...rate with a ... the part of ...t did not ...f foreign ...

... Mr. Kennedy ...ed to a ...erican ...ollapse ... per... ...hamb... ...link ...red-...

... in the face of danger have brought the empire to the present hazard. But for all that, but for public apathy in the last decade, England would have been so bristling with the defensive and offensive arms of war, and men fit to arm them, that no blitzkrieger would have dared to think of attack.

John F. Kennedy has written in Why England Slept so rational an explanation of national sins of omission as to give a short and direct answer to a question which must have puzzled most of the world. Incidentally, to judge from this first book, John F. Kennedy is a name to watch in the world of books and in world affairs from now on.

BOOKS OF THE TIMES

By THOMAS C. LINN

A STUDY of the reasons for Britain's lack of preparedness against German military might ought to interest many people in the United States, especially in Washington, D. C. For, as John F. Kennedy points out in his book "Why England Slept,"* that country has been the "testing ground" of democratic efforts to cope with totalitarian force. It is from Britain's experience that the United States must profit if democracy is to be maintained here against totalitarian threats.

"It [England] has been a case of a democratic form of government, with a capitalistic economy, trying to compete with the new totalitarian system, based on an economy of rigid state control. For a country whose government and economic structure is similar to England's and which may some day be similarly in competition with a dictatorship, there should be a valuable lesson."

* * *

Since John F. Kennedy is a son of Ambassador Joseph P. Kennedy, this book originated under fortunate auspices. For of all the Americans who have had advantageous positions for studying European affairs in the last few years, those in the American Embassy in London have been among the most favored. Not all young men enjoying such advantages, however, would have shown the will or ability to turn them to such useful literary ends. Young Mr. Kennedy also spent some time in the American Embassy in Paris, studied at the University of London, and is a cum laude graduate in international relations of Harvard University.

This is no time for any one to find fault with individual British statesmen for what they may have contributed to Britain's present plight. Mr. Kennedy is not interested in finding scapegoats but in pointing out for the education of his fellow-countrymen the reasons for Britain's tardy rearmament, so that similar mistakes may be avoided here.

* * *

This analysis considers the status of armament in England year by year from 1931, when the National Government came into office, to the present time. It traces the gradual change of temper in Britain from pacifism to war.

The basic reason for Britain's delayed rearmament, according to Mr. Kennedy, is inherent in the democratic form of government. Contrasting the weakness of democracy in competing with the totalitarian system, he writes, "Democracy is the superior form of government, because it is based on a respect for man as a reasonable being. For the long run, then, democracy is superior.

"But for the short run, democracy has great weaknesses. When it competes with a system of government which cares nothing for permanency, a system built primarily for war, democracy, which is built primarily for peace, is at a disadvantage. And democracy must recognize its weaknesses; it must learn to safeguard its institutions if it hopes to survive."

In democracies governments dare not act without the consent of the people, and the population of England swung slowly and reluctantly from its desire for disarmament of the Nineteen Twenties to its present war stride. The final and complete awakening to the acute unpreparedness of the empire did not come until after Munich. Only with war at the door did Britain's preparation for war begin with the earnestness which should have marked the effort years before.

For this tardiness Mr. Kennedy believes that no single man or group is to blame. The government, business and labor all had a share of responsibility. The government did not have the vision to foresee the crisis in the offing, business did not want to pay the taxes involved in extensive armament, and labor was loath to relinquish its rights until convinced that war was inevitable.

* * *

The tragedy is that England did not begin to rearm in 1934 instead of in 1936. Meantime Germany got a start which Mr. Kennedy believes fundamentally responsible for Munich and England's present difficulties. Munich, he thinks, was inevitable on the basis of British unpreparedness alone, but there was another consideration. "I believe," he writes, "Chamberlain was sincere in thinking that a great step had been taken towards healing one of Europe's fever sores. I believe that English public opinion was not sufficiently aroused to back him in a war."

Armament was retarded by various factors which were peculiar to England. Mr. Kennedy thinks that the country was unfortunate in its choice of men to head the government during this critical period, that there was a lack of progressive younger leadership caused by the loss of a generation in the World War, that the English parliamentary system increased the difficulty of rearmament as did the strong public sentiment in favor of the League of Nations, and, as did also "the closeness to the government of the English aristocracy, which was opposed strongly to war."

It is, of course, too early for any final appraisal of the men and the circumstances that shaped England's policy during the last decade. The information is by no means obtainable yet for such an undertaking. Mr. Kennedy has made a careful analysis from the records that are available. His factual and unemotional approach to the problem is praiseworthy, and his conclusions ought to be weighed carefully in this country. The new publishing firm of Wilfred Funk, Inc., has made an excellent choice for its first book.

*WHY ENGLAND SLEPT. By John F. Kennedy. Foreword by Henry R. Luce. 252 pages. Wilfred Funk, Inc. $2.

Inside Story

(AP Photo)

John F. Kennedy, son of the United States Ambassador Joseph P. Kennedy, envoy to Great Britain, has written the first publication of the new house of Willard Funk, "Why England Slept."

NO 5-6

December 5, 1940

Ambassador Joseph P. Kennedy
North Ocean Blvd.
Palm Beach, Florida

Dear Dad:

I received the letter from Simon and I am writing him myself and sending Luce one of the three pamphlets as he was quite bitter about Simon, ~~himself~~ and may find it of some interest.

I also received a rather unusual letter from Londonderry, a copy of which I am enclosing. I am also answering that. And lastly I received a very interesting letter from Liddel Hart. (Enclosure)

I am sending along to you a rough outline of some points that I feel it would be well for you to cover. It ~~really~~ only shows an approach to the problem, it is not meant to be a finished form. Part of it is in article form; in other parts I have just mentioned points you might answer. I don't present it in the form of a finished article as I first of all don't know what your view point is on some questions, and secondly I think the article should be well padded with stories of your experiences in England in order to give it an authenticity and interest.

Some points such as my mention of Alsop and Kintner you may want to leave out and undoubtedly you will prefer ~~a different~~ another approach to such questions as this, but it may serve to give you a different angle. ~~on the question.~~ I think it is right for you to do the article, at least one, in order to clear the record which has been somewhat twisted by Pearson and Allen and Alsop and Kintner, although I saw where Boake Carter wrote a couple of what I thought very good articles on your views how you felt it would be serious danger to America if there was a war at that time; that America's own defenses were completely down as well as England's; that England might have been bombed into submission overnight due to her complete lack of defenses and America would have been in an exposed and dangerous position. You might put in here that it was worth any risk for America to have a Europe at peace and therefore you supported Chamberlain."

Jack soon left California and returned to the East Coast. But it was not long before he was off again, this time on a trip to Latin America, where he toured, among other countries, Peru, Ecuador, and Colombia. But as 1941 progressed, it was clear to Jack Kennedy that the United States was going to have to play a role in the terrible war that had broken out in Europe. He joined the U.S. Navy and was dispatched in October 1941 to Washington, D.C., to work for the Office of Naval Intelligence. This was a heady position for a young man, but it left him entirely out of the action when the United States entered the war. Things got worse when he was transferred in January 1942 to a naval base in Charleston, South Carolina. He was confined to an office while brave men were fighting. He used his father's political influence to get himself out of Washington and into the Pacific theater.

Lieutenant J.G. Jack Kennedy and Ensign Joe Kennedy, May 4, 1942, in Palm Beach

In April 1943, Lieutenant Kennedy took command of a torpedo boat, PT-109, where his mission was to defend the Solomon Islands and to attempt to prevent the Japanese from supplying their bases. In early August, while Kennedy's ship was patrolling the Blackett Strait in the Solomons, a Japanese destroyer churning at 30 knots rammed the boat, slicing it in half and killing two crewmen. Kennedy was thrown to the deck, injuring his back. Nonetheless, the lieutenant swam 3 miles in the dark towing another, more seriously wounded sailor. He swam the breaststroke, the straps from his crewman's life preserver between his teeth, saving both their lives. That first night, with his crew safely tucked away on a tiny island, Lieutenant Kennedy swam back out into the darkened water alone, hoping to spot a passing PT boat, but his effort was to no avail. He led the crew to another island, where they ate coconuts. Jack Kennedy secretly raided a Japanese stash of water and candy bars, which he brought back to his men. After five days, they encountered natives. He scratched a message on a coconut and gave it to an islander: "Native knows posit . . . 11 alive need small boat Kennedy." This coconut—which sat atop Kennedy's desk in the Oval Office—is one of the most prized possessions in the Kennedy Library collection.

The native brought the coconut to an American base, and Kennedy and his crew were rescued. In time he was returned to the States sick with malaria, weighing a mere 127 pounds. His back had been seriously hurt, and he was admitted to the New England Baptist Hospital in Boston for surgery. Asked later how he had become a war hero, he replied: "It was easy—they sank my boat."

At the helm of PT–109

Jack, 1943

John F. Kennedy had been raised amid the greatest privilege. He had enjoyed enormous wealth and access to some of the most successful, influential people in the world. In his life, however, there was also more than his share of suffering and loss. While Jack was recovering, word came that his older brother Joe, a navy pilot, had been killed during a mission over Europe.

Joe Kennedy Sr. was devastated by the death. They all were. But the family patriarch made it very clear that they would forge ahead. "We've got to carry on," he said. "We must take care of the living." It was a notion that the Kennedy family would have to summon so many times through the years. Less than a month after Joe's death, word came that Kathleen Kennedy's husband, an Englishman named Lord Hartington, had been killed in action in France. And in 1948 Kathleen herself, Jack's beloved younger sister, died in a plane crash in France. Later in his life, of course, John F. Kennedy would suffer perhaps the most painful of all losses, the death of his infant son, Patrick, days after birth. Through it all, Jack Kennedy followed his father's dictum: He carried on.

And he did so even as he struggled throughout his life with debilitating, painful, and life-threatening physical maladies. "At least one half of the days that he spent on this earth were days of intense physical pain," Robert Kennedy said. While Rose Kennedy's index card began to record Jack's illnesses, navy reports from the war years provide fuller detail of his ailments. There are mentions of acute gastroenteritis, chronic colitis, a duodenal ulcer. One navy medical report crisply summarizes the PT-109 incident: "While on pt duty in the South Pacific, the patient's boat was rammed and sunk by a Jap DD at Vela Gulf, 1 August 1943. He spent over 50 hours in the water and went without food and drinking water for one week. Following this experience, his present abdominal

Joe Jr.'s plane reported lost in August 1944

symptoms started." Yet he bore it without complaint, and he did so during a time when there was a great deal of fear and ignorance concerning serious illness. For virtually his entire political career, he would conceal the true nature of his physical condition from the public, for discovery might well have meant political defeat.

His close friend from Choate, Lem Billings, observed that Jack Kennedy became more fatalistic after the deaths of his sister and brother and after he was diagnosed with Addison's disease, a disease of the adrenal glands characterized by extreme weakness, low blood pressure, and brownish discoloration of the skin. It was controlled through daily injec-

NMS—Form M
(1940)

REPORT OF MEDICAL SURVEY

Place U. S. Naval Hospital, Chelsea, Massachusetts Date 6 December 1944
From: *Board of Medical Survey.*
To: *Commanding Officer.*
For Transmission to the Bureau of Medicine and Surgery

Name KENNEDY, John Fitzgerald Rank or rate LT., USNR
Born: Place Massachusetts (Name of place and State or county) Date 29 May 1917
Enlisted or appointed: Date 1 October 1941 Place -
Total service: Navy 3 years 2 months Marine Corps - Army -

PRESENT HISTORY OF CASE

Admitted from SCTC, Miami, Fla. Date 11 June 1944
Diagnosis COLITIS, CHRONIC #381 (From Navy nomenclature, under which carried on sick list) Key letter - Specialty letter -
Disability is not (Is or is not) the result of his own misconduct and was (Was or was not) incurred in line of duty
Existed prior to enlistment No (Yes or No) If "Yes," was condition aggravated by service? (Yes or No)
Present condition Unfit for Service Probable future duration Permanent
Recommendation That he be ordered to appear before a Retiring Board.

FACTS ARE AS FOLLOWS:

This 27-year old Lt. USNR, with 2 years and 10 months' active service, was admitted to this hospital on 11 June 1944 with the complaints of pain in the lower back referred down the left leg. In addition he had persistent pain in the left lower quadrant.

By permission of the BuM&S he was granted leave to report to the Lahey Clinic. Following an air spinogram, Dr. James L. Poppen performed an operation for intervertebral disc. Investigation of the gastro-intestinal complaints by Dr. Sara M. Jordon, revealed, on x-ray examination, spasm and irritability of the duodenum without a finite ulcer crater but with a lipping of the base of the cap which was suggestive of a duodenal ulcer scar. Spasm of the colon was also demonstrated. Previously at Tulagi, on 23 November 1943 an x-ray examination revealed an early duodenal ulcer. During his stay at the Lahey Clinic he had an attack of Malaria, Benign, Tertian. He returned to this activity on 4 August 1944. The original complaints continued. An orthopedic consultant injected procaine into the left sciatic nerve with considerable relief resulting. The back and leg pain improved from that time, but the constant discomfort in the left lower quadrant remained. He was, therefore, surveyed for further treatment on 16 October 1944, which was approved.

Additional laboratory study at this activity showed blood smears negative for malarial parasites, an 8% eosinophilia on three occasions and six stool examinations negative for ova and parasites. An x-ray examination of the gall bladder showed normal function. Sigmoidoscopy was essentially normal except for very slight edema in the mucosa of the recto-sigmoid.

........, U. S. Navy. Senior Member of Board. ...., U. S. Navy. Member. ...., U. S. Navy. Member.

16—11583

NMS—Form M
(1940)

REPORT OF MEDICAL SURVEY PAGE.

Place U. S. Naval Hospital, Chelsea, Massachusetts (Name of hospital, ship, or station where survey is held) Date 6 December 1
From: *Board of Medical Survey.*
To: *Commanding Officer.*
For Transmission to the Bureau of Medicine and Surgery

Name KENNEDY, John Fitzgerald (In full, surname first) Rank or rate LT. USNR
Born: Place Massachusetts (Name of place and State or county) Date 29 May 1917
Enlisted or appointed: Date 1 October 1941 Place -
Total service: Navy 3 years 2 months Marine Corps - Army -

PRESENT HISTORY OF CASE

Admitted from SCTC, Miami, Fla. Date 11 June 1944
Diagnosis COLITIS, CHRONIC #381 (From navy nomenclature, under which carried on sick list) Key letter - Specialty letter -
Disability is not (Is or is not) the result of his own misconduct and was (Was or was not) incurred in line of duty
Existed prior to enlistment No (Yes or No) If "Yes," was condition aggravated by service? - (Yes or No)
Present condition Unfit for Service Probable future duration Permanent
Recommendation That he be ordered to appear before a Retiring Board.

FACTS ARE AS FOLLOWS: (Continued from Page One)

This officer's chief complaint continues to be pain in the left lower quadrant. According to his own accepted statement, for a period of two months in 1938, he had daily discomfort in the upper abdomen localized in the mid-epigastrium and described as a burning sensation. It had no direct relation to meals. By avoiding roughage and highly-seasoned foods, it gradually disappeared. X-ray examinations at the time were said to have shown irritation of the duodenum. It was not associated with lower abdominal cramps nor lower bowel disturbances. He further states that his present abdominal discomfort is different than that noted previous to enlistment.

While on PT duty in the South Pacific, the patient's boat was rammed and sunk by a Jap DD at Vela Gulf, 1 August 1943. He spent over 50 hours in the water and went without food or drinking water for one week. Following this experience, his present abdominal symptoms started.

He has failed to gain in appetite, strength or weight. It is the opinion of the Board of Medical Survey that this officer is unfit for service and it is recommended that he be rought before a Retiring Board.

S. McGINN R. T. DREW C. C. DERRICK
LT. COMDR. MC USNR, U. S. Navy. Senior Member of Board. LT. MC USNR, U. S. Navy. Member. LT. MC USNR, U. S. Navy. Member.

16—11583

A Naval medical report

tions of cortisone, but it could not be cured and was at the time potentially fatal.

"He just figured there was no sense in planning ahead anymore," Billings said. "The only thing that made sense . . . was to live for the moment, treating each day as if it were his last, demanding of life constant intensity, adventure and pleasure." And for Jack Kennedy pleasure often involved the company of beautiful young women. His charm, affability, and good looks made him extremely popular with women wherever he went, and he pursued romantic liaisons throughout his adult life.

"He always seemed so self-possessed, unruffled, equable, with a certain air of 'detachment' as though he were in the scene and living it fully and yet observing the scene with himself in it," his mother said. "I think by and large this was true. He did have an even temperament, I think that in part it was a quality he acquired because of ill health. Some people could have given in to self-pity, but Jack inured himself against misfortune and lived his life to its fullest."

And that meant being active. Doing. Being vigorous. It meant not sitting on the sidelines. After the war he thought he might teach and write, thought perhaps he could become a diplomat. He worked briefly for International News Service as a special correspondent. Reflecting his keen interest in international affairs, he covered the Potsdam conference and the founding conference of the United Nations. But journalism was too passive for him. He didn't want to merely observe and record events; he wanted to shape them. "I never wanted to be in politics until almost the time I ran," he said.

A political career had been preordained for Joe Kennedy. "We all liked politics but Joe seemed a natural to run for office," Jack said. "Obviously, you can't have a whole mess of Kennedys asking for votes. So when Joe was denied his chance, I wanted to run."

And run he did. In 1946 he declared his candidacy for the open U.S. House seat in the Massachusetts Eleventh Congressional District, which included parts of Boston and Cam-

432 words

WHY HARVARD MEN GO INTO POLITICS

- John F. Kennedy -

Isolation of the factors which governed one's choice of careers is almost always a speculative process, ~~tending to emphasize the senti-mental over the coincidental~~ -- but nowhere is this more true than in the political profession. There are no standard procedures for "going into politics" -- no formal rules of apprenticeship, no professional accrediting associations, no merit systems or farm teams ~~or officers candidate schools~~. The successful practitioner and the newly-elected freshman both owe their success at least in part to fluctuations of public opinion and economic conditions over which they had no control; and chance combinations of time and circumstance -- whether they involve vacancies in office, personal acquaintanceship, or "coat-tail" victories -- are frequently more important in launching political careers than formal preparation or philosophy.

Moreover, I know from my own experience that the initial determination of a political career is frequently influenced by the activi-ties and traditions of one's own family -- ~~the conversation at the dinner table, attendance at political rallies, admiration of the honor or acclaim bestowed upon one's father or grandfather, and inherited skills,~~ interests, ~~and even reputations and supporters.~~ A philosophy of public service, ~~more-over,~~ is more often inspired by one's religious and moral environment than his schooling.

Nevertheless formal education -- particularly of the type offered at Harvard -- plays an important role in nourishing the seed already bridge. Though he was somewhat shy at first, he quickly took to the campaign. Politics, after all, was in his blood. Both his grandfathers had been politicians. His paternal grandfather, Patrick "P.J." Kennedy, and his maternal grandfather, "Honey Fitz," had been elected to the Massachusetts Senate. P.J. had served five terms in the Massachusetts House and was later Boston's election commissioner and wire commissioner. Honey Fitz had been a member of the city council and served three terms in the Congress and two terms as mayor. Jack was running, in fact, for the very House seat his grandfather had once held. The seat opened up when the incumbent, legendary Boston political figure James Michael Curley, sought to return to the position of mayor of Boston. The Eleventh District included a few Brahmin pockets in Boston and intellectual precincts in Cambridge, but it was much more a gritty, working-class district populated by Irish and Italians living in cramped apartments. During the course of the campaign, Kennedy enlisted the help of Charlestown resident Dave Powers, a man who would remain at Kennedy's side for the rest of his life. Powers recalled that "there was a basic dignity in Jack Kennedy, a pride in being that appealed to every Irishman who was beginning to feel a little embarrassed about the sentimental, corny style of the typical Irish politician as the Irish themselves were becoming more middle class." Jack was aptly described later as having "a Harvard intellectualism and an Irish cultural heritage, making him perhaps the first Irish Brahmin in American politics."

The 1946 campaign

He also had the enormous benefit of his father's wealth. In this, his first campaign for public office, Jack Kennedy would enjoy a financial advantage over his opponents that would remain a factor in every other campaign of his political life. Joseph Kennedy spent liberally to help elect his son. Among his many expenditures was paying to print and distribute John Hersey's *New Yorker* article lauding Jack's courage in the PT-109 incident. With the slogan "The new generation offers a leader" and running heavily on his heroism during the war, John Kennedy was elected and entered the U.S. House in January 1947 at age twenty-nine.

Future *magazine*

Not long after his election, Congressman Kennedy was chosen by the U.S. Junior Chamber of Commerce as one of its ten outstanding young men of 1946. He was featured in an article in *Future* magazine "for his example that all young men owe their land a civic responsibility, and for his interest in veterans' housing." The magazine suggests that Jack Kennedy already had a place on the national political stage.

After the victory another politician congratulated Honey Fitz on the success of his grandson, saying he thought young Kennedy might go places. "Some day—who knows," the man said, "young Jack here may be Governor of the Commonwealth."

"Governor!" Honey Fitz replied. "Some day that young man will be President of the United States."

Within a year, while traveling in England, Congressman Kennedy suffered a physical collapse, a result of Addison's disease. The illness, which was kept secret, surely did not dampen his ambition. In 1952, after three terms in the House, Congressman Kennedy announced that he would run for the Senate against incumbent Henry Cabot Lodge, a venerable figure in Massachusetts who was considered all but unbeatable.

The family played a critical role, with Robert Kennedy as campaign manager and the Kennedy sisters along with Rose Kennedy hosting a series of tea parties throughout the state where large numbers of women would come and meet the candidate. During the course of the campaign, countless such

At a dinner party one evening, the handsome young congressman, one of Washington's most eligible bachelors, met Jacqueline Bouvier, a gorgeous twenty-one-year-old. As a girl Jackie had been a national equestrian champion, while in college she had been named "debutante of the Year," and won a prestigious writing award. To Jack Kennedy she was an irresistible combination of beauty, sophistication, and intellect. She was also Roman Catholic. They courted for two years and were married at St. Mary's Church in Newport on September 12, 1953. Their wedding attracted 800 guests and, according to the *New York Times*, "far surpassed the Astor-French wedding of 1934 in public interest."

For the occasion, the church had been decorated with pink gladioli and white chrysanthemums. Boston tenor Luigi Vena sang "Ave Maria," and a papal blessing was read. Following the forty-minute ceremony, the new couple emerged into a throng of 3,000 well-wishers to make their way with motorcycle escort to Hammersmith Farm. After two hours of greeting family and friends in a receiving line, the bridal couple joined the 1,200 invited guests for champagne and dancing to the music of Meyer Davis and his orchestra. After the couple cut a five-tier wedding cake, a luncheon of fruit cup, creamed chicken, and ice cream sculpted to resemble roses was served. Late in the afternoon Senator and Mrs. Kennedy departed Hammersmith Farm amid a shower of paper rose petals. They traveled to New York to spend the night at the Waldorf Astoria before continuing to Acapulco, Mexico, for a two-week honeymoon.

events were held at which the Kennedy women would act as hostesses and the handsome, single young congressman would sweep in, flashing that toothy smile, and charm them all.

The campaign was "a terrible grind," Kennedy later recalled. Lodge was favored not only because he had served the state well in the Senate but also because Dwight Eisenhower was expected to ride into the White House on a wave of Republican votes throughout the nation. John Kennedy had run for office three times and three times he had been successful, but as he waited for results on election night 1952, victory was by no means certain. That night was "one of the few times I remember seeing him really nervous," recalled his mother. Despite Eisenhower's overwhelming 208,000-vote margin in Massachusetts, Congressman Kennedy defeated Lodge by 70,000 votes in one of the biggest upsets of the political year.

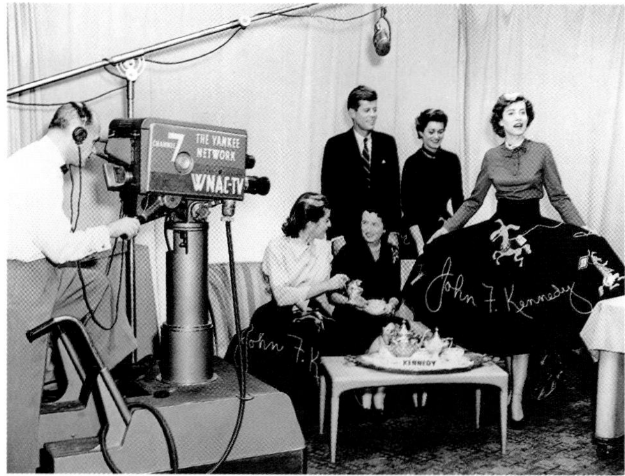

The 1952 campaign

He had been in the Senate less than two years when his back deteriorated to the point where he was in constant pain and required crutches to walk. Something had to be done. On October 21, 1954, at Manhattan's Hospital for Special Surgery, Senator Kennedy underwent a double fusion procedure of his spinal discs. The operation was long and quite difficult and involved inserting a steel plate into his back. Insertion of the plate, however, caused a staph infection, and Senator Kennedy fell gravely ill. For a time, he lay near death. He was again given the last rites of the Catholic Church.

Once again, however, as he had thirty-four years earlier when he had been so ill with scarlet fever, as he had seven years earlier when he had been near death from Addison's disease, John F. Kennedy struggled and survived. But his condition was so acute that he remained hospitalized for two months. He left the hospital in late December but returned in mid-February for yet another back operation, less serious than the first. And it was during his period of convalescence that he put together *Profiles in Courage,* a book about courageous acts by members of the Senate through history. The book was a commercial success and won the Pulitzer Prize in 1957. But even as it did so there were rumors that Kennedy himself had not written the book but had received considerable help from others, including Jacqueline Kennedy and Theodore Sorensen, a Senate staff member. The senator threatened libel and slander suits against those making such accusations.

In 1956, with Senator Kennedy's political star in rapid ascent, he was asked to give the nominating speech for presidential candidate Adlai Stevenson at the Democratic National Convention. Kennedy's speech sparked great enthusiasm among the delegates, not only for Stevenson but for Kennedy himself. When Stevenson threw the choice for vice president open to the convention, Senator Kennedy went after it and nearly won it. He was beaten on the second ballot by Estes Kefauver by just twenty votes. But the Stevenson-Kefauver ticket was easily defeated by President Eisenhower and his vice president, Richard M. Nixon.

"After the Democrats lost in '56 I began to think maybe I would run in '60," Kennedy recalled. It made perfect sense, for here was a young man who, at the age

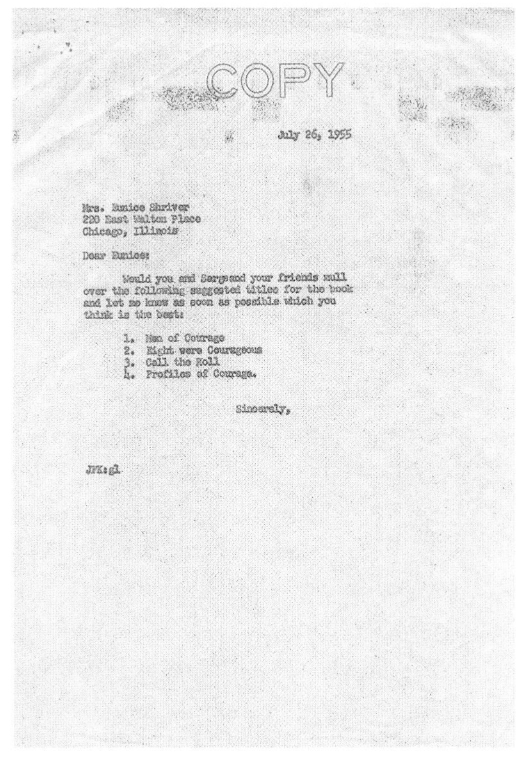

COPY

July 26, 1955

Mrs. Eunice Shriver
220 East Walton Place
Chicago, Illinois

Dear Eunice:

Would you and Sarge and your friends mull over the following suggested titles for the book and let me know as soon as possible which you think is the best:

1. Men of Courage
2. Eight were Courageous
3. Call the Roll
4. Profiles of Courage.

Sincerely,

JFK:gl

Searching for a title

Politics is a jungle – Torn between doing right thing & staying in office – between the local interest & the national interest – between the private good of the politician & the general good.

⊗ political Courage – Andrew Johnson sticking with Union in Tenn

General Awards.

Columbia University in the City of New York
NEW YORK 27, N. Y.
ADVISORY BOARD ON PULITZER PRIZES

May 7, 1957

Senator John F. Kennedy
Senate Office Building
Washington, D. C.

Dear Senator Kennedy:

I take very great pleasure in confirming the fact that the Trustees of Columbia University, on the nomination of the Advisory Board on the Pulitzer Prizes, have awarded the Pulitzer Prize in Biography or Autobiography, established under the will of the first Joseph Pulitzer, to you for "Profiles in Courage" for the year 1956.

In accordance with that award, I enclose the University's check for $500 as tangible evidence to you of the selection of your work.

With renewed congratulations, I am

Sincerely yours,

John Hohenberg

John Hohenberg
Secretary

JH/sl

Enclosure

Joseph P. Kennedy was a driven man. He was the product of immigrant parents who had come to America from Ireland in the middle of the nineteenth century to escape famine. Joseph Kennedy's father, P.J. Kennedy, was a tavern owner, successful enough—and his son bright enough—so that the boy went off to Harvard. But in the traditional Brahmin culture of old Boston, an Irish Catholic lad—whether a Harvard man or not—was unwelcome. The snubs he suffered were so painful that he would eventually move his family to New York.

Joseph Kennedy may not have been able to break into the Yankee social circles he coveted, but in business, where success came to those with brains, drive, and a daring spirit, Joe Kennedy excelled. He prospered as the owner of a sightseeing bus business, as a bank president, as the assistant manager of a shipyard. Soon his fortune mounted. As a Hollywood film producer, a Wall Street stock speculator, liquor importer, and financial consultant, he became one of the most successful businessmen in the country.

He also married well, choosing as his bride Rose Fitzgerald, the daughter of Boston mayor John "Honey Fitz" Fitzgerald. In all they would have nine children, five girls and four boys. Joe Kennedy demanded success of himself, in business and in politics as a major campaign adviser and fund-raiser for Franklin D. Roosevelt. When Roosevelt won, Joe Kennedy became chairman of the Securities and Exchange Commission and chairman of the U.S. Maritime Commission, and in 1938 he was appointed by Roosevelt to be the U.S. ambassador to Great Britain.

Joseph Kennedy Sr., by example, made clear that he expected success from his children as well, especially his sons. Joe and Rose Kennedy fostered an atmosphere of competitiveness within the family. There was a demand that whatever the children did—academics, sports, the arts—that they would drive themselves to excel. Slackers were frowned upon. Frequently, around the dinner table, issues of the day were discussed. The children, as they grew older, were expected to participate with intelligence and wit.

Joe Kennedy's wealth enabled the family to live well. They summered first in Hull, Massachusetts, on the south shore of Boston, and later in a magnificent, rambling home in Hyannis Port. In Bronxville, New York, where the family moved in 1927, when Jack was ten, there were cooks and servants, and a Rolls-Royce with a driver (which Bobby used for his paper route, until his parents found out about it). The children were sent to the finest schools and wanted for nothing.

of just thirty-nine, embodied the most intriguing combination of characteristics in the Democratic Party and perhaps in all of American politics at the time. He was a legitimate war hero and author of two books, one of which had just received the nation's highest literary award. He was the charismatic politician who had never lost an election, who had defeated the invincible Henry Cabot Lodge. He was a man of great wealth, a man with a demeanor of cool dispassion, married to a woman of uncommon elegance and glamour. He had about him an aura, a sense that he was a serious man; a man of accomplishment; a man who had been truly blessed; a man, as his father had put it, who could "go a long way"; a man perhaps capable of greatness.

The 1956 convention

WISCONSIN
HUMPHREY
ALL THE KENNEDYS
MAULDIN
©1960 St. Louis Post-Dispatch
"KEEP CIRCLING, KIDS. HE'LL THINK THERE ARE THOUSANDS OF US."

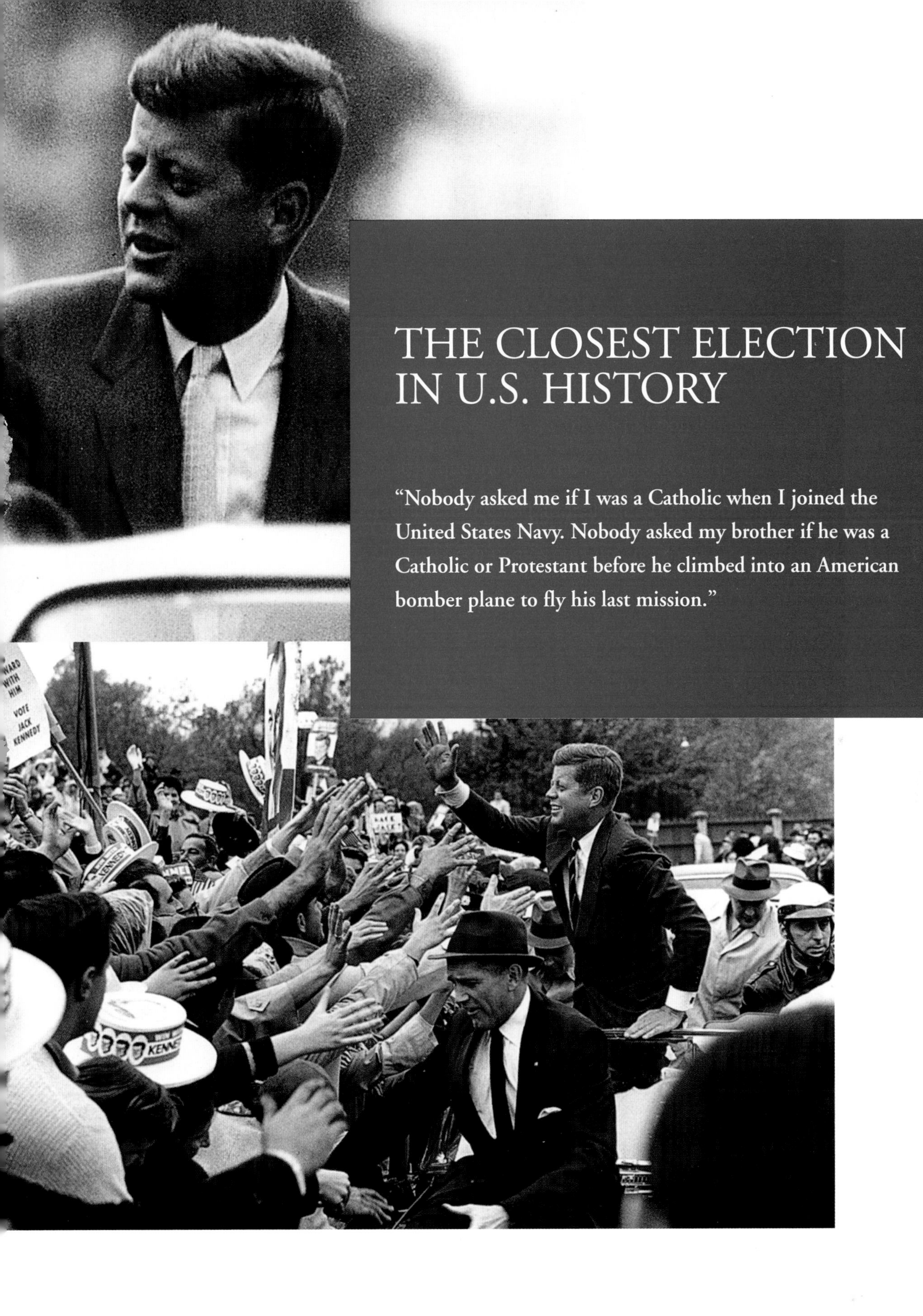

THE CLOSEST ELECTION IN U.S. HISTORY

"Nobody asked me if I was a Catholic when I joined the United States Navy. Nobody asked my brother if he was a Catholic or Protestant before he climbed into an American bomber plane to fly his last mission."

The archives of the John F. Kennedy Library offer eloquent and extensive testimony to the anti-Catholic bias that confronted Senator Kennedy in the presidential campaign of 1960. One bulging file after another preserves the collection of articles, pamphlets, letters, and resolutions attacking Kennedy because of his religion. In February 1960 one of Senator Kennedy's aides sought the counsel of a leading West Virginia politician concerning Kennedy's prospects in the state's pivotal presidential primary. The library preserves the memo in which the politician flatly predicted Kennedy would be "whipped" in West Virginia. Why? "Because the senator is a Roman Catholic."

Anti-Catholic literature from the 1960 campaign

Religious prejudice was nothing new to the Kennedys. Joe Kennedy had felt its sting in Boston back in the 1920s and before when Protestants excluded him from elite social circles. Joe Kennedy had solved that problem by packing up his family and moving to New York, where there were greater social and business opportunities and a more diverse culture. While the anti-Catholicism of 1960 was neither as virulent nor as overt as it had been during the 1920s, it was a powerful force nonetheless. Wisconsin, where Senator Kennedy would face his presidential campaign opponent Senator Hubert H. Humphrey of Minnesota, would be an important early test. And it would be particularly critical to watch how Kennedy fared in the state's predominantly Protestant congressional districts.

Senator Kennedy campaigned aggressively in Wisconsin, outspending Humphrey by a wide margin. Joseph P. Kennedy's wealth enabled his son to hire superior staffers, to create a stronger organization, and to lease his own private campaign airplane. On top of it all, perhaps in part because of it all, the press was charmed by Kennedy. It left Humphrey feeling like a "corner grocer running against a chain store."

Humphrey told the *Milwaukee Journal* that he sometimes read that his campaign was disorderly. "Thank God, thank God," he said. "Beware of these orderly campaigns. They are ordered, bought and paid for. We are not selling corn flakes or some Hollywood production."

Election night in Hyannis Port

Kennedy won the Wisconsin primary with 56 percent of the vote, carrying four predominantly Catholic congressional districts but losing in the four districts with Protestant majorities. Although the victory was important, the underlying message was that Protestant voters were not voting for him in anywhere near sufficient numbers for him to win a national election. Anti-Catholic bias had long been part of the American political culture and it was not just extremists who harbored the view that a Catholic should not be president. Many otherwise reasonable people feared Rome would hold undue sway over a Catholic president. New York governor Al Smith had run for president in 1928 and had been buried in an anti-Catholic landslide. That defeat had been so crushing that prominent Democratic Party leaders, many still active in 1960, remained fearful that a Catholic could not win a presidential election.

In politics one could not deal with religious bias by doing what Joe Kennedy had done three decades earlier—simply pulling up stakes and leaving. A candidate for president had to somehow confront the issue. West Virginia, where 95 percent of the population was non-Catholic, was an ideal place for a showdown. Senator Humphrey himself was a man of principle and tolerance, but his organizers in West Virginia were determined to make sure the state's voters kept religion in mind. They chose "Gimme That Old-Time Religion" as their campaign theme song. In the months leading up to the primary, Senator Kennedy held a comfortable lead in polls taken in West Virginia, but as the primary approached there was a significant shift against Kennedy. The candidate and his advisers were jarred by the numbers and groped for an explanation. They were told that when earlier polls had been conducted, few West Virginia voters had known Kennedy was Catholic. Now they did, and many didn't like it. In the face of declining poll numbers, the Kennedy forces redoubled their efforts, dispatching numerous family

Campaigning in West Virginia

members to campaign across the state. But as hard as the family worked, they encountered a persistent bias. "We've never had a Catholic president and I hope we never do," one voter said during the campaign. "Our people built this country. If they had wanted a Catholic to be president, they would have said so in the Constitution."

It was clear, as the primary approached, that the religious issue was affecting everything. Kennedy decided to meet it head-on by going on television to respond directly to the questions on the minds of many Protestants. The candidate appeared with Franklin D. Roosevelt Jr., who was Protestant and extremely popular in the state because of his beloved father. As Roosevelt posed questions, John Kennedy provided answers—well-crafted, reasonable answers. He spoke at length about the constitutional decision to separate church from state. He said that "when any man stands on the steps of the Capitol and takes the oath of office of president, he is swearing to support the separation of church and state; he puts one hand on the Bible and raises the other hand to God as he takes the oath. And if he breaks his oath, he is not only committing a crime against the Constitution, for which the Congress can impeach him—and should impeach him—but he is committing a sin against God."

Appearing on Face the Nation

After all he had been through in his young life, after all of the physical challenges and the difficulties of war and personal loss, John Kennedy said he could not believe that "I was denied the right to be president on the day I was baptized."

He took on the issue with a steely determination. "Nobody asked me if I was a Catholic when I joined the United States Navy," he said. "Nobody asked my brother if he was a Catholic or Protestant before he climbed into an

American bomber plane to fly his last mission." How could any reasonable person dispute an argument of such immense power? How could a war hero, the brother of a man who gave his life for his nation, be opposed purely on religious grounds?

This persuasive line of reasoning, along with money, put Kennedy in a strong position as primary day approached. The wealth of Joseph P. Kennedy had been a major factor in the success of his son's political career, and it would be a crucial asset in West Virginia. In the closing days of the primary, Kennedy's television commercials seemed omnipresent. Humphrey, in contrast, spent his own personal funds for a TV telethon that proved to be a comic disaster. He answered unscreened, hostile calls live, and he did so on a party line that was interrupted at one point.

Kennedy swept to an easy win in West Virginia, and when it was over he told reporters, "I think we have now buried the religious issue once and for all."

It would only be a matter of months before he would realize that had been nothing more than wishful thinking. But in the meantime West Virginia proved decisive in the race for the Democratic nomination. Humphrey withdrew from the contest and Kennedy went on to Los Angeles, where he was cheered as the party's nominee.

As Senator Kennedy arrived in Los Angeles to claim the Democratic nomination for president, there were signs of the turbulence in the world that he would soon have to face. Convention speakers talked of how the world had shrunk in the age of jet travel and proliferating nuclear weapons. The Congo was falling even as the Soviets gunned down a U.S. spy plane—a plane that was committing what the Soviets regarded as an act of war—with Soviet premier Nikita Khrushchev threatening retaliation if any more missions were flown over the USSR.

"I think the American people expect more from us than cries of indignation and attack," the nominee told the dele-

Thriving in the spotlight

gates. "The times are too grave, the challenge too urgent, the stakes too high to permit the customary passions of political debate. We are not here to curse the darkness, but to light the candle that can guide us through that darkness to a safe and sane future. As Winston Churchill said on taking office some twenty years ago: if we open a quarrel between the present and the past, we shall be in danger of losing the future. Today our concern must be with that future. For the world is changing. The old era is ending.

FOLLOWING PAGE: *An excerpt from Kennedy's speech to the Democratic National Convention in Los Angeles*

The Republican orators are fond of saying that experience in foreign policy is a major issue in this campaign. I agree. But the issue is not merely the experience of the candidates. It is the experience which the whole nation has gone through in the last eight years -- and what an experience it has been!

Never before ~~have we~~ has this country experienced such arrogant treatment at the hands of our enemy. Never before have we experienced such a critical decline in our prestige, driving our friends to neutralism, and neutrals to outright hostility. Never before have the tentacles of communism sunk so deeply into previously friendly

The old ways will not do. The problems are not all solved and the battles are not all won—and we stand today on the edge of a new frontier—the frontier of the 1960s, a frontier of unknown opportunities and perils, a frontier of unfulfilled hopes and threats."

The challenge upon breaking camp in Los Angeles was to create a coherent strategy for the general election, a strategy that understood the huge challenge of overcoming anti-Catholic bias. Meeting in Hyannis Port, the Kennedy team decided to focus on nine large states—New York, Pennsylvania, California, Michigan, Texas, Illinois, Ohio, New Jersey, and Massachusetts—with 237 of the 269 electoral votes needed to win. The strategy assumed that Kennedy's running mate, Senator Lyndon B. Johnson of Texas, would help win a few key southern states, including Texas.

Campaigning in Pennsylvania

John F. Kennedy was determined to set himself in sharp relief to the subdued style of the Eisenhower administration. While Republicans sought to portray Kennedy as too young and inexperienced, he sought to project an image of vigor and energy, style and verve. Over and over again throughout the campaign, he pledged to "get the country moving again." Not only would the faltering economy be reignited, but there would be a certain panache to the new administration. There was a palpable sense of excitement about Kennedy's campaign, about the man himself. He energized crowds that pressed in for a chance to shake his hand, to see him face-to-face.

As the party's nominee, he endorsed the Democratic platform calling for civil rights legislation, a program of medical care for the elderly, and an increase in federal aid to education. His most pointed rhetoric came on various foreign relations issues. He attacked Eisenhower and Nixon, charging that on their watch the Soviets had surged ahead of the United States in education, science, and technology. Most potent of all was his persistent accusation that a "missile gap" had developed between the U.S. and Soviet nuclear arsenals. Though Kennedy had been briefed by national security experts and knew that such a gap did not exist, he nonetheless saw it as a powerful political weapon and he raised the specter that the Russians had pulled ahead, that their stockpile was larger and more potent than America's.

"The enemy is the Communist system itself—implacable, insatiable, unceasing in its drive for world domination," the candidate said in a September speech. "This is not a struggle for supremacy of arms alone. It is also a struggle for supremacy between two conflicting ideologies: freedom under God versus ruthless, godless tyranny."

Republicans vehemently denied the existence of a missile gap, but Kennedy was determined to make his claim stick. And polls in the archives of the Kennedy Library showed it did. There was a broad perception in the land that this was no less than a life-or-death struggle. A Gallup poll during the campaign revealed that by a 47 percent to 33 percent margin Americans believed that the Soviets were ahead of the United States in the development of long-range missiles and rockets. Fully half of Americans polled believed war with the USSR was inevitable. The Soviet threat seemed so real that Gallup found seven in ten Americans favoring a law to require each community to build public bomb shelters.

While Kennedy sought to stay on the offensive, questions were raised that cast doubt on his preparedness for the White House. Many voters wondered whether Kennedy was elements

After discussions with ~~virtually~~ all of the Democratic Party leadership I have reached the conclusion that it would be the best judgment of the convention to nominate Senator Lyndon B. Johnson of Texas for the office of vice president.

His long experience dates back to the administrations of Franklin D. Roosevelt. On four separate occasions he has been chosen unanimously by his Senate colleagues for the Democratic leadership of that body. He has earned the endorsement of all 50 states through his vigorous and positive leadership.

I have said many times that in these days of great challenge, Americans must have a vice president capable of dealing with the grave problems confronting this nation and the free world. We need men of strength if we are to be strong and if we are to prevail and lead the world on the road of freedom ~~and liberty~~. Lyndon Johnson has demonstrated on many occasions his brilliant qualifications for the ~~highest~~ leadership we require today. I understand Governor David Lawrence of Pennsylvania will present his name in nomination, and that Senator Jackson of Washington and Gov. Williams [illegible] Illinois will second it. I hope the convention, ~~after careful deliberation~~, will nominate Senator Johnson.

Kennedy
September 6th 1962

too young and inexperienced to handle the presidency. A Gallup poll indicated that Americans believed that Nixon would be better able than Kennedy to deal with Khrushchev. Many voters expressed concern that Kennedy lacked experience in foreign affairs, a significant shortcoming in such perilous times. Nixon himself called JFK "rash" and "impulsive." Nixon talked of how he had engaged in debate with Khrushchev and of how "Mr. Khrushchev would make mincemeat" of Kennedy. Critics remarked that Kennedy had run only two enterprises of consequence in his life: a small Senate staff and PT-109, and the latter had been sunk.

The Kennedy campaign, in contrast, sought to portray the candidate as youthfully energetic rather than inexperienced. The campaign song was "A Man Who's Old Enough to Know But Young Enough to Do." More pointedly, the candidate responded to questions about his experience by

Fired up on the campaign trail in New York

saying that if "fourteen years in major elective office is insufficient experience, that rules out . . . all but a handful of American presidents, and every president of the twentieth century." And he sought to highlight the characteristics that voters liked about him—his intelligence and his energy.

Beyond talk of Kennedy's youth and inexperience, there remained a more fundamental question in the minds of many voters concerning his fitness for office, and that was the issue that Senator Kennedy thought he had answered once and for all in West Virginia: religion. One poll taken by an academic group found that Kennedy's Catholicism was mentioned more frequently than any other reason by those who planned to vote against him. In late summer, as the fall campaign was about to begin, the Kennedy forces heard ominous warnings about the religion issue, particularly from the Deep South. The very first week in September, the Reverend Norman Vincent Peale, an influential minister, brought together Protestant leaders to question publicly whether any Catholic could adequately fill the office of president.

During the West Virginia primary, Kennedy had confronted the issue head-on, and it had worked. He resolved to do the same again and accepted an invitation to address the Greater Houston Ministerial Association on September 12, just under two months prior to election day. He entered a room at the Rice Hotel packed with ministers in dark suits and grim expressions.

"I believe in an America where the separation of Church and State is absolute," he said, "where no Catholic prelate would tell the President (should he be a Catholic) how to act, and no Protestant minister would tell his parishioners for whom to vote, where no church or church school is granted any public funds or political preference; and where no man is denied public office merely because his religion differs from the President who might appoint him or the people who might elect him. That is the kind of America in which I believe. And it represents the kind of Presidency in which I believe—a great office that must be neither humbled by making it the instrument of any religious group, nor tarnished by arbitrarily withholding its occupancy from the members of any religious group. I believe in a President whose views on religion are his own private affairs, neither imposed upon him by the nation or imposed upon him as a condition to holding that office."

The question, he told the ministers, was "not what kind of church I believe in, for that should be important only to me, but what kind of America I believe in." He called for "an end to racial and religious discrimination in this country of ours."

As he answered questions, he was sincere and deft. Asked if he would accept the Church's direction in office, he was unequivocal in saying that to do so would be an "unfortunate breach—an interference with the American political system. I am confident there would be no such interference." He emphasized that he held a deep and abiding belief in religious freedom. When asked about the persecution of Protestant missionaries in the Catholic countries of Latin America—a topic about which these ministers were passionate—Kennedy answered: "One of the rights I consider to be important is the right of free religious practice, and I would hope that the President would stand for these rights all around the globe without regard to geography, religion, or. . ." His answer was cut short by sustained applause from the ministers. The hostility and tension had evaporated. So striking had been the turnaround among the ministers that the television networks broadcast excerpts from Kennedy's remarks the next day. And the Kennedy campaign used clips from it in paid commercials throughout the rest of the campaign.

During the ten-week general election campaign, John F. Kennedy traveled 77,000 miles to 237 cities in forty-four states. Although the stop in Houston would prove to be crucial, no campaign appearance could match in significance the series of televised debates between Kennedy and Nixon. Deservedly, they were destined to become part of American political lore, the most important political debates since Abraham Lincoln and Stephen Douglas came face-to-face in 1858.

Trailing in the polls, Kennedy challenged Nixon to debate the issues on television. Nixon's strategists opposed the idea, feeling their candidate had little to gain. But Nixon was confident in his experience, his grasp of the issues, and his skill as a debater. He accepted the challenge.

The first of the four encounters was set for September 26 in Chicago, aired in the time slot normally reserved for the *Andy Griffith Show*. Kennedy arrived in Chicago a day early with a team of advisers, including Ted Sorensen and Richard N. Goodwin, a Kennedy adviser and speechwriter. The team prepared fifteen pages of facts relating to a dozen subjects expected to come up. The morning of the debate, JFK was relaxed. He spoke to a union group before returning to his hotel for a nap and another review of his fact sheets.

Nixon's preparation did not go as smoothly. He had suffered a setback some weeks earlier when he had injured his knee, banging it on a car door while campaigning in North Carolina. Afterward Nixon had come down with a staph infection and been hospitalized from August 29 through September 9—a critical time at the outset of the fall campaign. After his release from the hospital, Nixon began a frantic sprint to make up for lost time. In the process he had grown exhausted and lost a good deal of weight. He appeared somewhat haggard. Rather than spending the day of the debate preparing, Nixon remained secluded in his hotel room. Even his own advisers could not reach him. To make matters worse, as he arrived at the studio for the debate, he again banged his knee on a car door. In the studio, small lights were set up to improve his appearance by illuminating the dark around his eyes. The lights were badly aimed, however, and failed to help.

During the debate Kennedy pressed his case that America could do better in recharging the economy, improving education, ministering to the poor and elderly, and fighting racial discrimination at home and tyranny abroad. Nixon agreed with many of Kennedy's goals but differed over how to achieve them. It was not so much what the candidates said, however, but how they *looked*. The film footage preserved by the John F. Kennedy Library reveals that on camera Nixon's skin was transparent and unattractive. His jowls

Television debates would prove to be pivotal

seemed to hang heavily. He sweat enough so that the Lazy Shave that had been applied to mask his heavy stubble began to run. Where Nixon appeared pale and uncertain, Kennedy appeared confident and informed. And the word "appeared" is crucial, for surveys showed that voters who listened to the debate on radio thought perhaps it had been about even. For those who saw it on television, however, there was no contest. And to Kennedy's eternal benefit, the television viewing audience included a staggering 70 million Americans, the largest political audience in U.S. history to that point. Historian Theodore H. White wrote of the vast audiences that watched the debates: "No larger assembly of human beings, their minds focused on one problem, has ever happened in history."

The impact of the debate was immediate and electrifying. After the first encounter the size of the crowds coming out to see Kennedy swelled and there was a mightier roar of approval. The debates revealed how each of the men performed under pressure. Kennedy's style was well suited to television. Perhaps most important, the debates demonstrated for all voters that Kennedy was not the woefully inexperienced young man the Republicans had tried to portray. By showing him cool under fire, the debates settled doubts about Kennedy's maturity and grasp of issues.

James Reston wrote in the *New York Times* that "there are those who feel that Mr. Nixon blundered it away by going on television with [Kennedy] and there may be something to this." On November 8, 1960, nearly 69 million Americans cast ballots in the presidential election. That night John F. Kennedy retreated to his home in Hyannis Port. During the course of the evening, he paced back and forth between his own home and that of his brother Robert, where Kennedy staffers were on phone lines to key states across the nation. At CBS an IBM 7090 whirred as it processed data from thousands upon thousands of precincts, but anyone expecting a quick verdict was bitterly disappointed. For the night dragged on and on, and still there was no definitive winner. Jacqueline Kennedy characterized the period between the time the polls closed and the results were in as "the longest night in history."

Showing the fatigue of the campaign days before the election

In the early morning hours, the Democratic nominee went to bed not knowing whether he had won or lost the presidency. But at 7:19 A.M. eastern time, John Fitzgerald Kennedy was declared the winner. At forty-three he would be the youngest U.S. president and the first Roman Catholic president ever. The final results showed that he won the closest election in the history of the United States: Out of nearly 69 million votes cast, Kennedy won by a margin of 118,555 votes—a mere two-tenths of a percent. He won 49.7 percent of the popular vote to 49.5 percent for Nixon. In the electoral college, however, Kennedy won by a comfortable margin, with 303 electoral votes to Nixon's 219. The disparity between the popular and electoral vote resulted from Kennedy victories in large industrial states rich in electoral votes. And though he won them by very small margins, the victor in any state receives all of that state's electoral votes. While Nixon took the farm states, Kennedy won New England, most of the Old South, and the crucial Mid-Atlantic states. Kennedy easily won among black and Jewish voters.

It was the ultimate irony, in a way, but John Kennedy won in part *because* he was Catholic. Many Catholic Democrats who had gone to Eisenhower in 1952 and 1956 voted for Kennedy. It is true that about 4.5 million Protestant Democrats defected to Nixon. But while Kennedy's Catholicism cost him more votes than it attracted, the Catholic votes he picked up were in key industrial states in the Northeast and Midwest, which proved decisive in garnering electoral votes.

Looking back on the campaign, Robert Kennedy considered his brother's speech to the ministers in Houston pivotal. As important as the appearance before the ministers

OPPOSITE PAGE: *The Invitation*

The Inaugural Committee

requests the honor of your presence

to attend and participate in the Inauguration of

John Fitzgerald Kennedy

as President of the United States of America

and

Lyndon Baines Johnson

as Vice President of the United States of America

on Friday the twentieth of January

one thousand nine hundred and sixty-one

in the City of Washington

Edward H. Foley

Chairman

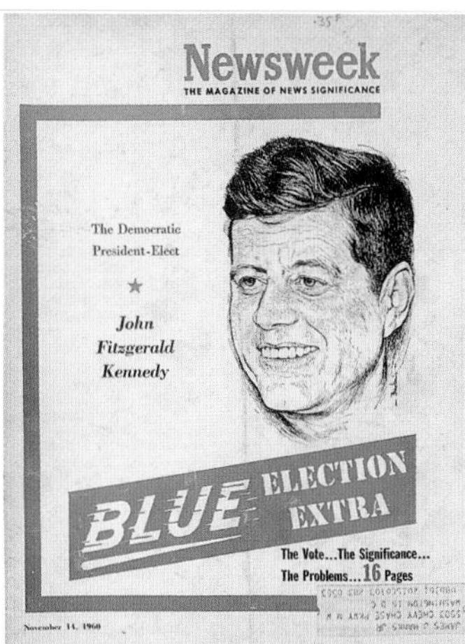

Coverage of the president-elect

had been, however, Robert Kennedy left no doubt as to what he considered the essential reason for his brother's victory: "I think that the most important part of the campaign was the debates," he said, "and, I think, the first debate particularly. [He] spent two days preparing for it. He went over questions and possible answers and over his opening statement. Nixon had built up, during the campaign, the idea that he was the only one who could stand up to Khrushchev, that a man of maturity was needed. That first debate indicated that not only could John Kennedy stand up to Nixon, he could better him, and so it destroyed the whole basis of Mr. Nixon's campaign in one night. I think that was extremely important also in giving [him] exposure to 70 million Americans, which he could never have received otherwise."

American politics had entered the television age, and John Fitzgerald Kennedy would be its first president. "It was TV more than anything else that turned the tide," the president-elect said the day after the election. In 1950 only 11 percent of American households owned television sets. But

FOLLOWING PAGES: *An early draft of the inaugural speech*

Today we sound the trumpet again, not as a call to arms, though arms we need – not a call to battle, though embattled we are, but a call to broader, more basic struggle against the common enemies of man – tyranny, poverty, disease, and war itself.

Can we forge against these enemies, a grand alliance north & south – east & west – that can ensure a more fruitful life for all men and women – Will you join in this historic struggle. To few generations has it been given in the long history of the world – to

ask not
what your country is going to do
for you - ask what you can do
for your country - My fellow
citizens of the world - ask not
what America will do for you - (or others)
ask rather what you [illegible] can do
for freedom. Ask of us -
the same high standards of
sacrifice and strength of heart
and soul that we seek from
you. ~~The alliance for~~
~~peace & progress will be forged~~

just a decade later an astonishing 88 percent of U.S. homes had TVs. Analysis of voters after the election found 57 percent of voters believed the debates had influenced their decision. An estimated 2 million votes for Kennedy came directly from the impact of the television debates.

Charges of vote fraud were raised against Kennedy in both Illinois and Texas. When Kennedy met Nixon in Florida after the campaign, Kennedy began by saying, "We still don't know who won the election." Kennedy was quite concerned that Nixon would call for a recount. That he did not showed considerable grace on his part.

John Kennedy had won, and suddenly he was confronted with the staggering responsibility that the job imposed. In a sense, the political campaign had pushed the reality of geopolitics into the background. The task had been to fight the political battles and try to win a campaign, a task very different from the challenge of leading a nation in time of peril.

PRESS CLUB LUNCHEON SPEECH, FRIDAY, JU

Some 170 years ago, when Gouverneur Morris w minister to Paris, a friend calculated that his here was roughly 6 hours in France for every one travelling here and back. Tomorrow, my own visi a close after only 3 days -- but it is an I, too, will have stayed here six times as long one round-trip flight.

I do not cite this comparison as proof of I cite it as proof of change. And the revolution in international travel and communication is among the least of ~~that~~ those changes which American foreign policy cannot ignore.

Among the earliest votes I cast in the Congress were those on behalf of the British Loan, the Truman Doctrine for Greece and Turkey, the Marshall Plan and later NATO. The United States

PERILOUS WORLD

"A cold winter."

After leading his loyal band of revolutionaries out of the countryside and marching boldly into Havana, Fidel Castro seized control of American mining, utility, and oil-refining facilities. For this, he was hailed by most Cubans, as he was reviled by Americans. It was one thing for leftist revolutions to sprout in Asia or Eastern Europe, but the existence of a Marxist regime a mere 90 miles from U.S. shores was far more troubling. The revolution drove thousands of Cubans, particularly businesspeople and landowners, from the country. Most fled to the United States, where they nursed an abiding hatred for Castro and plotted to take back their country.

During the presidential campaign, candidate Kennedy had been sharply critical of the Eisenhower administration for permitting "a Communist menace . . . only eight jet minutes from Florida." Everywhere he campaigned, voters were upset about Castro's takeover, about the existence of this revolutionary regime so close to the United States. In the final weeks of the campaign, Kennedy attacked Nixon for having supported a policy of "blunder, inaction, retreat, and failure." As a presidential candidate, Kennedy was free to criticize the handling of Cuba by U.S. officials. As president, however, Kennedy would have to take Cuba on as his own problem. The pressure on the president-elect to do something about Cuba began only nine days after the election, more than two months before his inaugural. On November 17 Allen Dulles, the CIA director, and Richard M. Bissell, CIA director of operations, flew to Palm Beach to brief Kennedy on the Cuban situation. The men informed the president-elect that under Eisenhower plans to mount an attack on Cuba had been in the works for some time. Under the tutelage of the CIA, Cuban exiles were training in Guatemala,

Fidel Castro

preparing for an assault. The plan was for the secret force of exiles, with U.S. support, to invade Cuba and attempt to spark a general uprising.

Kennedy shared the zeal of the exiles. In the fall he told aides, "There are two people I'd like to get out. Jimmy Hoffa and Castro. . . . Why doesn't he take off those fatigues? Doesn't he know the war is over?"

Dulles informed Kennedy that Russian military aid was pouring into Cuba and urged the president-elect to move quickly. When Kennedy said he needed to consider the options, Dulles replied, "That's understandable, Mr. President, but there isn't much time." Bissell and Dulles told Kennedy that the longer an invasion was delayed, the less likely it would be to succeed.

In private Dulles told members of the Senate that Cuba was "being rapidly absorbed into the Sino-Soviet bloc" and that it could soon become a "significant military power that could pose great security problems to the United States." By the eve of Kennedy's inaugural, Castro's regime supported revolutionaries in Panama, Nicaragua, the Dominican Republic, and Haiti, and U.S. intelligence officials feared the possibility that

CLASS OF SERVICE
This is a fast message unless its deferred character is indicated by the proper symbol.

WESTERN UNION
TELEGRAM
W. P. MARSHALL, PRESIDENT

SYMBOLS
DL = Day Letter
NL = Night Letter
LT = International Letter Telegram

The filing time shown in the date line on domestic telegrams is LOCAL TIME at point of origin. Time of receipt is LOCAL TIME at point of destination

BA204 SSH187
B NRA068 XV LONG GOVT PD=VJ NEWPORT RI 18 234P EDT=
THE HONORABLE JOHN F KENNEDY=
HYANNISPORT MASS=

I BELIEVE IT TO BE IN THE NATIONAL INTEREST, AND I HOPE IT CONFORMS TO YOUR DESIRE, FOR YOU, AS THE DULY DESINGATED CANDIDATE OF ONE OF THE MAJOR PARTIES FOR THE PRESIDENCY OF THE UNITED STATES, TO HAVE PERIODIC BRIEFINGS ON THE INTERNATIONAL SCENE FROM A RESPONSIBL OFFICIAL IN THE CENTRAL INTELLIGENCY AGENCY. ACTING ON THE ASSUMPTION THAT YOU LIKEWISE BELIVE SUCH BRIEFINGS T BE IN THE NATIONAL INTEREST, I HAVE ALREADY REQUEST THE DIRECTOR OF THE CENTRAL INTELLIGENCY AGENCY, ALLEN DULLE TO ARRANGE PROCEDURAL DETAILS WITH YOU OR WITH SOME DESIGNATED MEMBER OF YOUR STAFF.=

¶ BECAUSE OF THE SECRET CHARACTER OF THE INFORMATI THAT WOULD BE FURNISHED YOU, IT WOULD BE EXCLUSIVELY FOR YOUR PERSONAL KNOWLEDGE. OTHERWISE, HOWEVER, THE RECEIPT OF SUCH INFORMATION WOULD IMPOST NO RESTRICTION ON FULL AND FREE DISCUSSION.=

¶ ON THE ASSUMPTION THAT YOU DESIRE ME TO AUTHORIZ SIMILAR BRIEFINGS FOR THE HONORABLE LYNDON JOHNSON, YOUR VICE PRESIDENTIAL CANDIDATE, I AM OFFERING THEM TO HIM BY TELEGRAM TODAY, AND THESE BRIEFINGS WILL GO FORWARD UNLESS YOU ADVISE OF ANY VIEW TO THE CONTRARY THAT YOU MIGHT HAVE=

DWIGHT D EISENHOWER.

The briefings started early

The Communist threat was ever-present in the American media

one or more of those nations would follow the path of Cuba. In sum, Castro's Cuba was a destabilizing force in the backyard of the United States; a force that could not be tolerated. During a meeting with Eisenhower the day before the inauguration, Kennedy asked whether the United States should "support guerrilla operations in Cuba."

"To the utmost," Eisenhower replied. "We cannot let the present government there go on." Eisenhower told Kennedy that the CIA was doing a capable job in Cuba and it was Kennedy's responsibility to do "whatever is necessary."

In the days immediately after Kennedy's inaugural, the new president's top military and civilian aides reviewed the invasion plans initiated under Eisenhower. In a memo dated two weeks after the inauguration, February 6, 1961,

Khrushchev and an issue of Life

Kennedy asked, "Have we determined what we are going to do about Cuba? What approaches are we going to make to the Latin American governments on this matter? If there is a difference of opinion between the agencies I think [it] should be brought to my attention."

Two days later, McGeorge Bundy, special assistant to the president, told Kennedy that "Defense and CIA now feel quite enthusiastic about the invasion. . . . At the worst, they think the invaders would get into the mountains and at the best, they think they might get a full-fledged civil war in which we could then back the anti-Castro forces openly. State Department takes a much cooler view, primarily because of its belief that the political consequences would be very grave both in the United Nations and in Latin America."

Kennedy wanted to act, but he was not sure how. On March 11 Dulles and Bissell went to the White House and laid out a plan to attack Cuba with a series of air strikes and then to land an assault party near the small Cuban city of Trinidad. Kennedy didn't like it. "Too spectacular," he said. "It sounds like D-Day. You have to reduce the noise level of this thing."

The president wanted Castro out, but he wanted it accomplished so that it would appear that Cuban insurgents were wholly responsible for his ouster. As a result, throughout the operation's planning stages Kennedy whittled away at the size of the U.S. involvement. He told Bissell he did not want the world to know about "an invasion force sent by the Yankees." He dismissed the notion of an assault that would "put us in so openly, in view of the world situation." As proposed by the CIA the assault was "too much like a World War II invasion."

In response to the president's concerns, air support was canceled and naval support was pushed farther out to sea. Kennedy also wanted a more remote landing area and for the assault force to come ashore under cover of night. The president would not commit to military support to help establish a new government should the invasion succeed. "Under no circumstances!" he told his advisers. "The minute I land one Marine, we're in this thing up to our necks. I can't get the United States into a war and then lose it, no matter what it takes. I'm not going to risk an American Hungary. And that's what it could be, a . . . slaughter. Is that understood, gentlemen?"

The president was concerned about the international political ramifications if the United States were in any way involved in the assault. He worried that a U.S. misstep concerning Cuba might precipitate Soviet aggression in Berlin. This weighed heavily on Kennedy's mind. For an American president to lose Berlin would be a disaster, a humiliation throughout the world, and a crushing blow to U.S. relations with its European allies. And Kennedy understood that the world chessboard meant that U.S. aggression in Cuba could easily trigger Soviet aggression in Berlin. He worried also about the impact of an invasion in his own hemisphere, where Kennedy sought strengthened relations. He proposed the Alliance for Progress, which envisioned a ten-year, $209-billion program for economic and social improvement in Latin America. With the exception of Cuba, every Latin American republic signed on to the alliance. For the United States to storm ashore in Cuba would be viewed by other Latin American nations as the worst sort of bullying imperialism.

Though Kennedy was insistent that any U.S. involvement in the invasion be clandestine so that the United States could disown the action, the possibility of an invasion had become an open secret. Miami newspapers were reporting recruitment efforts among Cuban exiles, and a Guatemala City paper had months earlier reported that Cubans were training there for a possible U.S.-backed Cuban invasion.

While Kennedy was getting continuous pressure from the CIA to approve the plan, he sought the opinions of others. Two men were particularly critical of the idea, Dean Acheson, the former secretary of state under Truman, and Senator J. William Fulbright, chairman of the Senate Committee on Foreign Relations. On March 29, when Kennedy raised the topic, Acheson asked about troop strength. Kennedy said he expected Castro would mount a force of about 25,000 troops to oppose the assault army of 1,500. Acheson dryly replied that it was not necessary "to call Price, Waterhouse [accountants] to discover that 1,500 Cubans weren't as good as 25,000 Cubans."

Fulbright's response, while not as cutting, was more passionate. Fulbright worked with a member of his staff to write a memorandum to the president strongly opposing an invasion that he argued would violate the letter and spirit of the charter of the Organization of American States and "would be denounced from the Rio Grande to Patagonia as an example of imperialism." Fulbright added: "To give this activity even covert support is of a piece with the hypocrisy and cynicism for which the United States is constantly denouncing the Soviet Union in the United Nations and elsewhere. This point will not be lost on the rest of the world—nor on our own consciences." During a meeting the first week in April, Fulbright called the operation "wildly out of proportion to the threat" and a move that "would compromise our moral position in the world and make it impossible for us to protect treaty violations by the Communists."

But in the end Kennedy believed he had to act. The reassurances he received from the CIA and joint chiefs of staff outweighed the objections. The president thought he could not stand by and permit a Communist regime to flourish in Cuba.

Before dawn on April 17, 1961, 1,500 Cuban refugees went ashore at the Bay of Pigs with a mission to attract anti-Castro elements and incite a general uprising. In approving this mission, John Kennedy had relied heavily on intelligence reports that there were no Cuban military forces in the vicinity of the Bay of Pigs, that the Cuban populace would flock to the assistance of the invaders. But even as the rebels landed it became clear that something had gone quite wrong; intelligence reports had been disastrously inaccurate. Contrary to predictions, Cuban troops were in the area, and they were there in force. And there was not the slightest hint of an uprising against Castro. It was, in fact, John F. Kennedy's worst nightmare: slaughter. After just forty-eight hours, the rebels began their surrender. One hundred fourteen rebels had been killed and 1,189 captured.

The United States was humiliated before the world, the subject of widespread international condemnation. Anti-American demonstrations broke out in Moscow, Mexico City, Warsaw, Cairo, Tokyo, New Delhi, and elsewhere. Nikita

FROM THE DESK OF
HARRY S. TRUMAN

8-11-62

Privat & confidential.

Mr. President don't let these damned columnists and editorial writers discourage you.

In my opinion you are on the right track.

The President is just as great as the Congress—and really greater—when he exercises his Constitutional Prerogatives.

You are going through the same situations and troubles that Franklin Roosevelt, Abraham Lincoln and I had to meet.

Don't like to put myself in that high class—but I had a hell of a time.

You must 'em cuss 'em & give 'em hell and you'll win in 1964. H.S.T.

Khrushchev pounced on the opportunity to renounce the United States. "Mr. President," Khrushchev said, "you are taking a highly dangerous road. Think about it. . . . No one can have any commitment to defend rebels against the lawful government of a sovereign state like Cuba."

The opposite of what Kennedy had intended by the action occurred: Castro was strengthened. And if there had been any doubt about it before, there was none now: Cuba was entirely in the Soviet camp. For the young president, it was a crushing personal defeat. Not yet three months in office, he had made a decision that took a toll in human life, immeasurably strengthened Castro, and humiliated the nation. And it played directly to the fears some had had about Kennedy prior to the election, that he was too young, too inexperienced, too weak to lead a great nation.

On the day of the disaster, Jacqueline Kennedy accompanied her husband to the White House residence. Other than the 1954 back surgery in which he nearly lost his life, Mrs. Kennedy "had never seen him so depressed." He felt personally responsible for whatever hell the 1,200 rebels captured by Castro were facing in Cuban prisons. Soon after the debacle, the president met privately with his brother Robert. The president "kept shaking his head, rubbing his hands over his eyes. We'd been through a lot . . . together," Robert Kennedy recalled, "and he was more upset this time than he was any other."

Kennedy knew that his mistake had "unnecessarily worsened" relations with the Soviets, said his close adviser Theodore Sorensen, and it left the president feeling "depressed and lonely." Robert Kennedy said his brother "felt very strongly that the Cuba operation had materially affected . . . his standing as President and the standing of the United States in public opinion throughout the world. We were going to have a much harder role in providing leadership. The United States couldn't be trusted. The United States had blundered." The president told his brother that another incident like the Bay of Pigs would "destroy this administration."

Kennedy's friend Charles Spalding commented that in the aftermath of the invasion the Bay of Pigs "was the only thing on his mind. . . . Before the Bay of Pigs everything was a glorious adventure, onward and upward. Afterward, it was a series of ups and downs, with terrible pitfalls, suspicious everywhere, cautious of everything, questioning always."

Not long after the Bay of Pigs President Kennedy met with former vice president Nixon. "It really is true that foreign affairs is the only important issue for a president to handle, isn't it?" Kennedy said. "I mean, who gives a shit if the minimum wage is $1.15 or $1.25 in comparison to something like this?" In a private conversation, President Eisenhower bluntly told Kennedy that "the failure of the Bay of Pigs will embolden the Soviets to do something that they would not otherwise do."

Publicly, the president took full responsibility for the failure. Privately, he was determined to get to the bottom of what had gone wrong. One mistake he knew he had made was not including his most trusted confidant—his brother Robert—in on the deliberations. It was a mistake he would never repeat. Robert Kennedy, in fact, was one of the men the president assigned to investigate what had gone wrong. The results came as no great surprise to the president: He had been badly let down by the intelligence community, particularly the CIA. So shaken was his faith in these men that he said to his wife, "My God, the bunch of advisors we inherited. . . . Can you imagine being President and leaving behind . . . those people?"

Kennedy soon fired Dulles and Bissell. But he did not abandon the idea of harming Castro. The CIA engaged in a variety of covert schemes under Operation Mongoose, in which CIA agents attempted to sabotage Cuban sugar exports, damage Cuban imports, and run guns to opposition groups in Cuba. Many historians believe Operation Mongoose was initiated and supervised by the president and his brother Robert. The CIA also utilized organized crime groups that had been operating in Cuba before the revolution to try to kill Castro. Ironically, in the wake of the Bay of Pigs—the lowest point of his administration—the American people rallied to Kennedy's side, giving him a favorability rating of 82 percent, the apex of his popularity.

Just six weeks after the Bay of Pigs, President Kennedy was scheduled to attend the most important meetings of his young administration: two days of discussions with Soviet leader Nikita Khrushchev. Scheduled for June 3 and 4 in Vienna, the meetings were set so that the two men could discuss a number of pressing issues in person. In one sense the timing of the Vienna conference was unfortunate. The Soviets had just achieved another first in outer space: Cosmonaut Yuri Gagarin had completed an orbit of the earth, an event that suddenly stood as a symbol of Soviet superiority in science and technology. Communist insurgencies were also advancing in a number of nations around the world. The power and influence of the Communists had never been greater.

In the United States there was trepidation about the young president's sitting down with the veteran leader of the Soviets. Even a fellow Democrat, Senate Foreign Relations Committee chairman Fulbright, said there was "great nervousness" about Kennedy's meeting with Khrushchev.

But from President Kennedy's perspective there was another, more positive way to approach Vienna—as an opportunity for redemption, a chance to demonstrate that he belonged on the world stage. Kennedy worked diligently in preparing for the summit, discussing various topics with advisers and poring over briefing books that are preserved in the archives of the John F. Kennedy Library. "The president prepared more for those two talks than for anything in his life," said presidential press secretary Pierre Salinger. Kennedy was determined to impress Khrushchev that he was a man of substance, a confident man who did not need to turn to his advisers at each juncture in a conversation.

JFK was not in the best physical shape for the meetings. He was experiencing unusually severe back pain that required injections of Novocain, and he went so far as to employ more than one doctor at a time, receiving various treatments from each. Nonetheless, he was eager to discuss a number of topics, including Cuba and Berlin, Laos, space, and a nuclear test ban. Kennedy, in fact, had been led to believe that a breakthrough was possible on a nuclear test ban. A central stumbling block was the number of weapons inspections that would be permitted under a test ban agreement. The United States wanted as many as possible; the Soviets as few as possible. Word had reached Washington that Khrushchev might be prepared to agree to up to twenty inspections per year, a number that would all but assure approval on Capitol Hill of an agreement. The president knew that emerging from the summit with such a prize would be of historic significance. As much as anything, Kennedy wanted the opportunity to size up the Soviet chairman in person.

Almost from the start, however, it was clear that the chilly shadow of the Bay of Pigs was cast over the talks. Khrushchev, assuming from the beginning of the discussions that Kennedy would not be able to stand up to him, was extremely aggressive, convinced he could bully the young president.

The two men began their discussions in the elegant music room of the U.S. embassy in Vienna. Khrushchev prodded Kennedy on Cuba, saying that U.S. policies were pushing Castro inexorably into the arms of the Communists. The president countered that the Bay of Pigs was a

FOLLOWING PAGES: *Kennedy worked diligently to prepare for his meetings in Vienna with Khrushchev*

15

THE WHITE HOUSE

WASHINGTON

May 29, 1961

MEMORANDUM TO THE PRESIDENT:

Subject: Specific answers to your questions of May 29th relating to the USSR

First, on Berlin: At Tab A you will find some papers you asked for plus a general paper giving the State Department German desk views. The author, Hillenbrand, will be in Vienna, and is an able man. I'm asking him for better dope on the West German legal position.

I checked Walter Lippman's view with him again and it can be summarized as follows:

1. Stand absolutely firm on our right of access to Berlin and point out the extreme danger of any interference with it.

2. Avoid any actual negotiation at Vienna and aim to defer such negotiations beyond the German elections in September.

3. Do not foreclose the possibility that in return for detailed written guarantees of access to Berlin, we for our part might offer a practical de facto acceptance of the East German Republic (perhaps by associating it in the guarantee of access.) Lippmann thinks that without recognizing the GDR in formal terms, we can yet find ways of meeting what he thinks may be the fundamental Soviet impulse -- a need for security in Eastern Europe and the fear of what the post-Adenauer Germany might be like.

You will see that the differences between the Achesonians and Lippman do not turn on the specific issue of standing fast to defend our access to Berlin. They turn rather on whether there is any legitimate Soviet interest to which we can give some reassurance. At one extreme are those who feel that the central Soviet purpose is to drive us out of Berlin and destroy the European Alliance as a

TOP SECRET

consequence. On the other extreme are those who feel that if we think in terms of accommodation, we should be able to avoid a real crisis.

Secretary Rusk inclines to the harder view, while Thompson, as you know, believes we must explore the possibility of accomodation. But in practical terms, for Paris and Vienna, there may be no real difference between them. Rusk, for example, suggests that in talking with Khrushchev you may wish to begin by a strong statement on access to Berlin and go on to ask, as Thompson so often has in his conversations with Khrushchev, just what the Soviets really find so unsatisfactory, as a practical matter, in the present situation. There is a chance that you might draw him into some clearer statement of their purposes here. It's not a very good chance, though, because he will probably be cautious in tipping his hand, just as you must be.

My own summary is first that firmness on allied access to Berlin is indeed fundamental, and second that a willingness to hear the Soviet argument on other points will not be harmful. The one thing which must be avoided in both capitals is any conclusion that the United States is feeble on Berlin itself. What we might later be willing to consider with respect to such items as the Oder-Neisse line and a de facto acceptance of a divided Germany is matter for further discussion, and we ourselves might indeed have new proposals at a later time. (One which we like and Soviets do not is a free city of _all_ Berlin, and it's not unfair to mention that in Vienna if you want.)

Second, on the possibility of scientific proposals, I attach at Tab B a new and much improved memorandum from Wiesner's office. They put a priority on four possible areas of cooperation -- two in space and two in nuclear physics. Your own proposals to Khrushchev should probably not go further than to express your own interest and to suggest the matter be discussed at experts' meetings arranged through Ambassador Thompson. The practical process of scientific cooperation can be very difficult even with friends, and you will not want to get your own prestige hooked to specific negotiations that could be made sticky at any time by the Soviets.

result of Cuba's becoming a threat to U.S. security. Said Khrushchev: "Can six million people really be a threat to the mighty U.S.?" Couldn't the Soviets say the same thing about threats from Turkey and Iran, U.S. allies with American military bases?

Kennedy told Khrushchev that he wanted peace. But the president had long been deeply concerned about the possibility of miscalculation, and he told the Soviet leader that he thought there was a danger of war if either side were to miscalculate. In an effort to be direct, Kennedy said he had miscalculated on Cuba. Such talk angered Khrushchev. "Miscalculation! All I ever hear from your people and your news correspondents and your friends in Europe and every-

Kennedy and Khrushchev meet in Vienna

place else is that damned word miscalculation. . . . We don't make mistakes. We will not make war by mistake."

If there was to be war, by miscalculation or not, its most likely point of combustion was Berlin. Ever since the end of World War II, the Allies had shared custody of the city. East Berlin was under the Soviet umbrella; West Berlin, ruled democratically, was occupied by the Allies. This had become

---

Lighter Moments At Vienna Amid serious talk there was a lot of semi-serious joking. When Khrushchev called the USSR a young nation and the United States an old one, JFK quipped, "If you look across the table, you'll see that we're not so old." Khrushchev said to Kennedy, "We cast the deciding vote when you beat that son-of-a-bitch Nixon. We waited to release the spy pilots until after the election. So Nixon could not claim he knew how to deal with the Russians." At lunch after the meeting in Austria, Kennedy asked Khrushchev what the two medals that he wore were and Khrushchev answered, "Lenin Peace Prizes." "I hope you get to keep them," Kennedy replied. During a photo shoot, a photographer called out to Khrushchev, "Would you shake hands with Mr. Kennedy?" Nodding toward Mrs. Kennedy, Khrushchev replied, "I'd like to shake hands with her."

a huge problem for the Soviets, for they saw that each day 1,000 or more of the most skilled and educated workers from East Berlin crossed to the west in search of greater opportunities and an improved quality of life.

The United States and its allies wanted to settle the Berlin question via a plebiscite that would allow the city's residents to chose an all-German government if they so desired. The Soviets wanted no part of this, for they knew it would mean a loss of control. Khrushchev was direct. He told Kennedy that he wanted to settle the Berlin issue once and for all and he wanted to do it by the end of the calendar year. He was insistent: If the United States did not agree to a new deal, Khrushchev said he would sign a separate peace with East Germany. Such an agreement would put East Germans in control of access to West Berlin. The net result of such a move by the Russians would be to shut the Allies out of Berlin altogether.

"The USSR will sign a peace treaty with the German Democratic Republic [East Germany]," Khrushchev said. "The USSR would be prepared to join the U.S. in ensuring all the conditions necessary for preserving what the West calls West Berlin's freedom. However, if the U.S. rejects this proposal, the USSR will sign a peace treaty unilaterally and all right of access to Berlin will expire."

Kennedy was taken aback by the harshness of Khrushchev's position. It was a naked power play based on the Soviet belief that Kennedy was weak. The Russians believed that Kennedy had not mounted a full-scale assault on Cuba for fear of what the Soviets would do in Berlin, and thus Khrushchev was betting that if he boldly moved on Berlin, Kennedy would not risk nuclear war to defend the city. "Western Europe is vital to our national security and we have supported it in two wars," Kennedy said. "If we were to leave West Berlin, Europe would be abandoned as well. We cannot accept that."

Khrushchev was unrelenting. "The West has been saying that I might miscalculate, but ours is a joint account and each of us must see that there is no miscalculation. If the U.S. wants to start a war over Germany let it be so. If there is any madman who wants war, he should be put in a strait-jacket. So this is the Soviet position. The USSR will sign a peace treaty at the end of this year."

The president said that "this is an area where every President of the United States since World War II . . . has reaffirmed his faithfulness to his obligations. If we were expelled from that area and if we accepted the loss of our rights, no one would have any confidence in U.S. commitments and pledges. . . . If we were to accept the Soviet proposal, U.S. commitments would be regarded as a mere scrap of paper."

Khrushchev was so unreasonable at times that a joke was making the rounds in Vienna: "Khrushchev says, 'Give me your watch and your wallet.' Kennedy says: 'No.' Khrushchev says: 'Be reasonable. Let's negotiate. Just give me your wallet.'"

Khrushchev was clearly angry about Berlin and bluntly called it "the most dangerous spot in the world." He slammed his hand on the table in front of him and declared: "I want peace. But if you want war, that is your problem." Kennedy replied: "It is you, and not I, who wants to force a change."

The meetings ended on a somber note. Khrushchev insisted that "force would be met by force. If the U.S. wants war that's its problem. The decision to sign a peace treaty is firm and irrevocable and the Soviet Union will sign it in December if the U.S. refuses an interim agreement." Kennedy answered: "If that is true, it's going to be a cold winter."

Secretary of State Dean Rusk was stunned by the raw belligerence of the session. "In diplomacy, you almost never use the word war. Kennedy was very upset. . . . He wasn't prepared for the brutality of Khrushchev's presentation. . . . Khrushchev was trying to act like a bully."

The president was badly shaken by the experience. He left Khrushchev and went directly to a prearranged meeting with James Reston of the *New York Times.* Kennedy plopped into a chair and pulled his hat down over his eyes, sighing as he did so.

"Pretty rough?" asked Reston.

"Roughest thing in my life," Kennedy replied.

The president had gone to Vienna with the hope that he could regain his footing after the Bay of Pigs and perhaps achieve a breakthrough on a nuclear test ban. Not only had he not achieved either of those goals, but he left Vienna with the clear sense that Khrushchev would push the world to the brink and perhaps beyond in Berlin.

Deeply discouraged, Kennedy left Vienna and flew to London, where he met with Prime Minister Harold Macmillan. After the meeting the prime minister reported his impressions of JFK in a letter to the queen. "Rather stunned—baffled perhaps would be fairer," Macmillan wrote.

> Surprised by the almost brutal frankness of the Soviet leader. The Russians are (or affect to be) 'on top of the world.' They are now no longer frightened of aggression. They have at least as powerful nuclear forces as the West. They have a buoyant economy and will soon outmatch Capitalist society in the race for material wealth. . . .
>
> The President was completely overwhelmed by the ruthlessness and barbarity of the Russian Chairman. It reminded me in a way of Lord Halifax or Neville Chamberlain trying to hold a conversation with Herr Hitler. For the first time in his life Kennedy met a man who was impervious to his charm.

After Vienna there was no letup to the pressure of international events. Suddenly the talk of Vienna became the reality of confrontation in Berlin. Suddenly Berlin became the epicenter of the cold war—as Khrushchev put it, the most dangerous place on earth. If war were to break out, Berlin would be the most likely place. Khrushchev's threat to sign a treaty with the East Germans canceling the prevailing Berlin governance—including occupation rights for the Allies—would mean that access by the Allies to West Berlin would be blocked. This Kennedy would not accept. Berlin would now test the president's vow that the United States would "pay any price, bear any burden, meet any hardship, support any friend, oppose any foe to assure the survival and success of liberty." For at stake was nothing less than solemn commitments the United States had made to the defense of West Berlin, to ensuring freedom.

Kennedy's answer to Khrushchev's threat concerning Berlin came in a television address to the nation the evening he returned home from his European trip. As he prepared for his speech, Kennedy sought some statistics. He wanted to know how many Americans would die in an all-out nuclear exchange with the USSR. Without fallout shelters, about 79 million would perish, he was told. With a program of fallout shelters that number would fall to about 50 million. He asked about the number in the event a single enemy missile hit near a major city. Six hundred thousand, he was told. "That's the total number of casualties in the Civil War," he said, "and we haven't gotten over that in a hundred years."

Kennedy told columnist Joe Alsop that he thought there was a one-in-five chance of a nuclear exchange. As the president addressed the nation, the gravity of the Berlin situation was clear in both his manner and words. He said that the meetings with Khrushchev had been "a very sober two days" but that the discussions were "immensely useful." Striking his favorite theme, Kennedy said that the talks had lessened the possibility of a "dangerous misjudgment on either side."

In this respect something had been accomplished at Vienna. The two men had actually met face-to-face and begun to establish a relationship. And having established a relationship of sorts would prove critical in a later showdown.

The president immediately sought an increase in the defense budget and began pushing civil defense programs. Across the nation Americans were encouraged to build bomb shelters. Fallout shelters were planned in public and private places, food and water ordered for storage deep in train stations. Kennedy wanted the Soviets to take him seriously. He wanted them to believe that if they moved on Berlin, he would counter. He wanted them to believe that he would fulfill U.S. commitments no matter the price. In the parlance of the time, he wanted them to believe that he was prepared to launch a nuclear attack, to choose "holocaust over humiliation." The nation prepared as the president issued a message that the unthinkable was now possible.

Days after Kennedy's speech the Soviets released a threatening memorandum that had been kept secret since the Vienna meetings. The memorandum revealed to the world that the Soviets had set a Berlin deadline for year's end. To the United States, this was an act of provocation, a sure sign that the Soviets were ready for confrontation, that war was possible.

John F. Kennedy had learned his lesson from the Bay of Pigs. With Berlin he left nothing to underlings; he was in charge. He was so immersed in Berlin that a State Department official branded the president the department's Berlin desk officer. In early July Khrushchev, citing the increase in U.S. defense spending, announced a one-third increase in Soviet defense spending and suspension of the partial demobilization of the Red Army. Kennedy debated whether to proclaim a national emergency. The president approved a secret directive to NATO. "It must be clearly understood that tactical and strategic nuclear weapons would be used when it becomes necessary to do so to avoid being driven from the Continent." The truth was that the United States had few contingency plans in place that envisioned anything less than a massive assault on the Communist world—no planned military response short of nuclear weapons. McGeorge Bundy's analysis was that "the only plan the United States had for the use of strategic weapons was a massive, total, comprehensive, obliterating attack upon the Soviet Union. An attack on the Warsaw Pact countries and Red China [with] no provision for separating them out. An attack on everything Red."

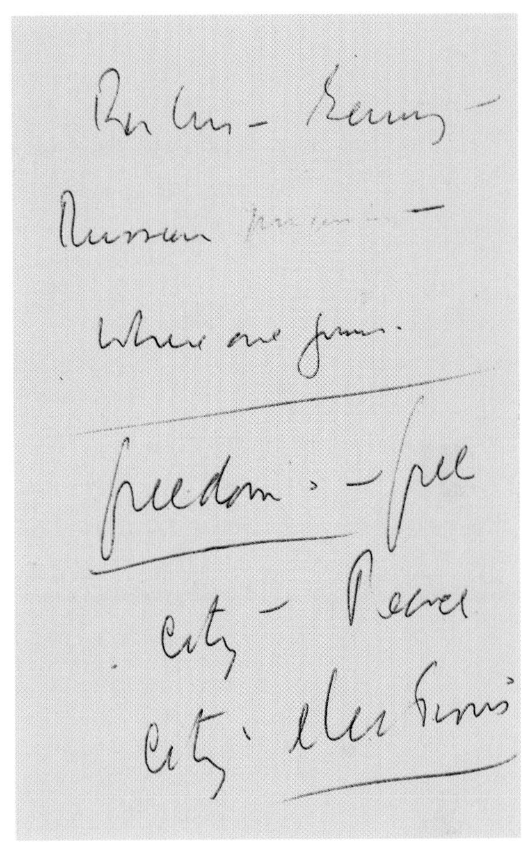

Kennedy's notes

JFK and Khrushchev were unyielding. Both talked of calling up reservists, mused about the perils of nuclear war, stepped up military spending. Throughout June and July, the two powers seemed to move ever closer to war. On July 25 Kennedy went on national television to discuss Berlin again. The president said that the Soviet leader "intends to bring to an end, through the stroke of a pen, first our legal rights to be in West Berlin—and secondly our ability to make good on our commitment to the two million free people in that city." Kennedy said that "we have given our word that an attack upon the city will be regarded as an attack upon us all. . . . We cannot and will not permit the Communists to drive us out of Berlin."

He listed the steps he was taking:

> One, I am tomorrow requesting the Congress for the current fiscal year an additional $3 billion 247 million of

Accordingly, I am now taking the following steps:

(1) I am tomorrow requesting of the Congress for the current fiscal year an additional $3,247,000,000 of appropriations for the military forces.

(2) To fill out our present Army Divisions, and to make more men available for prompt deployment, I am requesting an increase in the Army's total authorized strength from 875,000 to approximately 1 million men.

(3) I am requesting an increase of 29,000 and 63,000 men respectively in the active duty strength of the Navy and Air Force.

(4) To fulfill these manpower needs, I am ordering that our draft calls be doubled and tripled in the coming months; I am asking the Congress for authority to order to active duty certain ready reserve units and individual reservists, and to extend tours of duty; and, under that authority, I am planning to order to active duty a number of air transport squadrons and Air National Guard tactical air squadrons, to give us the airlift capacity and protection we may need. Other reserve forces will be called up if needed.

(5) Many ships and planes once headed for retirement are to be retained or reactivated, increasing our tactical airpower and our sea lift, airlift, and anti-submarine warfare capability. In addition, our strategic air power will be increased by delaying the deactivation of B-47 bombers.

(6) Finally, some $1.8 billion -- about half of the total sum -- is needed for the procurement of non-nuclear weapons, ammunition and equipment.

The details on all these requests will be presented to the Congress beginning tomorrow. Subsequent steps will be taken to suit subsequent needs. Comparable efforts for the common defense are being discussed with our NATO allies. For their commitment and interest are as precise as our own.

But let me add that I am well aware of the fact that many American families will bear the burden of these requests. Studies or careers will be interrupted; husbands and sons will be called away; incomes will be reduced. But these are burdens which must be borne if freedom is to be defended -- Americans have willingly borne them before -- and they will not flinch from the task now.

IV

We have another sober responsibility. To recognize the possibilities of nuclear war in the missile age, without our citizens knowing what they should do and where they should go if bombs begin to fall, would be a failure of responsibility. In May, I pledged a new start on Civil Defense. Last week, I assigned, on the recommendation of my Civil Defense director, basic responsibility in this program to the Secretary of Defense, to make certain it is administered and coordinated with our continental defense efforts at the highest civilian level. Tomorrow, I am requesting of the Congress new funds for the following immediate objectives: to identify and mark space in existing structures -- public and private -- that could be used for fall-out shelters in case of attack; to stock those shelters with food, water, first-aid kits, tools, sanitation facilities and other minimum essentials for survival; to increase their capacity; to improve our aid-raid warning and fall-out detection systems, including a new household warning system now under development; and to take other measures that will be effective at an early date to save millions of lives if needed. In addition, new Federal buildings will include space suitable for fall-out shelters, as well as normal use.

MORE

> appropriations for the Armed Forces. Two, to fill out our present Army divisions, and to make more men available for prompt deployment, I am requesting an increase in the Army's total authorized strength from 875,000 to approximately one million men. . . .
>
> Three times in my lifetime our country and Europe have been involved in major wars. In each case serious misjudgments were made on both sides of the intentions of others, which brought about great devastation.
>
> Now, in the thermonuclear age, any misjudgment on either side about the intentions of the other could rain more devastation in several hours than has been wrought in all the wars of human history.

He spoke of fallout shelters, of providing them with food and other "essentials for survival." This language was stunning, for it was the first time an American president had ever so bluntly warned the people to prepare for a nuclear exchange. Khrushchev read the speech as nothing less than a declaration of "preliminary war" on the Soviet Union.

The number of refugees streaming from East to West Berlin rose dramatically. Thirty-thousand fled in July alone. East Germany began to restrict exit, but that accelerated the exodus. The Soviets and the East Germans were desperate to stop the migration of people. On August 12 they acted. Communist Party brigades and East German soldiers blocked the border between East and West Berlin, shutting down roads, subways, elevated lines. On the 13th, shortly after midnight, East German troops occupied most of the crossing points on the East Berlin side of the border. They installed roadblocks, barricades, and barbed wired along the 27-mile border. Four days later crews began erecting the infamous concrete barrier, the Berlin Wall.

Kennedy was vacationing in Hyannis Port when he was

informed that the wall was being constructed. He ordered Secretary of State Rusk to proceed with his plans for the day—going to a baseball game. For his part, Kennedy intended to go sailing. Kennedy's goal was to do nothing that would elevate the construction of the wall to a dangerous international incident. For more than a week after the border between East and West Berlin was shut down, Kennedy made no public comment. As abhorrent as it might have been to Kennedy, he saw the wall as lessening the chances for confrontation in Berlin. The president's view was that Khrushchev had "closed the border to head off a confrontation, not cause one." He told advisers in private, "Why should Khrushchev put up a wall if he really intended to seize West Berlin? There wouldn't be any need of a wall if he occupied the whole city. This is his way out of his predicament. It's not a very nice solution, but a wall is a hell of a lot better than a war."

Early manifestation of the Berlin Wall

AD LIBBING POINTS:

1. Hit hard on theme of interdependence. Every one of the Allies on this North Atlantic Treaty Organization is necessary to the others.

2. Repeat the theme of confidence in the West — anti-Spenglerism. The West is on the rise. All we have to do is hold together. NATO is the fundamental organization for this holding together.

3. Note of confidence in the future of the North Atlantic Alliance.

4. It is appropriate that the North Atlantic Council be located in Paris. My visit with President de Gaulle — about which I am very much pleased — has as one main purpose: the strengthening of the Alliance, of our bonds with France. For I am convinced that the strength of the relations between my country and France and the strengthening of the Alliance are in the same direction.

5. The President might reassure the Council that if Mr. Rusk does not get here next Monday, a responsible officer will brief the Council on the President's meeting with Khrushchev.

6 Scientific discussion with Khruschev

Dear Mr.President,

At present I am on the shore of the Black Sea. When they write in the press that Khrushchov is resting on the Black Sea it may be said that this is correct and at the same time incorrect. This is indeed a wonderful place. As a former Naval officer you would surely appreciate the merits of these surroundings, the beauty of the sea and the grandeur of the Caucasian mountains. Under this bright Southern sun it is even somehow hard to believe that there still exist problems in the world which, due to lack of solutions, cast a sinister shadow on peaceful life, on the future of millions of people.

But as you will fully understand, I cannot at this time permit myself any relaxation. I am working, and here I work more fruitfully because my attention is not diverted to routine matters of which I have plenty, probably like you yourself do. Here I can concentrate on the main things.

His Excellency
Mr.John F.KENNEDY,
President of the United States of America
Washington, D.C.

With construction of the wall, West Berliners feared they might be abandoned by the Allies, consumed by the Communists. Kennedy dispatched two distinguished representatives to Berlin to demonstrate U.S. commitment—Vice President Johnson and General Lucius D. Clay, a man beloved by the Germans for his heroic role in the airlift crisis of 1948–1949. JFK accelerated the military buildup at home and sent a battle group of 1,500 troops down the autobahn from West Germany into Berlin. Vice President Johnson along with throngs of West Berlin citizens weeping tears of joy greeted the forces as saviors. Johnson told the crowd: "All the resources of the mightiest nation in the world stand behind you."

Construction of the wall halted the flow of people out of the eastern sector, thus solving the Soviet's most pressing problem in Berlin. Tensions eased throughout the summer but then heightened again in September when the Russians tested three hydrogen bombs over Siberia. Kennedy considered the testing an act of betrayal by Khrushchev. After three successive Soviet tests, Kennedy felt he had no choice but to order resumption of U.S. nuclear testing, albeit with a critical difference: The Soviets were testing their weapons in the atmosphere, while the United States was doing it in laboratories and underground.

In mid-October Khrushchev took a critical step that significantly improved the atmosphere in Berlin. He delivered a speech in which he said that Western powers were showing some understanding of the situation and were inclined to seek a solution to the German problem and the issue of West Berlin. Therefore, Khrushchev said, "we shall not insist on signing a peace treaty absolutely before December 31, 1961." In the end, the wall notwithstanding, Kennedy had emerged triumphant from the battle of Berlin. The United States and its allies had demonstrated resolve. Kennedy had stood his ground. He had preserved the freedom of West Berlin and avoided nuclear war.

The White House
Washington

1961 DEC 14 PM 9 54

WB215 PD

AV NEW YORK NY 14 413P EST

THE PRESIDENT

THE WHITE HOUSE

GRAVE CONCERN AND CONSIDERABLE SKEPTICISM AND SOME RESENTMENT HAVE ARISEN ACROSS THE COUNTRY SINCE THE NOVEMBER 27 ANNOUNCEMENT THAT AN AGREED-UPON DRAFT WAS READY OF AN ORDER PROHIBITING RACIAL DISCRIMINATION IN FEDERALLY ASSISTED HOUSING. THERE IS REAL FEAR THAT UNLESS IT IS ISSUED AT THIS TIME IT MAY NOT BE ISSUED. THE MILLIONS WHOSE HIGH HOPES WERE ENCOURAGED BY THE CLEAR COMMITMENT OF THE ADMINISTRATION FEEL THAT THE REDEMPTION OF A 1960 PROMISE SHOULD NOT REST UPON ANTICIPATED DEVELOPMENTS IN 1962. IF THE HOLIDAY CANNOT BE COMPLETELY MERRY FOR ALL OF US BECAUSE OF THE THREATS TO PEACE IT CAN BE MADE AN OCCASION FOR DEEPLY FELT THANKS AND QUIET JOY ON THE PART OF A SUBSTANTIAL SEGMENT OF THE POPULATION BY AN ACTION OF A PRESIDENT WHO HAS DEMONSTRATED HIS ALLEGIANCE TO THE BETHLEHEM TRUTH THAT THERE MUST BE ROOM AT THE INN

ROY WILKINS.

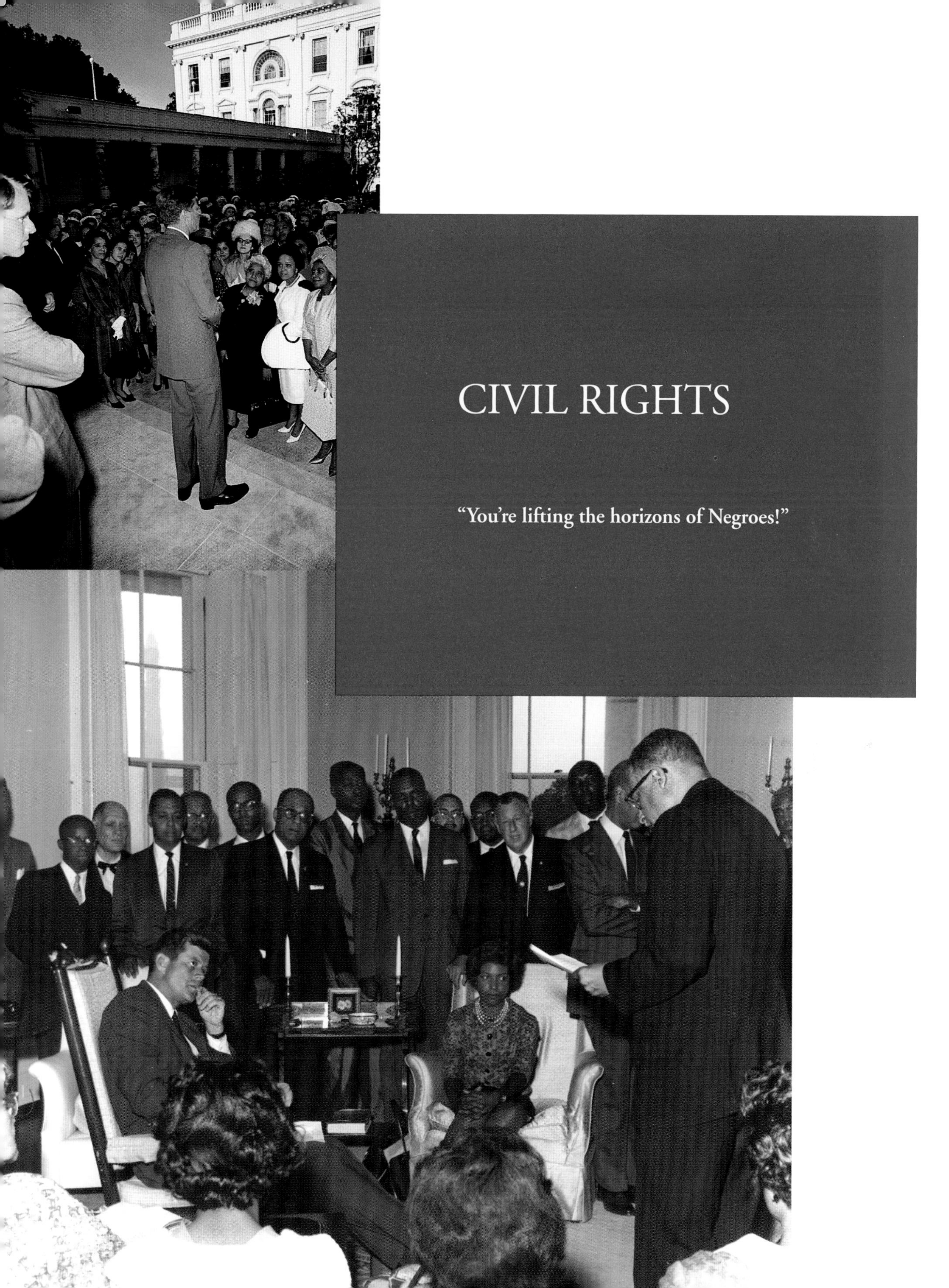

CIVIL RIGHTS

"You're lifting the horizons of Negroes!"

Coretta Scott King feared her husband would be murdered. When Martin Luther King Jr. was sentenced to six months hard labor for a traffic violation, Mrs. King believed he would tumble into the recesses of the Georgia state penal system never to come out alive. Her fears were shared by many American Negroes. Mrs. King was five months pregnant at the time, and though she had lived with the fright and peril of having a husband who was emerging as the most prominent civil rights advocate in the nation, this was the penal system of the state of Georgia. King's sentence came during the third week of October 1960, a mere two weeks before a presidential election that was expected to be tight and in which both parties were competing for the Negro vote. Some of Kennedy's campaign workers had been urging the candidate to make a gesture of some kind that would appeal to Negro voters. His brother-in-law Sargent Shriver suggested that Kennedy call Mrs. King and comfort her.

"Negroes don't expect everything will change tomorrow, no matter who's elected," said Shriver. "But they do want to know whether you care. If you telephone Mrs. King, they will know you understand and will help. You will reach their hearts and give support to a pregnant woman who's afraid her husband will be killed."

"Get her on the phone," Kennedy said, and Shriver did.

"I want to express to you my concern about your husband," Kennedy told Mrs. King. "I know this must be very hard for you. I understand you are expecting a baby and I just wanted you to know that I was thinking about you and Dr. King. If there is anything I can do to help, please feel free to call on me."

Mrs. King was deeply moved by the call, and she said so publicly. Her father-in-law, the Reverend Martin Luther King Sr., an influential voice among Negroes, switched from Nixon to Kennedy on the strength of that call alone. "I had expected to vote against Senator Kennedy because of his religion," said the senior King. "But now he can be my president, Catholic or whatever he is. It took courage to call my daughter-in-law at a time like this. He has the moral courage to stand up for what he knows is right. . . . I've got all my votes and I've got a suitcase and I'm going to take them up there and dump them in his lap." The Reverend Ralph David Abernathy, a leading civil rights activist, exulted over the call, saying that Kennedy had done "something great and wonderful."

Rev. Martin Luther King and Coretta Scott King

Robert Kennedy was furious when he later heard about the call, for he feared it was a grave political miscalculation that could cost his brother votes in key southern states. But when word of the call reached the press, the reaction of Negroes was one of overwhelming support for JFK. (Seeing this, Robert Kennedy went so far as to call the judge in the case and ask for King's release.)

Dr. King himself, upon his triumphant release from prison, said, "I am deeply indebted to Senator Kennedy, who served as a great force in making my release possible. It took a lot of courage for Senator Kennedy to do this . . . for him to be that courageous shows that he is really acting upon principle and not expediency."

The call to Mrs. King would prove to be pivotal, for in the closest presidential election in history, Kennedy carried an overwhelming 70 percent of the Negro vote.

When John F. Kennedy entered the White House, the expectations for what he would accomplish on civil rights could hardly have been higher. Civil rights leaders expected the new president to deliver quickly on his campaign promise to eliminate discrimination in federally subsidized housing. They expected the president to support comprehensive civil rights legislation. They expected, in

American Justice on Trial

MRS. MARTIN LUTHER KING:

"It certainly made me feel good that he called me personally and let me know how he felt. Senator Kennedy said he was very much concerned about both of us. He said this must be hard on me. He wanted me to know he was thinking about us and he would do all he could to help.

"I told him I appreciated it and hoped he would help. I had the feeling that if he was that much concerned he would do what he could so that Mr. King would be let out of jail.

"I have heard nothing from the Vice President or anyone on his staff. *Mr. Nixon has been very quiet."*

REV. MARTIN LUTHER KING, SR.:

"I had expected to vote against Senator Kennedy because of his religion. But now he can be my President, Catholic or whatever he is.

"It took courage to call my daughter-in-law at a time like this. He has the moral courage to stand up for what he knows is right. He has shown his sympathy and concern and his respect for the Constitutional rights of all Americans.

"I've got all my votes and I've got a suitcase and I'm going to take them up there and dump them in his lap."

REV. RALPH ABERNATHY

President, Montgomery Improvement Association; Secretary-Treasurer, Southern Christian Leadership Conference

"I earnestly and sincerely feel that it is time for all of us to take off our Nixon buttons. I wish to make it crystal clear that I am not hog-tied to any party. My first concern is for the 350-year long struggle of our people.

"Now I have made up my mind to vote for Senator Kennedy because I am convinced he is concerned about our struggle.

"Senator Kennedy did something great and wonderful when he personally called Mrs. Coretta King and helped free Dr. Martin Luther King. This was the kind of act I was waiting for. It was not just Dr. King on trial—America was on trial.

"Mr. Nixon could have helped, but he took no step in this direction. It is my understanding that he refused even to comment on the case.

"I learned a long time ago that one kindness deserves another. Since Mr. Nixon has been silent through all this, I am going to return his silence when I go into the voting booth.

"Senator Kennedy showed his great concern for humanity when he acted first without counting the cost. He risked his political welfare in the South. We must offset whatever loss he may sustain.

"He has my wholehearted support because

Dr. Martin Luther King, Jr.

"I am deeply indebted to Senator Kennedy who served as a great force in making my release possible. It took a lot of courage for Senator Kennedy to do this, especially in Georgia. For him to be that courageous shows that he is really acting upon principle and not expediency. He did it because of his great concern and his humanitarian bent.

"I hold Senator Kennedy in very high esteem. I am convinced he will seek to exercise the power of his office to fully implement the civil rights plank of his party's platform.

"I never intend to be a religious bigot. I never intend to reject a man running for President of the United States just because he is a Catholic. Religious bigotry is as immoral, un-democratic, un-American and un-Christian as racial bigotry."

Negro leaders were effusive in their praise of Kennedy after his phone call to Mrs. King

short, that Kennedy's actions would show that he was on their side, that their cause was his. His sympathies certainly lay with Negro Americans. He had been president for barely an hour when he watched the inaugural parade and bridled at the absence of any Negroes in the detachment marching from the Coast Guard Academy. "Call the commandant," the president snapped, "and tell him I don't ever want to see that happen again."

But when John F. Kennedy took the oath of office, he was almost entirely preoccupied with the danger of the world, with the Communist threat and the possibility of nuclear confrontation, with the very survival of the nation. No other issue—not civil rights, not taxes, not the economy generally—even came close to capturing Kennedy's time and attention.

Practical political considerations also played a critical role in the president's thinking on civil rights. Having served in both the House and Senate, Kennedy fully understood the political realities he faced. Though his own party held a sixty-five-to-thirty-five-seat majority in the Senate and a 263-to-174 majority in the House, he knew from experience that real congressional power lay with conservative southern committee chairmen in the Senate and a coalition of Republicans and southern Democrats in the House. While he was pushed hard and early by civil rights leaders to propose comprehensive civil rights legislation, Kennedy knew he needed the full support of key House and Senate members to pass legislation for a military buildup, for more weapons systems. The president had a general timetable in mind for civil rights: He would take some steps during his first term, but then, after a solid reelection, he would be in a position to make significant strides.

He also did not believe the country was quite ready for rapid change and did not want to be perceived among key southerners on Capitol Hill or among the American people as prematurely pushing a civil rights agenda. "First things first," said presidential confidante Theodore Sorensen in the early days of the administration. "He concentrates on what he has to concentrate on." And that meant the international situation, particularly Cuba, Berlin, Khrushchev, and the growing Communist threat. Civil rights leaders were sympathetic to the president's position. They understood that the world was a dangerous place and knew that Kennedy had to focus a good deal of attention on the world stage. Still, they wanted progress, and when little came in the early days, they were frustrated. Very soon after the election, it became clear to Roy Wilkins, head of the NAACP and one of the most prominent civil rights leaders of the time, that "Kennedy had no intention of beginning his new administration with a full-scale legislative program for civil rights."

Roy Wilkins

Kennedy urged patience. Kennedy Library records contain the blunt reply to the president from baseball great Jackie Robinson, a Republican then in private business. "I would like to be patient, Mr. President," Robinson wrote to Kennedy just a few weeks into the new administration, "but patience has [cost] us years in our struggle for human dignity." When leaders from the 1961 NAACP convention in Washington were invited to meet with the president in the White House, they asked that he propose and support comprehensive civil rights legislation. But the president said no. "We remain convinced that legislation is not the way," he said. "At least it is not advisable at this time."

Wilkins and other leaders were disappointed: "We wanted Congress and the White House to come out of hiding and line up alongside the Supreme Court on segregation. We thought we had had a clear promise from the

Democrats and from Kennedy himself to do just that, but now he was backing down. We were off to a very bad start with Kennedy."

Rather than seeing it as "backing down," Kennedy viewed his caution on civil rights as entirely rational given the harsh political realities on Capitol Hill and with the cold war. Barely a month into office, Kennedy met with Father Theodore Hesburgh, then president of the University of Notre Dame and chairman of the U.S. Civil Rights Commission. Father Hesburgh pointed out to Kennedy that the Alabama National Guard was entirely segregated.

"Look, father," Kennedy said, "I may have to send the Alabama National Guard to Berlin tomorrow and I don't want to have to do it in the middle of a revolution at home."

By April Roy Wilkins was moved to write a personal note to Harris Wofford, a friend and Kennedy's adviser on civil rights. Wilkins recognized Kennedy's attention to the international situation: "We do have a difference with the Kennedy Administration and perhaps that difference is rooted in the purpose of the NAACP as contrasted with the purpose of the government of all the people in a time of world crisis." This was an important acknowledgment of the position the president was in. Nonetheless, Wilkins was frustrated. "The Kennedy Administration has done with Negro citizens what it has done with a vast number of Americans:

Meeting with NAACP leaders in the summer of 1961

it has charmed them. It has intrigued them. Every seventy-two hours it has delighted them. On the Negro question it has smoothed Unguentine on a stinging burn even though for a moment (or for perhaps a year) it cannot do anything about a broken pelvis."

Just a month before Kennedy took office, the U.S. Supreme Court ruled that segregation was illegal in facilities serving interstate travelers. As a result, segregation was banned in places such as bus terminal waiting rooms, bathrooms, and restaurants in terminals used by buses traveling interstate. The Freedom Riders challenged restrictions that remained in spite of the Supreme Court ruling. Interracial groups of Freedom Riders intended to travel via Trailways and Greyhound buses throughout the Deep South. "We propose to challenge, en route, every form of segregation met by the bus passenger," James Farmer of the Congress of Racial Equality (CORE), the Freedom Ride organizer, wrote to Kennedy. "We are experienced in, and dedicated to, the Gandhian principles of non-violence."

The Freedom Riders departed Washington by bus on May 4, 1961. For ten days, they were merely anonymous travelers, but on May 14 they made news across America. On that day, as seven Freedom Riders traveled through Alabama, their bus was attacked. Farmer dispatched an urgent telegram to the president:

> Today a Greyhound bus travelling from Atlanta to Birmingham was ambushed outside of Anniston, Alabama, by fifty white men, its tires slashed, windows smashed, tear gas hurled inside and the bus finally set afire and gutted by flames. . . .
>
> One hour later, seven other interstate freedom riders on a Trailways bus also at Anniston, Alabama, were

a national organization with affiliated local groups working

CONGRESS OF RACIAL EQUALITY
CORE

to abolish racial discrimination by direct, nonviolent methods

38 PARK ROW
NEW YORK 38, NEW YORK
COrtlandt 7-0035

Unacknowledged

GENERAL

HU2-6

April 26, 1961

The President
The White House
1600 Pennsylvania Avenue, N. W.
Washington, D. C.

My dear Mr. President:

We expect you will be interested in our Freedom Ride, 1961. It is designed to forward the completion of integrated bus service and accomodations in the Deep South.

About fifteen CORE members will travel as inter-state passengers on Greyhound and Trailways routes. We leave Washington early in May and, travelling through Virginia, North and South Carolina, Georgia, Alabama and Mississippi, plan to arrive in New Orleans on Wednesday, May 17th.

The group is interracial. Two-thirds are Southerners. Three are women. We propose to challenge, en route, every form of segregation met by the bus passenger. We are experienced in, and dedicated to, the Gandhian principles of non-violence.

Our plans are entirely open. Further information is available to all.

Freedom Ride is an appeal to the best in all Americans. We travel peaceably to persuade them that Jim Crow betrays democracy. It degrades democracy at home. It debases democracy abroad. We feel that there is no way to overstate the danger that denial of democratic and constitutional rights brings to our beloved country.

And so we feel it our duty to affirm our principles by asserting our rights. With the survival of democracy at stake, there is an imperative, immediate need for acts of self-determination. "Abandon your animosities and make your sons Americans," said Robert E. Lee. Freedom Ride would make that, "All your sons -- NOW!"

Sincerely yours,

James Farmer
James Farmer
National Director

JF:nm
encs.

> severely beaten by eight hoodlums inside the bus after Negro passengers failed to move to rear seats when ordered to do so by the bus driver. . . . Arriving in Birmingham the CORE freedom riders were again attacked by a mob and at least one freedom rider hospitalized with severe cuts. . . .
>
> Federal investigation and intervention urgently required. Equally imperative that moral force of your office be exerted. The president must speak.

Soon other Freedom Riders were attacked and beaten in Birmingham. Kennedy was angry about the Freedom Rides in part because he believed that the spectacle of violence against black Americans embarrassed the nation before the world. Kennedy asked his civil rights adviser, Harris Wofford, "Can't you get your goddamned friends off those buses? Stop them." The president believed that the disruption caused by the Freedom Riders in the South would make it more difficult for him to deal with key southerners in the Congress. Robert Kennedy agreed with his brother, saying to Wofford, "I wonder whether [the Freedom Riders] have the best interest of their country at heart. . . . The president is going abroad and this is all embarrassing him." A May Gallup Poll showed that nearly two-thirds of all Americans disapproved of the Freedom Riders.

Kennedy nonetheless recognized that the Freedom Riders had the law of the land squarely on their side. The president assigned his most trusted adviser, his brother Robert, to monitor the situation closely. Robert Kennedy sent his administrative assistant, John Seigenthaler, the only southerner in his office, to Birmingham. When Seigenthaler asked Robert Kennedy what he wanted him to do, the attorney general replied: "Hold their hands and let them know we care." In Montgomery, Seigenthaler was beaten bloody and unconscious.

The president responded by dispatching U.S. marshals to protect the Freedom Riders. When a Freedom Riders' bus was stopped, Robert Kennedy telephoned an official at the bus company in Birmingham. "Mr. Cruit, this is Robert Kennedy," said the attorney general. "Isn't there some way we can get this bus down to Montgomery?"

"No, sir," Cruit said, adding that the drivers were fearful for their lives and "refused to drive."

"Do you have anybody else that can drive this bus?" Kennedy asked. "Any other driver."

"No," said Cruit.

Kennedy was angry.

"Mr. Cruit," he said, "I think if I were you I would get a driver of one of the colored buses and have them take the bus down. You can get one of them, can't you?"

"No," replied Cruit.

"Well, hell, you can look for one, can't you? After all, these people have tickets and are entitled to transportation to continue the trip . . . to Montgomery."

But Cruit persisted in saying that there were no drivers available.

"Do you know how to drive a bus?" Kennedy asked.

"No," said Cruit.

"Well, surely somebody in the damn bus company can drive a bus, can't they?"

When Cruit still would not budge, Kennedy said: "Mr. Cruit, I think you . . . had better be getting in touch with Mr. Greyhound or whoever Greyhound is. . . . I am—the government—is going to be very much upset if this group does not get to continue their trip. . . . Somebody better get in the damn bus and get it going and get these people on their way."

While the Freedom Riders were continuing their challenge down South, Kennedy met at the White House with a group of people involved with the Peace Corps, including Harry Belafonte, a popular black entertainer, who asked the president to be more outspoken in support of the Freedom Riders. During the same meeting, Eugene Rostow, the dean of Yale Law School, looked at the president and flatly said:

"There is a need now for moral leadership." This angered Kennedy. "Have you read my statement in the newspapers?" Kennedy replied.

The president was feeling put upon. Here he was getting ready for one of the most important meetings of his life—his Vienna summit with Khrushchev was just weeks away—and he was being hectored at home. When the group had left, Kennedy vented his anger on Wofford. "What in the world does he think I should do?" Kennedy asked. "Doesn't he know I've done more for civil rights than any president in American history? How could any man have done more than I've done?"

Meeting with Whitney Young and Henry Steeger (right), both of the Urban League

Toward the end of the president's first year in office, civil rights leaders were growing increasingly impatient with what they perceived to be the president's unwillingness to follow through on his campaign promise to abolish discrimination in federally funded housing "with the stroke of a pen." A campaign mocking the president's promise had already begun, and thousands of pens were mailed to the White House in protest. In November 1961 some civil rights leaders left a White House meeting with Kennedy carrying the clear impression that the order was on the eve of being issued. In mid-December, when the order was not forthcoming, Roy Wilkins sent a frankly worded telegram to the president:

> Grave concern and considerable skepticism and some resentment have arisen across the country since the

November 27 announcement that an agreed-upon draft was ready of an order prohibiting racial discrimination in federally assisted housing. There is real fear that unless it is issued at this time it may not be issued. The millions whose high hopes were encouraged by the clear commitment of the administration feel that the redemption of a 1960 promise should not rest upon anticipated developments in 1962.

If the criticism from Wilkins was bad, there was more to come. In March 1962 Martin Luther King Jr. offered his assessment of Kennedy in an article in the *Nation* titled "Report on Civil Rights; Fumbling on the New Frontier." According to King:

> The Kennedy administration in 1961 waged an essentially cautious and defensive struggle for civil rights. . . . As the year unfolded, Executive initiative became increasingly feeble, and the chilling prospect emerged of a general Administration retreat. In backing away from an executive order to end discrimination in housing, the President did more to undermine confidence in his intentions than could be offset by a series of smaller accomplishments during the year. He has begun 1962 with a show of renewed aggressiveness; one can only hope that it will be sustained.
>
> The year 1961 was characterized by inadequacy and incompleteness in [civil rights]. . . . It is not only that the Administration too often retreated in haste from a battlefield which it has proclaimed a field of honor, but—more significantly—its basic strategic goals have been narrowed.

Kennedy nonetheless stayed his cautious course. He continued to express frustration that he was being pushed too hard on civil rights and that the country wasn't ready for action that overreached. Kennedy felt he knew the Hill well enough to know that the perception that he was being

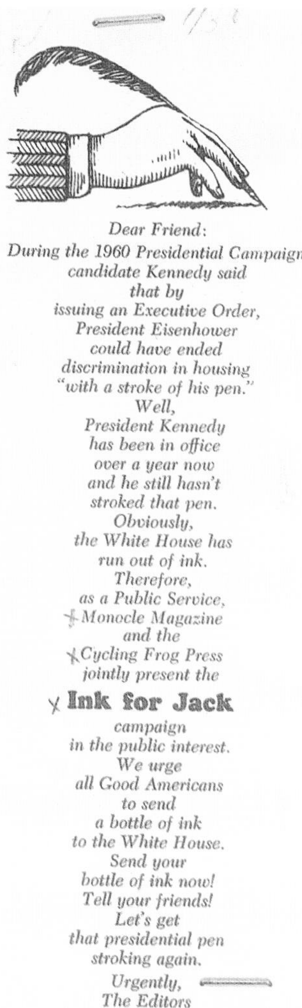
Dear Friend:
During the 1960 Presidential Campaign, candidate Kennedy said that by issuing an Executive Order, President Eisenhower could have ended discrimination in housing "with a stroke of his pen." Well, President Kennedy has been in office over a year now and he still hasn't stroked that pen. Obviously, the White House has run out of ink. Therefore, as a Public Service, Monocle Magazine and the Cycling Frog Press jointly present the

Ink for Jack

campaign in the public interest. We urge all Good Americans to send a bottle of ink to the White House. Send your bottle of ink now! Tell your friends! Let's get that presidential pen stroking again.

Urgently,
The Editors

Civil rights advocates sent pens and ink to the White House, urging President Kennedy to sign an anti-discrimination order overly aggressive with a civil rights agenda could badly harm his ability to work with congressional leaders. When members of the U.S. Civil Rights Commission told him that it intended to open public hearings on complaints of racial discrimination in Mississippi, Kennedy asked the commission not to proceed. "You're making my life difficult," the president said to the chairman.

Assistant Press Secretary Andy Hatcher helps JFK prepare for civil rights Address to the Nation

The president expressed his frustration one day to Louis Martin, the publisher of a chain of Negro newspapers in Chicago and the president's single Negro adviser. "Negroes are getting ideas they didn't have before," Martin told the president.

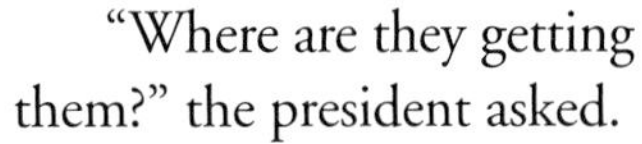

"Where are they getting them?" the president asked.

"From you!" Martin replied. "You're lifting the horizons of Negroes!"

One of the ideas Negroes were getting was that they were entitled to an education. James Meredith longed to go to the University of Mississippi and earn a college degree, but his admission had been barred by state officials because of his race. Meredith had gone to court and won a judicial order requiring the state of Mississippi to enroll him at the university.

For Mississippi governor Ross Barnett, this was too much. He could not permit integration of the university on his watch. He could not appear to capitulate to the federal government. Were he to do so, he would have a revolution on his hands. He explained this to Robert Kennedy when the attorney general called to try to persuade Barnett to register Meredith at the university. Robert Kennedy said he understood the governor's political problems, but he also said that the law of the land was the law of the land and had to be upheld.

On September 26, 1962, Meredith was taken to the state capitol by two agents of the U.S. government. The agents asked state officials to register Meredith, but they refused. The next day the agents drove Meredith to Oxford, home of the university, and again sought to register Meredith. Again they were refused.

Robert Kennedy tried to work out a deal with the governor. Kennedy proposed that the agents would bring Meredith back the next day accompanied by twenty or so armed federal marshals. Then the governor himself would attempt to turn Meredith away. This would help the governor politically by showing all of Mississippi that he was willing to stand up to the federal government and against the Negroes. At that point, under Robert Kennedy's proposal, a federal marshal would draw a gun and demand that Meredith be enrolled, leaving Governor Barnett no choice in the matter. But just when Robert Kennedy thought he had a deal, Barnett balked. He said one drawn gun would not be enough. All of the marshals would have to draw their guns. Robert Kennedy refused.

James Meredith

President Kennedy himself called Barnett and tried to convince him that there was no possible alternative to registering Meredith. It had to be done, the president said, so let's make sure it's done peacefully.

The Kennedy brothers understood politics. Robert

1. Will he get him in — Court —
2. Will he [illegible] — [illegible]
3. Will he maintain law & order

Points to be covered in conversation with Governor Barnett:

Can you maintain law + order —

1. Will he cooperate through the law enforcement officials in the State in seeing that Meredith can safely enter the university?

   The Court has ordered that Meredith enter the university and the Court ordered him to cooperate. Does he intend to follow the Court order?

   In other words, will he cooperate with us in meeting our responsibilities?

2. If he won't cooperate in getting Meredith in, will he actively try to oppose Meredith from going in? (If the answer to #1 is "yes", of course we don't have to go on to #2.)

   In other words, will he interpose himself physically or use the physical force of the law enforcement officers of the State to prevent Meredith from entering the university peacefully and safely?

   If the anwer to #2 is that he will obstruct him from entering the university, then if the Federal Government makes an effort to carry out the order of the Court, will he assure us there will be no violence or no disorder? What action will his own police take and other law enforcement officers under his command? Will he cooperate to prevent mobs and disorder? (Last Thursday night he indicated initially there would be no disorder, yet he told the Attorney General subsequently if the Marshalls had come to the university 40 or 50 people would be killed. Will that be the situation next week when Meredith attempts to enter the University?)

3. Does he have the power and will he exert the power to preserve law and order in the area of Oxford, Mississippi, when Meredith enters the University??

Kennedy called Barnett and said that he had tape-recorded all of the conversations with Barnett, discussions in which the governor had discussed settling the Meredith affair. If the tapes were to be made public, it would reveal that in private Barnett had not been as staunch as he was in public. "We've got it all down, governor," the attorney general said to Barnett. And Robert Kennedy threatened to release the tapes if Barnett didn't cooperate. The governor said that federal agents should secretly move Meredith on to the Oxford campus. In the meantime, Barnett would lead demonstrations against Meredith in the state capitol. Meredith was brought to the campus as the president signed an order for troops to go into Mississippi and enforce the will of the court. Three hundred federal marshals assembled on the campus to ensure Meredith could attend classes. But a couple thousand protesters chanting "Go to hell, JFK!" gathered to prevent him from entering a classroom.

The president went on national television and said that Meredith had been enrolled at the university. A riot broke out. Tear gas was fired into the rioters; shots rang out. The National Guard was called in. The Kennedy Library displays a federal marshal's crumpled helmet, which looks as if it had been beaten with a baseball bat. The president got on the phone to his secretary of the army and angrily demanded that troops be moved into Oxford immediately. By dawn the next day, there were 23,000 soldiers around Oxford. There had been 200 arrests. Two hundred marshals and soldiers were injured. Two men were dead.

That morning, James Meredith attended his first class at the University of Mississippi. Less than two months later, President Kennedy signed an executive order prohibiting discrimination in federally subsidized housing. The order did not cover privately funded housing and thus fell short of what civil rights leaders wanted and felt Kennedy had promised in 1960. But the decision reflected what Kennedy believed was politically possible at that moment. It was a start.

The President
Remarks
Nobel Prize Dinner
April 29, 1962

I am proud to welcome
Nobel Prize in the Western H
history of this house we have
a concentration of genius and

The Nobel Prize, of co
general. It knows no geograph
brisk disregard for his fellow
took care to specify in his wi
desire that, in the awarding o
be paid to the nationality of the candidates, that is to
the most desrving be awarded the prize, whether he
Scandanavian or not...".

Nobel's passion was to honor men and women w
mankind in the fields of science and in literature and
cause of peace. His faith was that the spirit of inqu
the extension of knowledge would best guarantee the f
welfare of humanity. "Knowledge", said Plato t
soul". We must all agree with Nobel that the
pursuit of knowledge has always been-- and always be-- the
mainspring of human Progress.

THE POWER OF SYMBOLS

"Landing a man on the moon and returning him safely to earth."

Near the end of a grueling day of campaigning in the fall of 1960, an exhausted John Kennedy was hours behind schedule as he arrived for his last stop, at the University of Michigan. It was nearly 2 A.M. when the candidate finally pulled into the campus. Surely the crowd that had gathered hours earlier would have dispersed, the students back in their rooms, asleep, or off partying. But Kennedy was greeted by a throng of 10,000 students who had waited for hours to hear him speak. Kennedy was inspired by their exuberance, fueled by their energy, and asked whether they would be willing to serve their country overseas as ambassadors at the grassroots level. Would they be willing to go off as representatives of the United States to help people in foreign lands? The crowd roared its approval with such assurance that Kennedy was moved to propose a new volunteer program, one that would draw on the talents and idealism of Americans in all walks of life. Within days University of Michigan students had circulated a petition in support of Kennedy's proposal signed by hundreds of prospective volunteers.

The original idea had been proposed by Senator Hubert Humphrey, and Kennedy recognized the symbolic potential of such a program. Barely six weeks into his presidency, Kennedy issued an executive order creating the Peace Corps on March 1, 1961. And the president signaled that he would take a personal interest in the program when he appointed as the Peace Corps head his brother-in-law Sargent Shriver. The official mandate stated that Peace Corps volunteers would "live at the same level as the citizens of the countries which they are sent to, doing the same work, eating the same food, speaking the same language."

The Peace Corps is born—Sargeant Shriver and, to JFK's right, Senator Hubert Humphrey

Shriver laid out the program's objectives to the president at the start. The Peace Corps would seek to promote the development of nations and regions that played a critical role in various parts of the world, promote cooperation among nations, create goodwill toward the United States, and help Americans gain a better understanding of the realities in other countries. The Peace Corps would beat the Communists at their own game by winning the hearts and minds of people aspiring to improve the quality of their lives and the lives of their children.

Within months Americans from many walks of life, most of them young college graduates, were at work in the African bush and in the slums and outlands of Latin America and Asia, applying their skills and their zeal to a wide variety of self-help projects. They worked shoulder to shoulder with local citizens to construct roads, develop water and sewage systems, provide prenatal and medical care, and improve farming methods. The president said the initial reaction to the program was proof that "we have in this country an immense reservoir of dedicated men and women willing to devote their energies and time and toil to the cause of world peace and human progress."

The President with a Peace Corps volunteer

Perhaps more than any other initiative, the Peace Corps evoked the energetic spirit embodied in Kennedy's New Frontier. It refocused the suspicious, inward-looking stare of the cold war and reached out to embrace the world. More than any other program, the Peace Corps tapped into a rich vein of idealism among the young people of America. Peace Corps volunteers took on the Communists in critical places around the globe, competing not with weapons but with medicine, agricultural techniques, road-building, and schoolbooks. In just two years the program grew tenfold, from 500 trainees to 5,000. And just a year later 10,000

Peace Corps volunteers were laboring in more than sixty nations throughout the world.

The Peace Corps projected precisely the image of America that Kennedy wanted to convey—youth, energy, involvement throughout the world. It also helped to project just such an image for the president himself. But John Kennedy was far too sophisticated to leave the creation of that image to chance. He was surely one of the most skilled image-builders ever to occupy the White House.

After the president had been in office for just over a year, *U.S. News and World Report* undertook an analysis of the Kennedy image-building techniques. "Reporters cannot remember when a president was so concerned with what was written or said about him," the magazine observed.

The White House employed a carrot-and-stick approach with journalists: The carrot was private discussions with the president; the stick was being ignored or browbeaten by Kennedy staffers or even the president himself. "There are times," the article noted, "when reporters have been cut off from all news sources at the White House because of an item that did not win approval. Presidential aides have refused to see or talk with these reporters. This punishment sometimes goes on for weeks."

Not only was a substantial staff devoted to press relations, but "almost every official on the White House staff does his bit at one time or another in trying to get friendly stories published or spread across the television and radio networks," *U.S. News* reported. Staffers were so

Addressing Peace Corps volunteers

aggressive that they would sometimes "suggest the exact language the president would like to see in a story. If the language does not appear as dictated, there are likely to be telephone calls. It is not unusual for a White House aide to ask to see a story before it is printed."

The president was at his confident best during press conferences

Sometimes a reporter who had written an article the president did not like would be summoned to the Oval Office for criticism directly from Kennedy himself. Publishers from newspapers throughout the nation were brought to the White House in small groups for lengthy private luncheons with the president. "Everything is handled in such an informal manner that you feel at ease," said one publisher after such a luncheon. "The president asked us for our opinions on a number of matters. He told us that he liked to have as much background as possible before making a decision. The president speaks so frankly about things that you get a feeling he trusts you and that he is taking you into his confidence."

Central to the creation of the Kennedy image was the use of television. The president well understood how pivotal the role of television had been in getting him to the White House. He made sure that extensive use of the medium would promote his programs and ideas to the broadest possible audiences. The Peace Corps was an ideal story for television, for it allowed networks to journey to exotic locations and send home images of bright young Americans helping needy people of other lands. The story was real and tangible and beamed into tens of millions of homes.

Kennedy became the first American president to make extensive use of live televised news conferences as well. This decision was risky, for it could expose the president's mistakes to instant public notice. (Eisenhower, for example, had been asked at just such a conference in August 1960 to name a major contribution Nixon had made to the administration. "If you give me a week, I might think of one," Ike said, thus embarrassing his party's presidential nominee.) But Kennedy believed in his own ability to step before live cameras and handle, or if necessary finesse, any question with grace. He had been in office for only a matter of days when he held his first broadcast press conference, on January 25, 1961. The new president appeared in the amphitheater of the State Department and with poise and confidence calmly answered each question put to him. The combination of the president's knowledge of the issues, self-confidence, beguiling wit, and telegenic good looks made the event an instant hit. During his first ninety days in office, Kennedy held ten televised press

A televised press conference

conferences, an extraordinarily high number. At certain times Kennedy even permitted television crews to follow him through the day, filming him for television specials. A program called "Crisis" focused on the president and his brother working on civil rights. Another, "A Conversation with the President," was aired on all the major networks and attracted a huge audience. Barely three months into his term *Life* magazine called Kennedy "the most accessible American president in memory."

Peace Corps volunteers embodied the youth and energy Kennedy sought to project

Pierre Salinger would later observe that "never before had the American people had such an intimate glimpse of a president: his personality, his mind at work, his sense of history—and his sense of humor." After one televised event, the president said, "We couldn't survive without TV."

Some of the most dramatic footage of the Kennedy years would involve the race for space. While Peace Corps volunteers labored on the ground, a much larger cold war competition was taking place far above the earth in the newest of all frontiers, outer space. Where the Peace Corps was a grassroots initiative to win favor in the far reaches of the world, the space race involved the latest science and technology, the expenditure of billions of dollars, and nothing less than the global reputations of the nations involved. And the undisputed leaders in the race for space were the Soviets. Their launch in 1957 of the *Sputnik* satellite convinced the world that the Soviets held a substantial scientific and technological lead over the rest of the developed nations, the United States included.

The Soviets' crowning achievement came less than three months after President Kennedy had been in office, when cosmonaut Yuri Gagarin was launched into a 108-minute space flight, during which he completed a single orbit of the earth. Gagarin's flight stunned America. It left the nation feeling, in the words of *Time* magazine, "frustration, shame," and even "fury."

President Kennedy was shaken. "Is there anyplace we can catch them?" Kennedy asked Vice President Johnson, chairman of the U.S. Space Council. "What can we do? Are we working twenty-four hours a day? Can we go around the moon before them? Can we put a man on the moon before them? Can we leapfrog? If somebody can just tell me how to catch up! Let's find somebody, anybody. I don't care if it's the janitor over there, if he knows how."

Kennedy called in Wernher von Braun, the German scientist living in the United States designing rockets for the army. Von Braun, in fact, had designed the missile that launched the very first U.S. satellite into space. "Can we beat the Russians?" Kennedy asked von Braun.

"We have a sporting chance," replied the scientist. "With an all-out crash program I think we could accomplish this objective in 1967/68."

Advisers told the president that the cost of an all-out space race with the Soviets would be astronomical and with no guarantee whatsoever that the United States would win. They said there was no better than a fifty-fifty chance of beating the USSR to the moon. The cost, in fact, would far exceed any results that would justify such expenditures on scientific grounds. Yet Kennedy was absolutely determined to forge ahead, for if the scientists knew their field, he knew his, and he understood the political significance worldwide of the space race. And there was no mistaking that the overriding consideration for such an initiative would have to be its political significance. Vice President Johnson wrote to the president that "in the eyes of the world, first in space means first, period."

Kennedy agreed. He also made the decision to take a calculated risk and permit live television to cover U.S. space launches. This was in sharp contrast to Soviet practices, which were highly secretive. When a Soviet cosmonaut was burned and died only weeks before the Gagarin flight, the incident was concealed. The planned launching of an American flight, however, would be on live TV for all the world to see. The flight of Alan Shepard, who was launched into space on May 5, 1961, was a success, and it put the United States back into competition. The Soviets were still ahead, but at least the Americans were in the race.

In a speech on May 25, 1961, dubbed his second State of the Union address, President Kennedy emphasized the importance of space. "If we are to win the battle that is now going on around the world between freedom and tyranny, the dramatic achievements in space which occurred in recent weeks should have made it clear to us all, as did the *Sputnik* in 1957, the impact of this adventure on the minds of men everywhere. I believe this nation should commit itself to achieving the goal, before this decade is out, of landing a man on the moon and returning him safely to earth. No single space project in this period will be more impressive to mankind."

Vice President Johnson wrote a memo to Kennedy stating, "This country should be realistic and recognize that other nations, regardless of their appreciation of our idealistic values, will tend to align themselves with the country which they believe will be the world leader—the winner in the long run. Dramatic accomplishments in space are being increasingly identified as a major indicator of world leadership."

Greeting astronaut Alan Shepard

The political significance of space was reflected in a conversation Kennedy had with the president of Tunisia after Shepard's flight. As they talked, Kennedy posed a hypothetical question to the Tunisian leader: Should Kennedy give Tunisia an additional $1 billion in aid each year? Or should Kennedy put that money into the space race? The Tunisian replied: "I wish I could tell you to put it in foreign aid, but I cannot."

JFK went to Congress seeking large sums for the space program: $562 million in the next fiscal year and a total of somewhere between $7 and 9 billion. U.S. scientists worked furiously throughout the remainder of 1961, thinking perhaps that in December they might be ready to launch a man into space and orbit the earth. But that timetable proved overly optimistic. Nonetheless, by February 20, 1962, the Americans were ready. That morning the president was one of about 100 million Americans watching television. The screen displayed a massive Atlas rocket—an intercontinental ballistic missile that would typically carry a nuclear warhead—on its pad at Cape Canaveral, Florida. Atop the rocket, as it stood poised for launch, astronaut John Glenn was strapped into a cramped capsule.

With John Glenn after the historic flight

At 9:36 A.M. eastern time, Americans stopped what they were doing and watched. In New York's Grand Central Terminal, 15,000 people stood silently, watching a massive screen, as *Friendship 7*

Glenn showing Kennedy Friendship 7

lifted ever so slowly from its pad and rose majestically into the sky. John Glenn, an ideal representative of America—clean-cut, enthusiastic, accomplished—circled the earth three times in just under five hours. Kennedy spoke with Glenn by telephone that afternoon, after the astronaut had been scooped out of the sea. The president, along with the rest of the country, basked in the glory of Glenn's magnificent flight. It presaged better days ahead for the nation and its young leader.

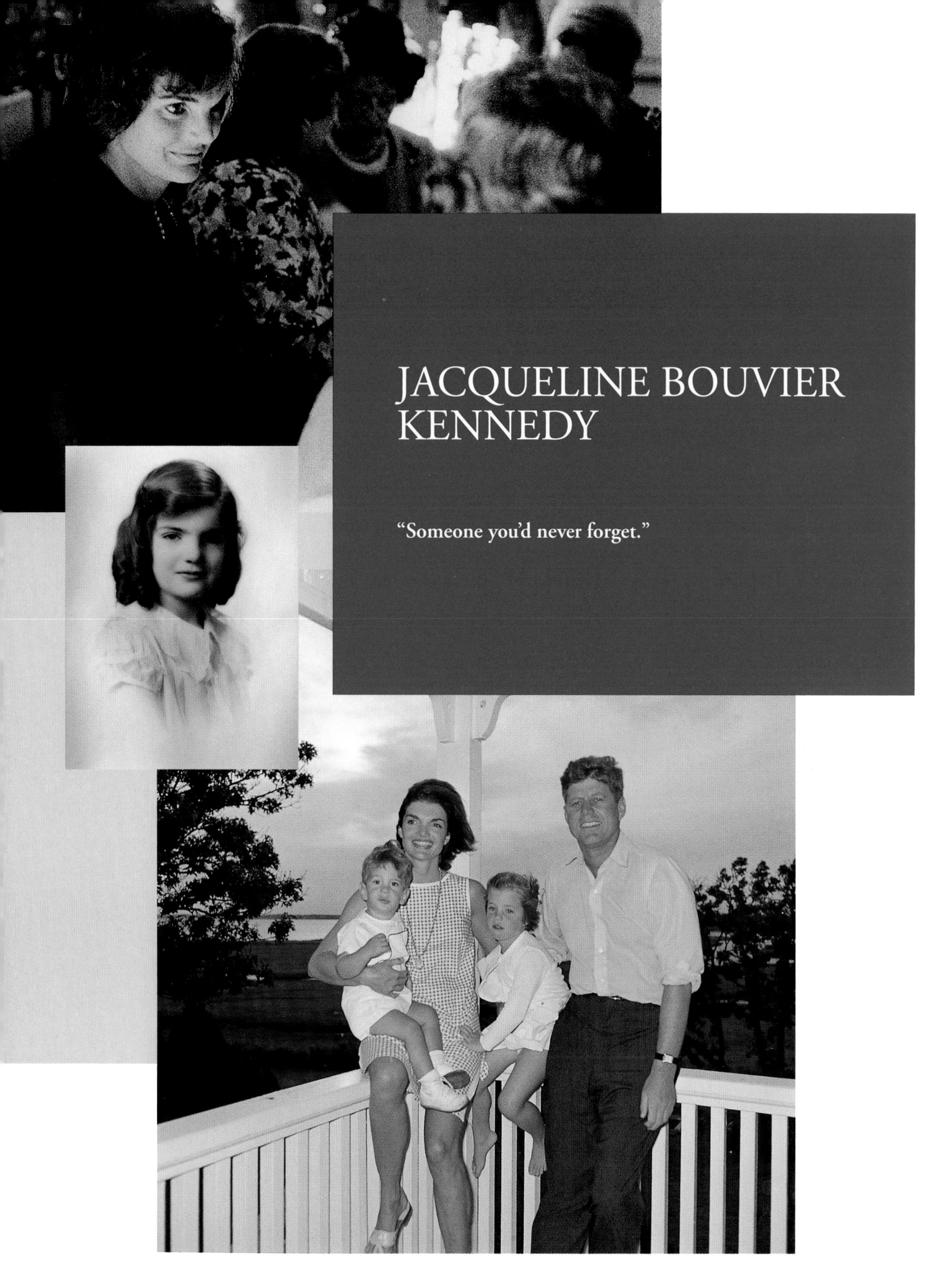

JACQUELINE BOUVIER KENNEDY

"Someone you'd never forget."

From the beginning, there was something about her, something that set her apart. Placed upon a horse at age one, she quickly became a prodigy. By age seven she had accomplished the astonishing feat of winning not one but two national equestrian championships. Of all the beautiful, poised, and talented girls introduced to American society in 1947, young Jacqueline Bouvier was chosen as the "debutante of the year." When *Vogue* held the Prix de Paris, a writing competition for women college students nationwide, Jacqueline Bouvier won first prize. There was something about her that transcended any specific achievement or attribute, something that was more than all of them combined. It was true that she was strikingly beautiful—slender and lovely with an almost ethereal quality. She was as sophisticated as she was attractive, fluent in French, comfortable in Spanish and Italian. She was possessed of a strong intellect and a fine aesthetic sensibility. Jackie was barely a teenager, but even at that point her art teacher recognized that she was special. Said the teacher: "She was someone you'd never forget."

Jacqueline Lee Bouvier was born on July 28, 1929, in Southampton, New York. Her father was a successful Wall Street broker of French ancestry. Her mother, Janet Norton Lee, was an accomplished equestrian. Jackie grew up amid privilege and affluence in New York City and Long Island. By the time she turned twelve, her parents had divorced. Two years later her mother married Hugh D. Auchincloss Jr. and they moved to McLean, Virginia. The family summered at Hammersmith Farm, the spectacular Auchincloss estate over-

Age 2

looking Narragansett Bay in Newport, Rhode Island.

Age 3

Early on riding was her passion. An article in the *New York Times* in 1940 reported that "Jacqueline Bouvier, an eleven year old equestrienne from East Hampton, Long Island, scored a double victory in the horsemanship competition. Miss Bouvier achieved a rare distinction. The occasions are few when a young rider wins both contests in the same show."

Jackie attended private schools, where she was a good student and popular with other girls. She was considered "very lively and full of mischief." When she graduated from Miss Porter's, an exclusive girl's prep school in Farmington, Connecticut, in 1947, she was known among her classmates for her keen wit. She said in her yearbook that her ambition was "not to be a housewife."

At Vassar, where she studied history, literature, art, and French, she was selected by the Hearst newspaper chain as the nation's debutante of the year. "America is a country of traditions," wrote columnist Igor Cassini. "Every four years we elect a President, every two years our congressmen. And every year a new Queen of Debutantes is crowned. The Queen Deb of the year for 1947 is Jacqueline Bouvier, a regal brunette who has classic features and the daintiness of Dresden porcelain. She has poise, is soft-spoken and intelligent, everything the leading debutante should be. Her background is strictly Old Guard."

Age 12

Reflecting on his selection, Cassini later said that "I usually tried to choose one of the prettier, flashier society girls. Jackie wasn't flashy, and she didn't make her debut at any of the classic cotillions. Yet I felt something very special in her, an understated elegance. . . . Although shy and extremely private, she stood out in a crowd. She had that certain something. I don't know precisely what word to use to describe this quality: beauty, charm, charisma, style, any or all of the above. Whatever it happened to be, she had it."

In the late 1950s

For her junior year, she traveled to Paris for what would be a defining experience studying at the Sorbonne. After Paris she returned to the United States to study French literature at George Washington University. While there she entered the Vogue Prix de Paris contest. Her essay read in part:

> As to physical appearance, I am tall, 5'7", with brown hair, a square face and eyes so unfortunately far apart that it takes three weeks to have a pair of glasses made with a bridge wide enough to fit over my nose. I do not have a sensational figure but can look slim if I pick the right clothes. I flatter myself on being able at times to walk out of the house looking like the poor man's Paris copy, but often my mother will run up to inform me that my left stocking seam is crooked or the right-hand top coat button is about to fall off. This, I realize, is the Unforgivable Sin.
>
> I lived in New York City until I was thirteen and spent the summers in the country. I hated dolls, loved horses and dogs and had skinned knees and braces on my teeth for what must have seemed an interminable length of time to my family.
>
> I read a lot when I was little, much of which was too old for me. There were Chekov and Shaw in the room where I had to take naps and I never slept but sat on the

1st Prize

VOGUE'S PRIX DE PARIS

Please, will you fill out this questionnaire and return it as soon as possible to Vogue's Prix de Paris Director, 420 Lexington Avenue, New York 17, N. Y.?

Name of entrant Jacqueline Bouvier College George Washington University

Permanent home address Merrywood, (street) McLean (city) (zone) Virginia (state)

Date of birth July (month) 28 (day) 1929 (year)

1. Where have you travelled? British Isles, France, Spain, Italy, Switzerland, Austria, Germany, Belgium

2. Name of high school or "prep" school Miss Porter's School, Farmington, Conn.

3.* What is your major? it was English, is now French Your minor? Art

4. Do you read or speak any foreign languages? read and speak French, read Spanish

5. In what extra-curricular activities have you engaged during your college days?
Dance Group, College Paper, Art Club, designing costumes for Dramatic Club

6. Do you type? Yes Take shorthand? no Ever done any public speaking? took a course in it in high school, have not spoken since.
W.P.M. ____ W.P.M. ____

7. In what type of work are you most interested?

√√ Fashion
____ Merchandising
√√ Interior Decorating
____ Copy Writing
√√ Feature Writing
√ Photography (though I dont know anything about it)
____ Layout
____ Production

Other: ____

8. Have you had any business or fashion experience? If so, please describe:

Where did You Work	For How Long	Type of Work
a)		
b)		
c)		

* If you have had any specialized art or photography training, please explain below:
I took two years of studio art at Vassar. We learned the techniques of charcoal and pastel drawing, watercolor, gouache and oil painting.

> window sill reading, then scrubbed the soles of my feet so the nurse would not see I had been out of bed. My heroes were Byron, Mowgli, Robin Hood, Little Lord Fauntleroy's grandfather and Scarlett O'Hara.
>
> Growing up was not too painful a process. It happened gradually over the three years I spent at boarding school trying to imitate the girls who had callers every Saturday. I passed the finish line when I learned to smoke, in the balcony of the Normandie theatre in New York from a girl who pressed a Longfellow upon me then led me from the theatre when the usher told her that other people could not hear the film with so much coughing going on.
>
> I spent two years at Vassar and still cannot quite decide whether I liked it or not. I wish I had worked harder and gone away less on weekends. Last winter I took my Junior Year in Paris and spent the vacation in Austria and Spain. I loved it more than any year of my life. . . . I learned not to be ashamed of a real hunger for knowledge, something I had always tried to hide, and I came home glad to start in here again but with a love for Europe that I am afraid will never leave me.
>
> . . . I have studied art, here and in Paris, and I love to go to Art Exhibits and paint things that my mother doesn't put in the closet until a month after I have given them to her at Christmas. I have written a children's book for my younger brother and sister as it amuses me to make up fairy tales and illustrate them. I love to ride and to fox hunt. I will drop everything any time to read a book on ballet.

After graduation from college, Jacqueline socialized in elite Washington circles. It was at a Georgetown dinner party, in May 1951, that she met Congressman John Kennedy, then serving his third term in the House.

In January 1952 Jackie took a job with the Washington *Times-Herald* as the "inquiring camera girl," a position that required her to roam the streets of the city and elicit comments from people on a wide variety of topics. She would snap photographs to run with the quotations. In April 1953 she included in her column both Vice President Nixon and her husband-to-be, then a U.S. senator.

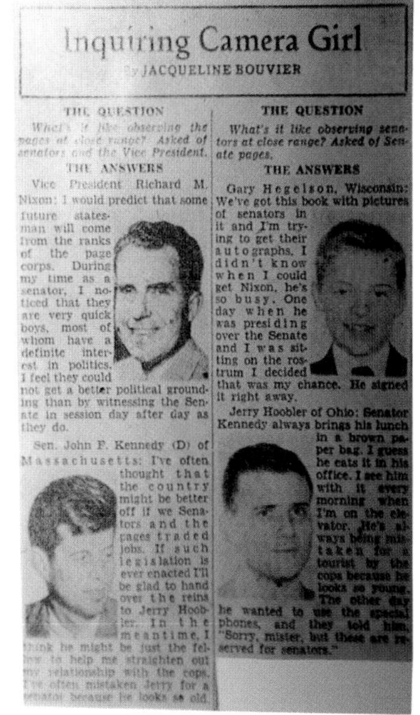

Inquiring Camera Girl

By JACQUELINE BOUVIER

THE QUESTION

What's it like observing the pages at close range? Asked of senators and the Vice President.

THE ANSWERS

Vice President Richard M. Nixon: I would predict that some future statesman will come from the ranks of the page corps. During my time as a senator, I noticed that they are very quick boys, most of whom have a definite interest in politics. I feel they could not get a better political grounding than by witnessing the Senate in session day after day as they do.

Sen. John F. Kennedy (D) of Massachusetts: I've often thought that the country might be better off if we Senators and the pages traded jobs. If such legislation is ever enacted I'll be glad to hand over the reins to Jerry Hoobler. In the meantime, I think he might be just the fellow to help me straighten out my relationship with the cops. I've often mistaken Jerry for a senator because he looks so old.

THE QUESTION

What's it like observing senators at close range? Asked of Senate pages.

THE ANSWERS

Gary Hegelson, Wisconsin: We've got this book with pictures of senators in it and I'm trying to get their autographs. I didn't know when I could get Nixon, he's so busy. One day when he was presiding over the Senate and I was sitting on the rostrum I decided that was my chance. He signed it right away.

Jerry Hoobler of Ohio: Senator Kennedy always brings his lunch in a brown paper bag. I guess he eats it in his office. I see him with it every morning when I'm on the elevator. He's always being mistaken for a tourist by the cops because he looks so young. The other day he wanted to use the special phones, and they told him, "Sorry, mister, but these are reserved for senators."

Jackie Bouvier and John Kennedy married on September 12, 1953, and though they were among the most attractive, successful, and envied couples in Washington, it was not long before they faced adversity. Senator Kennedy's back deteriorated so markedly that he needed major surgery and nearly lost his life in the operation. His wife suffered through the ordeal at his side. When follow-up surgery was necessary in 1955, Senator Kennedy spent his convalescence working on *Profiles in Courage.* Mrs. Kennedy assisted him in the preparation of the book. A love of books, in fact, was one of their most abiding common interests. Upon its publication in 1956, Kennedy dedicated *Profiles* to Jackie, writing that "this book would not have been possible without the encouragement, assistance and criticism offered from the very beginning by my wife, Jacqueline, whose help during all the days of my convalescence, I cannot ever adequately acknowledge."

The Inquiring Camera Girl's work and camera

In the summer of 1956, during the seventh month of pregnancy, Mrs. Kennedy delivered a baby girl by Cesarean section.

Jackie and Caroline at Hyannis Port

Sadly, the child was stillborn. The following year, in November 1957, the Kennedys were blessed with a daughter, Caroline. Three years later, only days after her husband won the presidential election, Mrs. Kennedy gave birth to a son, John. It was a difficult pregnancy resulting in a Cesarean delivery.

One of the youngest first ladies ever, Jacqueline Kennedy was just thirty-one years old when she moved into the White House. In spite of her youth, however, she was essentially bedridden for months after the birth of her son.

After the election, she and her husband flew to her father-in-law's home in Palm Beach, where they spent much of the transition period. While her husband was putting together a cabinet, she struggled to recover and at the same time planned what was to become a massive restoration of the White House. As the inauguration approached, her physical condition improved, but she was not yet entirely healthy.

"By Inauguration Day," recalled Rose Kennedy, "Jackie was still suffering from physical and nervous exhaustion. (The month after the baby's birth had been the opposite of recuperation.) Jackie missed all the gala events she had wanted to share with Jack. She did go to the inaugural gala, but had to go home in the first intermission."

After the inaugural parade, she returned to the White House to lie down and found herself unable to get up. A physician was summoned, and she was soon back on her feet. Later that night, however, moving from one celebratory event to another, "I just crumpled. All my strength was finally gone! So I went home and Jack went on with the others."

But soon enough she was able to participate more fully in the social life of the capitol. She and her husband were, of course, the most sought-after guests in a very social city. Early in the administration the Kennedys accepted an invitation to dinner at the home of Senator John Sherman Cooper of Kentucky. Mrs. Cooper recalled the scene as guests gathered in preparation for the Kennedys' arrival: "Everyone thought they looked out of this world, so beautiful, both of them, and enveloped in radiance which seemed almost tangible."

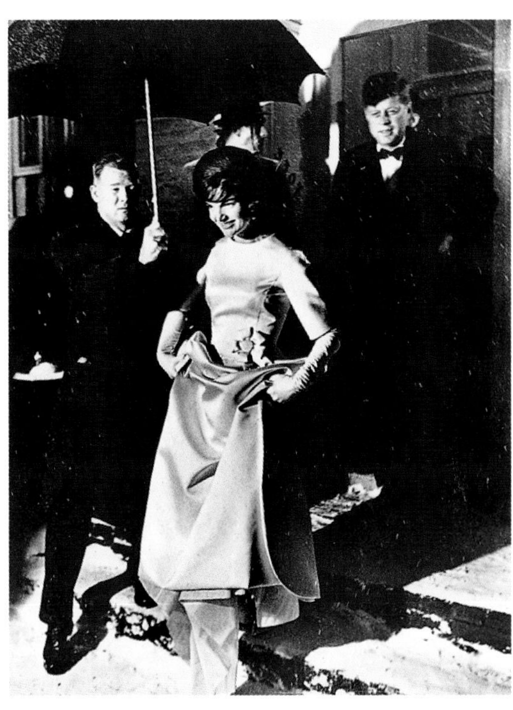

Heading out to celebrate on the eve of the inauguration

The first lady was alarmed by what she considered to be the deplorable condition of a national treasure as precious as the White House. She was aghast to find cheap furniture throughout. Where, she wondered, were all the authentic American and European pieces that had once graced this home? Where were the furnishings and decorative arts emblematic of a great nation? Of its history?

"The White House always looked so sad," she said.

"I always loved beautiful houses; all the time I was in Europe I had gone out of my way to see so many. So I suppose that when I knew I would be living there it wasn't a matter of wanting to restore it or not, it was something that had to be done. . . . It would be a sacrilege merely to 'redecorate'—a word I hate—It must be *restored*

Before a State Dinner

and that has nothing to do with decoration. That is a question of scholarship."

The project was too vast and required too much expertise for Mrs. Kennedy to undertake on her own. Thus, only a month into her husband's term she created the White House Fine Arts Association to oversee the restoration and ensure that only the finest works and artifacts, fully authenticated, would be chosen for use in the White House. She drew from various experts in historic preservation and decorative arts. She also created the position of White House curator and pushed legislation establishing museum status for the presidential home. Mrs. Kennedy herself led the experts on forays into the White House basement and storage rooms as well as government warehouses in search of the finest pieces. She wanted nothing less than a White House that would showcase the best examples of American art and taste.

The First Lady with Charles Collingwood, CBS correspondent, during taping of a tour of the White House

A year after beginning her ambitious project, Mrs. Kennedy was done. The results were to be featured in a program that would be aired on CBS and then repeated four nights later by both ABC and NBC. To produce this special, CBS brought a crew of forty and massive amounts of equipment into the White House for filming. Mrs. Kennedy rehearsed for a day and then over two days the show was filmed and subsequently edited down to a one-hour format. Remarkably, Mrs. Kennedy did not work from a script. She ad-libbed the entire program and in the process demonstrated an intimate familiarity with the history of each furnishing and artifact. She moved from room to room explaining the history of various pieces, their origin, and artistic significance. She then taped the program in Spanish and French for overseas distribution.

"A Tour of the White House with Mrs. John F. Kennedy" aired on February 14 and again on February 18, 1962. In all the program attracted 56 million viewers. The reaction from throughout the nation was wildly positive. The Academy of Television Arts and Sciences thought the broadcast worthy of an Emmy award. The academy cited the first lady for her "gracious invitation, extended to millions of Americans, to see the White House and through this tour to learn of the historical and cultural background of this national monument, for making history a living thing and for making the entire country feel at home."

Jacqueline Kennedy was passionately devoted to the arts, and she wanted to share that passion with the American people. Ever since she was a child, she had loved ballet—she had danced beautifully herself. She was an able writer, a lover of poetry, and a talented artist. She painted *The White House Long Ago* and gave it to her husband, who hung it in the Oval Office. She wanted to make a statement about her values by inviting leading cultural figures to the White House. Her very first invitation went to George Balanchine, the brilliant, Russian-born director of the New York City Ballet. He came for tea, and she asked how he thought she could be most effective in promoting the arts. Balanchine replied that she should strive to help the country "to distinguish between material things and things of the spirit—art, beauty."

And so she did. Of the 175 public appearances outside the White House Jacqueline Kennedy made during her husband's administration, nearly every one was at a cultural event. In the White House she hung work by Cézanne. Among the guests she invited to the presidential home were writers Saul Bellow, Arthur Miller, Archibald MacLeish, Tennessee Williams, Thornton Wilder, and Paddy Chayef-

Pablo Casals at the White House

sky and artists Mark Rothko and Andrew Wyeth. She hosted some of the giants of the classical music world, including Igor Stravinsky, Aaron Copeland, Leonard Bernstein, and, for one of the most memorable evenings of the Kennedy years, Pablo Casals.

> "It was very cold that evening, but Jacqueline Kennedy insisted on accompanying Marita and me to our car," Casals recalled. "She was without a coat—she was wearing an evening dress—and I was afraid she might catch cold. I asked her please not to come outside. But she said, 'The president would want me to—and I myself want to.' She stood there, in the cold, waiting as we drove away."

She felt strongly that the arts had long been underappreciated in America. In a letter to a government official, she wrote: "President Kennedy and I shared the conviction that the artist should be honored by society, and all of this had to do with calling attention to what was finest in America, what should be esteemed and honored. The arts had been treated as a stepchild in the United States." Inspired by his wife, the president said: "I have called for a higher degree of physical fitness in our nation. It is only natural that I should call for the kind of intellectual and spiritual fitness which underlies the flowering of the arts."

New York Times columnist Charlotte Curtis observed that Mrs. Kennedy stood for a "sensitivity to art and beauty despite pragmatic politics, nuclear tests, and the cold war. She is one of the few independent spirits left in an age of conformity." The *New York Times* offered the view that Mrs. Kennedy was "well qualified for the role of unofficial Minister of Culture" of the United States. She wanted to send a message to Americans and the world that the power and majesty of the human mind mattered greatly to her and her husband. Toward that end she hosted a dinner in late April 1962 honoring all forty-nine Nobel Prize winners residing in the Western Hemisphere. For this occasion, the first lady persuaded Ernest Hemingway's widow to allow one of his unpublished works to be read that night.

John Glenn, the astronaut, who became a friend of Mrs. Kennedy's, observed her intellectual breadth up close. "Whenever there was a discussion going on about the Far East or Mideast or Russia, or any world affairs, she was very well informed and could hold her own in any conversation. She never made any public knowledge of this, and it wasn't the way most people viewed her. Behind the scenes, once you got beyond this veneer that she had been pigeonholed in, you realized this."

Like her husband, she had been a lover of books ever since childhood. One of the first things she noticed about the White House upon reviewing photographs of various rooms during the transition period was a dearth of bookshelves. "Doesn't any president *ever* read?" she remarked. "No bookcases, *anywhere*."

When she wanted to familiarize a White House gardener with the flowers she particularly liked, she gave him "several books from her collection on still-life art and a marvelous ancient tome on Flemish flower arrangements borrowed from Mrs. Mellon." She also had a small personal library devoted to books on ballet. At one time she had considered becoming a children's book author. She had, in fact, been in correspondence with Ludwig Bemelmans, author of the Madeline series, about collaboration on a children's book set in the White House. Sadly, he died in midproject in the fall of 1962.

But she successfully published a guidebook about the White House detailing its restoration and providing background information about the building and the many artifacts within. She supervised every detail of the book's preparation, and it was an instant hit.

For all of her love of art and beauty, for all of her devotion to matters of the intellect, Jacqueline Kennedy was a levelheaded woman. She was precise and determined in her ways. She was not at all shy about expressing her opinions privately on certain matters. After all of the work she put into the White House itself, she was greatly frustrated by the lack of progress on beautifying the grounds. She fired off a memorandum to the White House chief usher on the matter:

> Mr. West,
>
> The White House lawns are a disgrace. I am sure that you are working on them—but something truly drastic must be done by Fall.
>
> 1. It is a sea of brown as one looks across the South Lawn.
>
> 2. Clover, weeds and crab grass are mixed in.
>
> 3. On the hillsides there is a completely different type of stringy, long green grass.—It is driving the president crazy—and I agree with him. In Glen Ora [a Virginia country estate the Kennedy's rented] where we have one man who cuts the lawn every two weeks, it looks like

THE WHITE HOUSE

WASHINGTON

This guidebook is for all of the people who visit the White House each year.

It was planned - at first - for the children. It seemed such a shame that they should have nothing to take away with them, to help sort out the impressions received on an often crowded visit. It was hoped that they would go over the book at home and read more about the Presidents who interested them most. Its purpose was to stimulate their sense of history and their pride in their country.

But as research went on and so many little-known facts were gleaned from forgotten papers, it was decided to make it a book that could be of profit to adults and scholars also.

On the theory that it never hurts a child to read something that may be above his head, and that books written down for children often do not awaken a dormant curiosity, this guidebook took its present form.

I hope our young visitors will vindicate this theory, find pleasure in the book, and know that they were its inspiration.

To their elders, may it remind you that many First Families loved this house - and that each and every one left something of themselves behind in it - as you do now by the effort you have made to come here.

Jacqueline Kennedy

THE WHITE HOUSE

WASHINGTON

February 14, 1962

MEMO TO EVELYN LINCOLN:

1. Reminder for The President to inscribe to Prime Minister Nehru, a leather bound copy of, "To Turn the Tide" plus all his other books.

2. Reminder to have The President sign a copy of his book, "To Turn the Tide", for Ambassador and Mrs. Galbraith. (leather-bound)

3. Reminder to have The President sign a copy of his book, "To Turn the Tide", for General Ayub Khan.

These books will be taken in advance to India as presents. (Febr. 24th)

LB

> green velvet—and this place does not look as well as cow-fields in Virginia.
>
> Months ago the complaint of crab grass came up—the lawns are now worse than ever—and patches of soggy, dying expensive turf are not solving the question. This summer please solve this. . . .
>
> I have never bothered much about lawns—but every place I have lived—with a part-time gardener—the lawn has been beautiful—so surely with twelve gardeners that is possible at the White House—
>
> By the East Wing—the hill and gardens are truly atrocious.

She was customarily very precise in laying out what she wanted done. In anticipation of a visit from her father-in-law, she sent a memorandum to a staffperson detailing nine tasks. Number eight on the list of nine reads: "Drink tray put it on Mr. K's side—but in dining room on a suitcase stand . . . he just has make-believe cocktails [because of his paralysis]. Tray should have Gin & Tonic, Coke, Ginger Ale, Rum, Scotch, Ice, cocktail, shaker, Lemon juice—(I think this comes in a mix already in a bottle)."

So meticulously did she plan that before departing for a trip to India and Pakistan, she wrote out postcards and asked a White House staff member to deliver them to Caroline and John each day. "I have numbered these cards. Could you give one each day to the children—in order of numbers—and put stamps on them first as they want to believe it was mailed."

The chief usher, West, observed that "she had a will of iron with more determination than anyone I have ever met. Yet she was so soft-spoken, so deft and subtle, that she could impose that will upon people without their ever knowing it."

When she undertook a project, she dove in and worked diligently until completion. Such was the case when she received the news that there were plans in the works to demolish the nineteenth-century townhouses on Lafayette Square across from the White House and replace them with modern government office buildings. Her sense of historical preservation was deeply offended, and she swung into action. She was told repeatedly that it was too late, that plans were well on the way to being implemented. But she would not yield. "The wreckers haven't started yet and until they do, it can be saved," she said. And save them she did, helping to create an alternative plan that allowed the area to maintain its historical identity.

Through it all—as she worked on White House restoration and historic preservation, as she promoted the arts, as she traveled abroad—her popularity rose. The fashion industry grew obsessed with her simple, elegant taste, and she was featured in countless fashion magazines. She made numerous appearances on her own for a wide variety of cultural causes. She accompanied her husband on visits to

The First Lady reviews plans for redevelopment of Lafayette Square

Emperor Haile Salasse of Ethiopia

Canada, Austria, United Kingdom, Venezuela, Colombia, and Mexico. In the process she became one of the most beloved celebrities in the world. Communist students at a university in Venezuela displayed a sign: "KENNEDY—NO; JACQUELINE—YES." In Colombia there appeared a poster: "Yankee go home, Jackie come back." When she traveled to India, without her husband, an Indian woman "who walked sixteen miles to see her said that Jackie was 'Durga, the goddess of power.'"

The highlight of her international travel was a visit to France in June 1961. Prior to her trip she had been interviewed for French television, and she had spoken fluent French: "I was at the Sorbonne, and then I went [to France] almost every summer. . . . I was in France as a child, as a tourist, as a student, and now I am going with my husband on an official visit. I love France." It was, after all, the home of her paternal ancestors. Arriving with her husband, she was greeted as a national hero. Clearly aware of her overwhelming popularity, the president jokingly introduced himself at one event as "the man who accompanied Jacqueline Kennedy to Paris."

During a glittering dinner at Versailles, she acted as translator between her husband and Charles de Gaulle, and after talking with her at some length in French, de Gaulle said to JFK that she knew more about the history of France than most French citizens. Charlotte Curtis of the *New York Times* wrote that Mrs. Kennedy "stands for . . . foreign languages and an effort to understand foreign people in a country that tends to think it is the only country and that English is the only language."

High praise came as well from an unlikely source: Nikita Khrushchev, who met her in Vienna when he behaved so brutally toward the president. "Kennedy's wife . . . was youthful, energetic and pleasant, and I liked her very much," Khrushchev said. "She knew how to make jokes and was, as our people say, quick with her tongue. In other words, she had no trouble finding the right word to cut you short if you weren't careful with her. . . . Even in small talk she demonstrated her intelligence."

An indication of how she was perceived came in Vienna when the president and the first lady pulled into an estate where they were to join the Soviet delegation in a formal dinner. From out of the crowd came an excited voice: "The American princess!"

For all the grandeur of their life in the White House, the Kennedys endured some turbulent times in their relationship. John Kennedy was frustrated by what he considered his wife's excessive spending, especially on clothes. Far more troubling, however, was Jacqueline Kennedy's personal pain at the knowledge of her husband's active interest in other women.

Their most tragic moment together involved their third child, Patrick Bouvier Kennedy. He was a mere 4 pounds, 10 ounces when he was born on August 7, 1963, at Otis Air Force Base hospital on Cape Cod. Patrick suffered from a severe lung problem and was rushed to Children's Hospital in Boston. Kennedy's secretary, Evelyn Lincoln, was with the president at the hospital. "He was holding Patrick's hand," she recalled, "and the nurse said, 'He's gone.' And tears came into his eyes." Patrick's life lasted but three days. British prime minister Macmillan sent a handwritten note to the president: "The burdens of public affairs are more or less tolerable, because they are, in a sense, impersonal. But private grief is poignant and cruel."

Richard Cardinal Cushing, the archbishop of Boston, described the funeral:

OPPOSITE: *The First Lady worked to save the ancient Egyptian Temple at Abu Simbel*

1. Memo to JFK

Abou Simbel Temple

Agnelli's request: Gianni Agnelli is interested because a FIAT engineer has invented a way to cut entire temple out & float it on new lake. ~~[illegible]~~ It will cost 30 million. Italy has ~~[illegible]~~ offered 3 million which is more than her share in Unesco – FIAT however offered to subcontract it all to Westinghouse – thinking money could be raised that way – but they were not interested.

US cannot pay: I said US could not possibly pay the difference. It would be a miracle if they could even pay 3 million – as there was an 8 billion tax cut planned this year and unsympathetic chairmen of Rules & Appropriations Committees – so just to give up hope of getting the money from us.

President's support desired: Agnelli said in that case – if the President would just indicate his interest in saving the temples – it would be the greatest help and they could then approach Foundations & other members of Unesco.

Importance of Abou Simbel – It is the major temple of the Nile – 13th century B.C. It would be like letting the Parthenon be flooded. On it is the oldest Greek inscription in the world – which is sort of a Rosetta stone.

2

President's 1961 speech: April 7 1961 JFK asks for 2.5 million to save temples of Philae. This was done. Abu Simbel was not discussed at that time as no definite plan had been devised to save it.
JFK said "By thus contributing to ~~[illegible]~~ ~~[illegible]~~ the preservation of past civilisations
...w & enrich our OWN."

...vince US of possibility of saving
...gypt could be used – though
...e needed.

...tical argument carries more
... one. The Russians are
...tly in economic enterprise.
... US could show they care
... – and realize the importance
...imony of Egypt. –

...e to Nasser – as he promised
... them in Yemen & South Arabia
...gypt 30 million dollars s–
...ady repaid this debt.

... a his support in 2 ways.
...port – or in a later special

3

message. But the later message dealing solely with
Abu Simbel might be too vulnerable to poli...
~~[illegible]~~ –

e) Deadline – March 1963 is the lates...
a decision can be taken. ...
will be too late. So if the...
could say he is in favor of...
temples BEFORE March...
~~[illegible]~~ even though US can't...
it would spur the movement to...
to save them.

f) Contact Man...

Opinions of Mrs Kenned...
Italian...
temple should ...
get $30 million ...
satisfied with ...
support. Ther...
of the money...

> The family wanted the Mass of the Angels offered as part of the services. . . . The little chapel in the Archbishop's Residence accommodates about sixteen people. Only the members of the family were present. Jacqueline was too sick. . . . I wrote a special prayer that I gave to Jacqueline after I read it at the end of the mass. Then they all filed out, and for the second time I saw tears in the eyes of Jack Kennedy. . . . He was the last of the family to leave the little chapel. I was behind him. The casket was there. It was in a white marble case. The president was so overwhelmed with grief that he literally put his arms around that casket as though he was carrying it out.

Cardinal Cushing said to the president, "Jack, you better go along. Death isn't the end of it all, but the beginning."

The first lady worked diligently to protect the family's privacy, especially for Caroline and John. The children had a small play area on the White House grounds, but she realized that it was visible from the line where tourists waited for White House tours. She drew a map indicating the point of visibility and asked White House staff to have bushes planted there. She was vigilant about making sure the children were not photographed too often. *Look* photographer Stanley Tretick remembered that "Mrs. Kennedy had a way that strikes terror into your heart. She was a very strong minded girl and tough." At one event, said Tretick, "she caught my eye and said, 'Oh, now you're not here to photograph us, are you Stanley? . . . Or Caroline either?'"

When she and her husband built a country home in Virginia, she would not permit it to be photographed. "It's the only house Jack and I ever built together, and I designed it all myself," she said. "I don't want it to be exploited and photographed all over the place."

One price she paid for being Jackie Kennedy was that

she became the object of great jealousy. Tish Baldridge, a staffer and friend of the first lady, said she knew precisely why tongues wagged. "Of course, they're all jealous of her—she's young, beautiful, intelligent and rich, and besides all this, she's married to Jack Kennedy!"

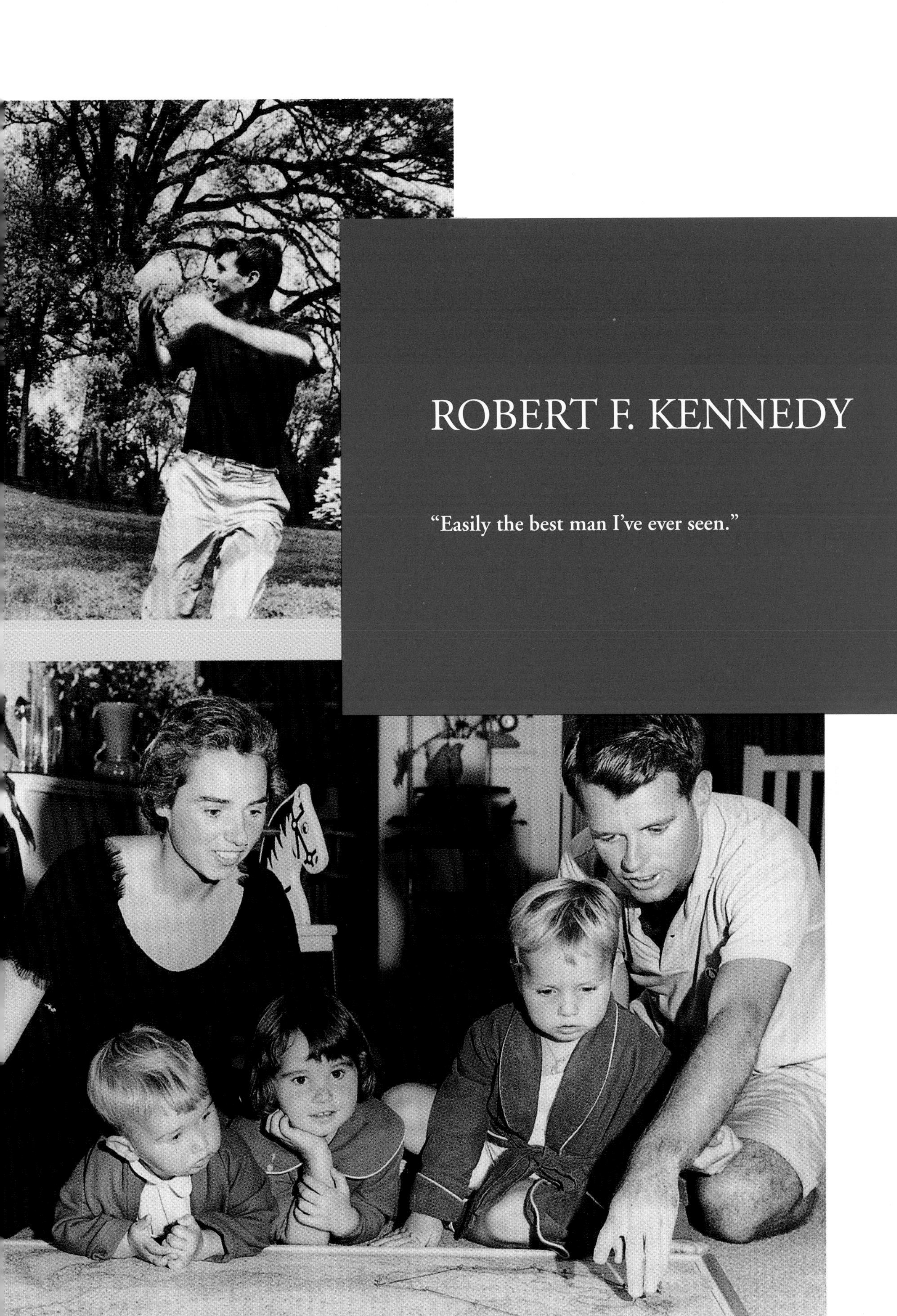

ROBERT F. KENNEDY

"Easily the best man I've ever seen."

Robert Kennedy was there as best man at his brother John's wedding. He was the man John Kennedy relied upon to guide his first run for the Senate, to lead his campaign for the presidency. Robert Kennedy was the first person President Kennedy called when learning of the Soviet missiles in Cuba. He was there for every major decision except the greatest disaster of the administration—the Bay of Pigs—and from that bitter lesson John Kennedy learned never again to do anything important without him.

"I should have had him involved from the beginning," the president lamented.

After the Bay of Pigs, although his official portfolio was exclusively domestic, Robert Kennedy became central to his brother's foreign policy apparatus. Vice President Johnson saw how important Robert Kennedy was. "It's not McNamara, the Chiefs of Staff, or anyone else like that. Bobby is first in, last out. And Bobby is the boy he listens to."

Robert Kennedy was not merely the most influential person in the administration of President Kennedy; he was arguably the most influential adviser to any president ever. Historian Michael Beschloss observed that "Robert Kennedy became his brother's trouble-shooter, lightning rod, spokesman, adviser, no-man, eyes and ears . . . whiphand overseer of the FBI and CIA, and tribune of presidential wishes and thoughts that the President would not let himself be heard to speak." Robert Kennedy was the sole adviser, wrote Beschloss, "who operated almost purely from the presidential point of view and with only the President's welfare at heart, undiluted by the aspirations of State, Defense, or the NSC staff."

They were different men in their ways. Because he was eight years older than his brother, John Kennedy had been away from home for much of the time that Robert was growing up. Jack had gone off to Choate when Bobby was only six years old. It was not merely a difference in age, however, but a difference in nature and character as well.

Robert had a tougher, more pugnacious exterior than his brother. "I was the seventh of nine children, and when you come from that far down you have to struggle," Bobby said.

Where John Kennedy was cool and cerebral, Robert was passionate and emotional. Where John was effortlessly smooth with strangers, Robert was uneasy and shy. He was often abrupt, seeming preoccupied. Where there was a sense of ease about John Kennedy, about Robert there was an almost tangible intensity. "Bobby is more direct than Jack," their father once said. "Jack has always been one to persuade people what to do. . . . [Bobby] resembles me much more than any of the other children."

Robert Kennedy was born on November 20, 1925. He graduated from Milton Academy, an exclusive private school

Jack and Bobby at the U.S. Embassy residence in London

just outside Boston, then went on to Harvard and the University of Virginia Law School. Like his brother before him, Robert Kennedy was attracted to Washington, but not initially as an elected official. Instead, he joined the Department of Justice in the Truman administration, then left to run his brother's 1952 campaign for the Senate. After the campaign Robert Kennedy returned to Washington to work for Senator Joseph McCarthy of Wisconsin as assistant counsel to the Permanent Subcommittee on Investigations. "At that time, I thought there was a serious internal security threat to the United States," he later said. "I felt at that time that Joe McCarthy seemed to be the only one who was doing anything about it."

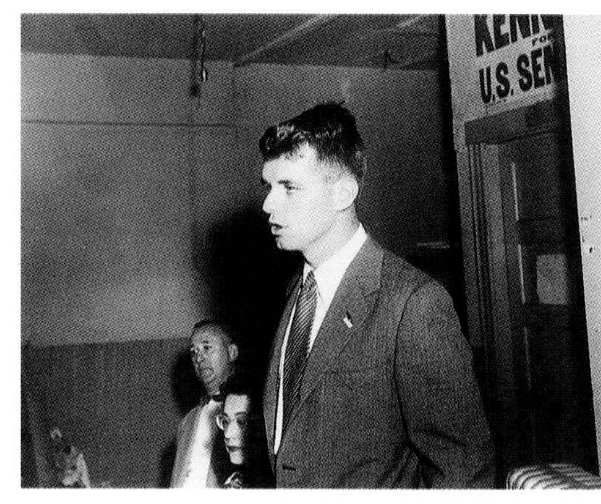

RFK as manager of Jack's 1952 Senate campaign

He left that job in 1956 to join the Stevenson presidential campaign. If his brother was to run nationwide at some point, it was important for Bobby to have experienced a presidential race from the inside. But he was very disappointed in Stevenson as a candidate. "People around Stevenson lost confidence in him," Bobby said. "There was no sort of enthusiasm about Stevenson personally." The experience nonetheless proved quite valuable. "Nobody asked me anything" during the Stevenson campaign, Robert said, "nobody wanted me to do anything, nobody consulted me. So I had time to watch everything. I filled complete notebooks with notes on how a Presidential campaign should be run."

Following Stevenson's loss, Robert Kennedy went back to work for the Senate Permanent Subcommittee on Investigations, where he focused on the influence of organized crime within the labor movement. His experiences over the next couple of years led him to write *The Enemy Within,* a book about corruption spreading from the underworld into labor, business, and politics. By the time he had completed the book in 1959, his brother had decided he was running for president and Robert Kennedy took over the campaign. He was John Kennedy's "first and only choice for campaign manager." His job was to organize, lead, and inspire. For his part, the candidate knew that all he had to do was concentrate on his role and the rest of the campaign details would be taken care of. "I don't have to think about organization," JFK said. "I just show up. [Bobby is] the hardest worker. He's the greatest organizer."

When president-elect Kennedy went through the process of selecting his cabinet, Robert Kennedy was by his side conferring, advising, debating. Robert Kennedy wanted to bring "new faces to government, men who believe their jobs go on forever, not just from nine to five." With most of the major cabinet jobs filled, JFK turned to the position of attorney general. This was the point at which the president-elect's father, Joseph P. Kennedy, stepped forward. He wanted Bobby appointed attorney general, and he would not take no for an answer. "I want Bobby there," the father told John Kennedy. "It's the only thing I'm asking for and I want it."

Joe Kennedy anticipated the difficult times ahead, and he knew, instinctively and from experience, that the president would need someone close by in whom he had complete and absolute trust. That could only be a family member. It could only be Bobby.

But Robert Kennedy resisted the idea. "He fought it until he drove Jack and me crazy," Joseph Kennedy said. And Bobby was not alone. There were many—staunch Kennedy supporters among them—who thought this level of nepotism was a terrible mistake. "A lot of people in our own

The brothers at a White House ceremony

camp fought it, too, and agreed with him," said the father. "They wanted to see him go back to Boston and become Senator. Not me!"

On December 15 John Kennedy asked Bobby to come to breakfast at his Georgetown home. They talked about what Bobby might do. There was discussion of a subcabinet position at the Department of Defense. There was discussion of attorney general. Bobby thought it politically risky, arguing that the next attorney general would have to take strong stands on civil rights matters, stands that would surely alienate many voters. If someone unrelated to the president were attorney general, perhaps he could absorb greater political heat. Bobby worried that if he were chosen it might result in the president's taking greater political blame for civil rights decisions. Bobby said he was considering returning to Massachusetts and perhaps running for governor.

"No," John Kennedy said. "You will be attorney general. I need you. . . . I need someone I know to talk to in this government."

Fletcher Knebel is reporting
that you told him that
if you were elected
President you would not
appoint any relative
to the White House staff.
Is this right?

Note from Evelyn Lincoln, the President's secretary, to JFK

Robert Kennedy's desk at the Department of Justice (as displayed at the Kennedy Library)

And so Robert Kennedy would do what his brother and father asked. When the time came to go outside John Kennedy's home and announce the appointment to the press, "he told me to go upstairs and comb my hair," Robert Kennedy said. "I said it was the first time the President had ever told the Attorney General to comb his hair before they made an announcement. And then when we were outside he said, 'don't smile too much or they'll think we're happy about the appointment.'"

The choice triggered immediate controversy. Many critics charged that Robert Kennedy was woefully lacking in the experience needed to run the Justice Department. Vice President Johnson recalled Senator Richard Russell's fury at the appointment. Said Johnson: "He thinks it's a disgrace for a kid who's never practiced law to be appointed." John Kennedy tried to use humor to defuse some of the criticism: "I can't see that it's wrong to give him a little legal experience before he goes out to practice law."

But Robert Kennedy knew that the critics would be silenced only by performance, and so it was that he dove into the job with all of the intensity he possessed. He began by recruiting energetic young lawyers who shared his passionate desire to use the law for social good. He chose young men and women from the finest law schools, people willing to work day and night, people who would follow wherever he led. From the start he targeted organized crime as no other attorney general ever had. From his work in the Senate and his experience writing *The Enemy Within,* Robert Kennedy was already intimately familiar with the problem of organized crime in the United States, and he was determined to attack it with a vengeance: "To meet the challenge of our times, so that we can later look back upon this era not as one of which we need be ashamed but as a turning point on the way to a better America, we must first defeat the enemy within."

Through speeches and writing, he alerted the country to the existence of a "private government of organized crime with an annual income of billions, resting on a base of human suffering and moral corrosion." He established the first coordinated program involving all twenty-six federal law enforcement agencies to investigate organized crime, overcoming FBI indifference to the pursuit of racketeers. He significantly increased funds and manpower for the department's Organized Crime Section, assigned a special team of prosecutors to handle the entire process of investigating and prosecuting cases against

Robert Kennedy with two men he was at odds with—J. Edgar Hoover, the FBI Director, and (below) Jimmy Hoffa, Teamsters boss

key racketeers, and successfully lobbied Congress for legislation expanding federal powers against organized crime. The attorney general's war on organized crime caused sharp disputes with FBI director J. Edgar Hoover. Hoover was obsessed not with organized crime but with what he perceived to be a grave Communist threat within the nation. In 1959 the FBI New York office had over 400 agents working on communism, four on organized crime. Robert Kennedy not only had a very different substantive agenda from Hoover, but the attorney general made no secret of his intense personal dislike of the FBI director. Convictions of racketeers by the Organized Crime Section and the Tax Division steadily increased: 96 in 1961, 373 in 1963. And Robert Kennedy went after the biggest catch of them all, Jimmy Hoffa, indicting the Teamsters leader on charges of jury tampering in 1963.

Robert Kennedy staked out a strong position on the plight of poor people in the federal courts. He wanted to level the playing field so that the poor would not be at such a disadvantage when it came to "bail, the cost of defense counsel, the cost of appeals." He discovered that many poor defendants remained in jail for months at a time because they could not "afford to pay for . . . freedom." At the attorney general's initiative, the National Conference on Bail and Criminal Justice was convened, and Congress eventually passed the federal Bail Reform Act. Though it was controversial, Robert Kennedy lent strong support to James V. Bennett, the progressive director of the Bureau of Prisons, who set up halfway houses, planned youth centers for young offenders, and attacked inequality in sentencing.

He brought a passionate intensity to the subject of civil rights. The attorney general thought integration should begin with example. When he found only ten black lawyers among the Justice Department's 955, he called for "thorough integration" of all the department's offices and wrote leading law schools asking for their best black graduates. In the spring of 1961, for example, he wrote to Eugene Rostow, dean of Yale Law School, that

> since coming to the Department of Justice I have noticed that there are few Negro lawyers employed here.
>
> I have no desire to employ anyone on the basis of his race. We are looking for qualified people here in the Department of Justice and ability is the primary consideration.
>
> However, I am anxious to take some steps to break down the barrier which apparently existed. With this in mind I am writing to ask you to furnish me with the names of qualified Negro attorneys of your acquaintance who might be interested in coming into the Dept. We also are interested in encouraging promising law students to consider making a career here.

As he delved more deeply into civil rights, the attorney general saw voting rights as critically important. "From the vote, from participation in the elections, flow all other rights," he said. He also believed that "nobody could really oppose voting." His goal was to register 100 people a day. That was the key to opening the door to all of what they wanted to accomplish in education, housing, jobs, and public accommodation. As the president's point man on civil rights, Robert Kennedy faced a major challenge when the Freedom Riders set out on their historic journey in May 1961. When the Freedom Riders were assaulted and beaten along their route, Kennedy was incensed. He exhibited a natural empathy for the underdog, and in this case he came to "an enormous anger, as if he had been down in Montgomery himself and been hit." When it was clear that local authorities were not acting with sufficient strength to keep the peace, Robert Kennedy dispatched 500 federal marshals.

But the political instincts that compelled him to protect his brother collided with his view of the Freedom Riders.

The attorney general felt strongly that they had made their point and that by continuing their protests they risked embarrassing the president on the eve of his Vienna meeting with Khrushchev.

Relations between civil rights leaders and the Kennedy Justice Department were not always harmonious, but there was a working relationship more often than not. As the Freedom Riders pushed on, Robert Kennedy pressed for the Interstate Commerce Commission to issue orders ending segregation in bus terminals; the commission did so in September 1961.

In June 1962 the attorney general faced another civil rights crisis. James Meredith, through a federal court order, had won the right to attend the University of Mississippi.

The Attorney General and the Vice-President with civil rights leaders in the Rose Garden after meeting with the President

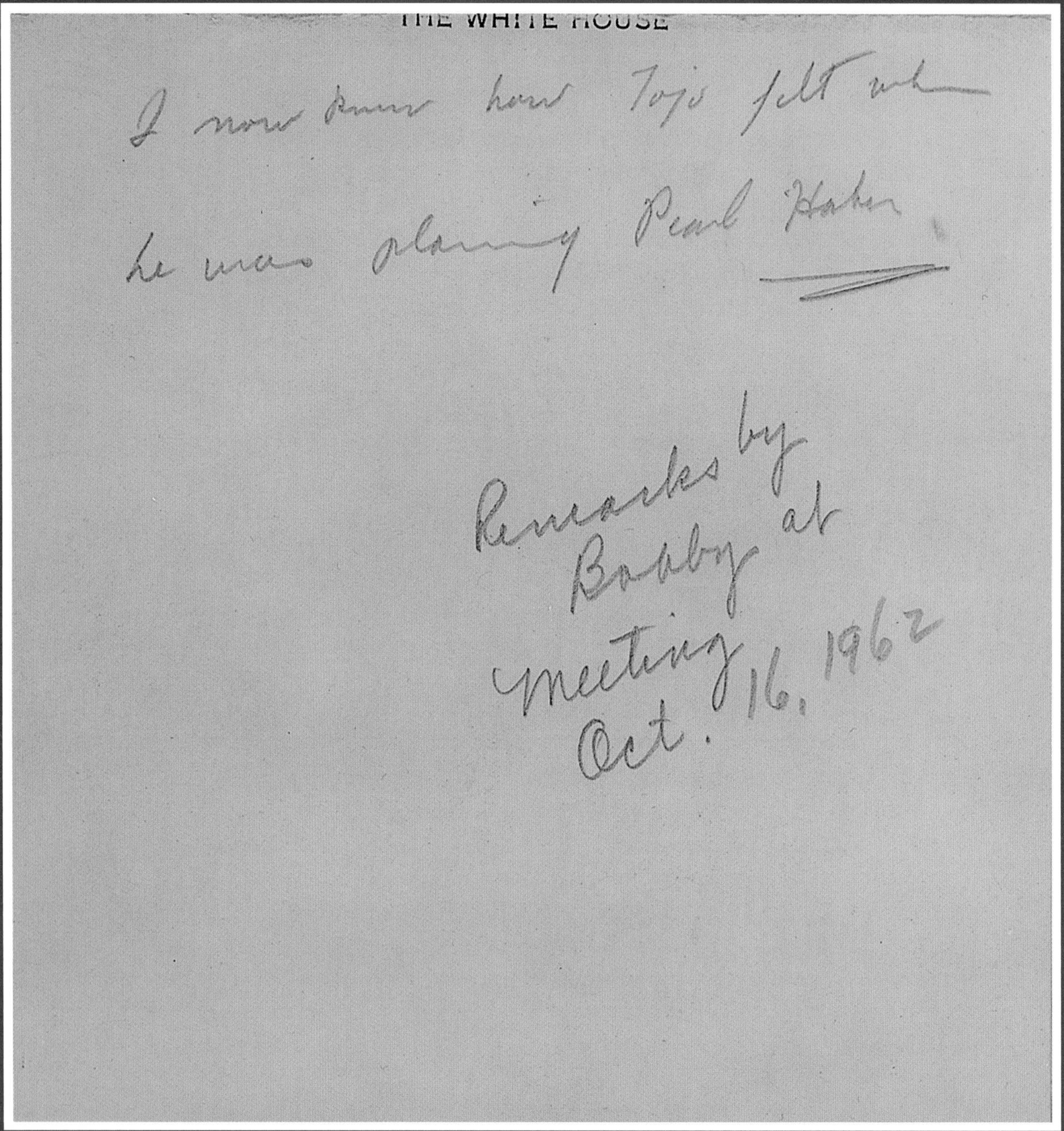

THE WHITE HOUSE

I now know how Tojo felt when

he was planning Pearl Harbor

Remarks by Bobby at meeting Oct. 16. 1962

But when time came for fall enrollment, Governor Barnett vowed that he would not "surrender to the evil and illegal forces of tyranny." Robert Kennedy flew to Mississippi to meet with Barnett. "I have a responsibility to enforce the laws of the United States," he told the governor. "The orders of the court are going to be upheld. As I told you, you are a citizen not only of the State of Mississippi but also of the United States."

Fierce resistance to Meredith's enrollment grew. Whites traveled from across the state to join in blocking his entrance to the university. In preparation for what seemed inevitable violence, the attorney general met with the joint chiefs of staff. "Maps of Mississippi were improbably unrolled in the Pentagon War Room," recalled Arthur Schlesinger Jr. Finally, after a call from the president, Governor Barnett relented and Meredith was registered. But violence erupted and the army was called in.

The brothers confer during a Senate hearing in 1957

Robert Kennedy learned a crucial lesson from the Mississippi experience. He knew that in the future hard work to prepare for integration could pay off in averting the most extreme reactions. When time came in 1963 to integrate the University of Alabama, he mounted a campaign to build support for the move. A key initiative was enlisting the support of business leaders from throughout the state. "We wrote down the names of every company with more than 100 employees," Robert Kennedy said. "A cabinet member called . . . every one of them."

The attorney general went to Alabama and told Governor George Wallace that he had a responsibility to see that the integrity of the courts was maintained and that "all of the force behind the Federal Government will be used to that end." When black students arrived to register, Wallace blocked their entrance. JFK called up the National Guard; Wallace backed down; the students registered.

When the president introduced comprehensive civil rights legislation in 1963, the attorney general led the fight on Capitol Hill. Testifying before the Senate Commerce Committee, he said that "the question is whether we, in this position of dominance, are going to have not the charity but the wisdom to stop penalizing our fellow citizens whose only fault or sin is that they were born. That . . . is why Congress should enact this bill, and should do it in this session."

Although it was highly unusual for an attorney general to be so involved, after the Bay of Pigs President Kennedy consulted his brother on every major decision, including matters of foreign policy. His first role in foreign affairs was

Ethel and Robert Kennedy in West Berlin

as a member of a small study group created to analyze why the Bay of Pigs had been such a failure. In the course of that work, Robert Kennedy developed a powerful connection to the 1,189 members of the Cuban brigade who had been captured during the mission. Over time, working through intermediaries, Robert Kennedy negotiated for the release of the captives, paying millions to the Cubans in cash and material goods, including medical supplies and tractors. On December 24 the prisoners arrived in Miami, where they were met by Robert Kennedy.

The successful release of the Cuban brigade, however, did nothing to deter Robert's determined opposition to Fidel Castro. The attorney general, in fact, played a key leadership role in the CIA's Operation Mongoose, an ongoing effort to undermine Castro by engaging in espionage, contaminating sugar exports, and printing counterfeit currency. The controversy surrounding Mongoose and its tactics would prove to be a stain on Robert Kennedy's reputation.

Robert Kennedy was an important ambassador on his brother's behalf. In February 1962 Robert traveled to fourteen countries, including Japan, Indonesia, India, Italy, West Germany, and France. During the trip he negotiated with foreign leaders; met with newspaper editors, clergymen, union representatives, and local politicians; and debated college students, workers, and intellectuals critical of the United States.

The president told a friend: "Bobby's easily the best man I've ever seen."

MRBM FIELD LAUNCH SITE
SAN CRISTOBAL NO 1
14 OCTOBER 1962
ERECTOR/LAUNCHER EQUIPMENT
ERECTOR/LAUNCHER EQUIPMENT
8 MISSILE TRAILERS

THE CUBAN MISSILE CRISIS

"We're eyeball to eyeball."

What was to be the turning point of the Kennedy administration—the event that fundamentally altered the course of his presidency and changed the way historians viewed his performance—was initiated, ironically, by the leader of the Soviet Union. Nikita Khrushchev expected President Kennedy to invade Cuba and drive Fidel Castro from office some time before the end of 1962. As Khrushchev thought about the Cuban situation, he had a daring idea for how to deter Kennedy from an invasion while at the same time demonstrating to the world that the United States was not superior to the Soviets in missile power. Khrushchev would secretly send nuclear missiles to Cuba, installing them before the United States could detect them. Khrushchev's hope was that when the missiles were in place, the United States would rethink any plans it might have for an invasion. The Soviets already had defensive surface-to-air missiles in Cuba in case of attack. But offensive nuclear warheads were of an entirely different magnitude. Placing missiles in Cuba was hardly an act of war, Khrushchev reasoned. It was, he believed, quite comparable to the United States' placing its missiles in Turkey. The United States called its missiles in Turkey "defensive," and so too would Khrushchev call his Cuban missiles "defensive." The Americans, Khrushchev said, "would learn just what it feels like to have enemy missiles pointing at you."

In late August 1962, the CIA was aware that "something new and different" was going on in Cuba. There was a buildup of Soviet personnel and a growing array of surface-to-air missiles and other defensive weapons. The first week of September Robert Kennedy, at his brother's behest, conveyed a message to Russian ambassador Anatoly Dobrynin. Robert Kennedy said the president was "deeply concerned" about the buildup in Cuba. Dobrynin sought to reassure the attorney general that the Russians had no offensive intentions. He said everything being done in Cuba was purely for defensive purposes and that Khrushchev had said there would be no "ground to ground missiles or offensive missiles placed in Cuba."

The activity drew the scrutiny of congressional Republicans angry at the existence of a Communist regime in Cuba. The Republicans wanted action, and they wanted it quickly. With midterm congressional elections approaching, the Republicans seized the issue of Cuba as though it were a political club and pounded away on the president. Republicans attacked Kennedy just as he had once gone after the Eisenhower administration in the campaign. A Communist regime ruled in Cuba, just 90 miles from the United States, and the president, his critics charged, was doing nothing about it. The Republican National Committee vowed that Cuba would be the major issue in the midterm congressional elections. In September Republican senator Homer Capehart of Indiana called for an invasion of Cuba to topple Castro and communism. That same month a Gallup poll revealed that seven out of ten Americans who were "informed" on the issue wanted some action.

President Kennedy confers in the Oval Office with Foreign Minister Gromyko (just to JFK's right) and with Ambassador Dobrynin (seated in the middle of the sofa)

The president issued a clear warning to Khrushchev in mid-September: Soviet buildup in Cuba would mean that the United States would do "whatever must be done to protect its own security and that of its allies." Khrushchev countered that an American attack on Cuba would mean war.

The rhetoric of a campaign season was suddenly overshadowed by the real-

U-2 reconnaissance photo of Cuban missile site

ity of the cold war. On October 14, 1962, an American U-2 reconnaissance plane, flying 70,000 feet over western Cuba, took a series of photographs of an area near San Cristobal. The following day, once U.S. photo interpreters had had an opportunity to study the pictures, the conclusion was inescapable: The Soviets were installing offensive nuclear missiles in Cuba. They were doing so after Khrushchev had stated explicitly that this would not happen. They were doing so after Ambassador Dobrynin had stated explicitly that this would not happen. They were doing so after having lied about it in the most bald-faced and public way possible. The discovery precipitated thirteen of the most perilous days in world history.

Monday, October 15

JFK was in his bedroom reading newspapers and sipping coffee when McGeorge Bundy, one of his senior advisers, arrived with the photos at 8:45 A.M.

"Mr. President," said Bundy, "there is now hard photographic evidence, which you will see, that the Russians have offensive missiles in Cuba."

JFK, listing the names of the men he wanted present, directed Bundy to convene a meeting right away. The president then picked up the phone and called his brother at the Justice Department. "We have some big trouble," John Kennedy said. "I want you over here."

Kennedy was determined first and foremost to get the missiles out of Cuba. He would settle for nothing less. A guiding principle, from the start, was Kennedy's determination not to trap Khrushchev; not to force the Russian leader into a corner that might precipitate an emotional or irrational response. He wanted to give Khrushchev breathing room. Kennedy was also intent on keeping the existence of the missiles as secret as possible. As long as the news did not leak, Kennedy would have time, and he knew he would need time. This was not an environment in which a hasty decision would be wise.

What would come to be known as Ex Comm, the Executive Committee of the National Security Council, convened at 11:30 A.M. in the cabinet room. Those present in addition to the president, his brother, and Bundy were Vice-President Johnson; Secretary of State Dean Rusk; Secretary of Defense Robert McNamara; CIA director John McCone; presidential aide Theodore Sorensen; General Maxwell Taylor, the chairman of the joint chiefs of staff; and a number of other national security and intelligence officials. A series of easels displayed aerial photographs showing two types of Soviet missiles, one with a range of about 630 miles, the other with a range of 1,100 miles.

"Is this ready to be fired?" the president asked.

No, came the reply.

"How long have we got . . .? How long before it can be fired?" he asked.

General Marshall Carter, deputy director of the CIA, estimated a week, maybe two.

The photos showed approximately sixteen Soviet ballistic missiles in the vicinity of launchpads that were under construction.

"What is the reason for the Russians to set this up . . .?" Kennedy asked. "It must be that they're not satisfied with their ICBMs [intercontinental ballistic missiles]."

"Khrushchev knows that we have a substantial nuclear superiority," said Rusk. "We don't really live under fear of his nuclear weapons to the extent that he . . . has to live under fear of ours. Also, we have nuclear weapons nearby, in Turkey and places like that."

The U.S. arsenal of nuclear warheads was far superior to that of the Soviets. Khrushchev may have been attempting to close the gap by setting up medium- and intermediate-range missiles in Cuba rather than trying to supplement the Soviet stock of ICBMs. It was clear Khrushchev was gambling, thinking perhaps that the last Cuba experience for JFK had shaken the young president, that Kennedy was weak, lacking in judgment and backbone.

Rusk said there were two broad choices: to attack Cuba or to open discussions with the Soviets and U.S. allies. JFK's initial instinct was to mount an air attack to destroy the missiles and their sites before construction was complete and the missiles were mounted on their launchpads, ready for firing. But it was too early for such action. Kennedy instructed McNamara to continue U-2 surveillance and said the group would gather again at six that evening.

Upstairs in the White House, the president talked with Adlai Stevenson, his ambassador to the United Nations. "We'll have to do something quickly," Kennedy said. "I suppose the alternatives are to go in by air and wipe them out, or to take other steps to render the weapons inoperable." Stevenson urged the president to explore other means before deciding on such an attack. Early that evening, when the group reconvened, General Carter said additional U-2 photographs had identified four more medium-range missiles. There was a sense in the room that an attack would be necessary. Robert Kennedy suggested the possibility of staging an event reminiscent of the sinking of the *Maine* that would give the United States a pretext for an assault on Cuba. But the president held back. He had long feared as he told Khrushchev in Vienna, that a nuclear exchange could occur through miscalculation. With Kennedy, it was not posturing. He had a profound fear that a misreading of intentions by one nation could lead to war. He also wanted to make sure that the man seated in his position in the Kremlin was not forced into a corner where fear and instinct could cause him to lash out.

The President, McNamara, and Roswell Gilpatrick during the missile crisis

By the end of the evening meeting, it was clear that the human cost of an immediate air strike—the deaths of Soviet troops and technicians—could well be high enough to bring retaliation from Moscow.

Wednesday, October 17

At the Ex Comm meeting, CIA director McCone advised Kennedy to attack. Robert Kennedy spoke in opposition to an air strike, arguing that it would be a "Pearl Harbor in reverse." The United States, he said, did not engage in sneak attacks. Ted Sorensen handed the president a summary of the options that had been discussed at Ex Comm thus far. "The following possible tracks or courses of action have each been considered," Sorensen wrote:

> Track A—Political action, pressure and warning, followed by a military strike if satisfaction is not received.
>
> Track B—A military strike without prior warning, pressure or action, accompanied by messages making clear the limited nature of this action.
>
> Track C—Political action, pressure and warning, followed by a total naval blockade . . . and either a Congressional Declaration of War on Cuba or the Cuban Resolution of the 87th Congress.
>
> Track D—Full-scale invasion, to "take Cuba away from Castro."

That morning the *Washington Post* carried a Gallup poll indicating that 51 percent of the American people believed an attack on Cuba would lead to World War III. General Curtis LeMay during the meeting that day told the president he favored bombing. Kennedy asked LeMay how he thought the Soviets would respond to such an attack. The general said the Soviets would do nothing. JFK's confidence in his generals had declined markedly after the Bay of Pigs. There were some—such as Maxwell Taylor and Marshall Carter—in whom he had a great deal of confidence. But there were others, LeMay among them, whom he thought were foolish. "Are you trying to tell me that they'll let us bomb their missiles, and kill a lot of Russians and then do nothing? If they don't do anything in Cuba, then they'll certainly do something in Berlin."

The president found LeMay's answer absurd. Back at his office he remarked to an aide: "Can you imagine LeMay saying a thing like that?" He said that "if we listen to [the

TCS - 10/17/62

1. It is generally agreed that Soviet MRBM's -- offensive weapons -- are now in Cuba. While only one complex of three sites and no nuclear warheads have been spotted, it must be assumed that this is the beginning of a larger build-up.

2. It is generally agreed that these missiles, even when fully operational, do not significantly alter the balance of power -- i.e., they do not significantly increase the potential megatonnage capable of being unleashed on American soil, even after a surprise American nuclear strike. The Soviet purpose in making this move is not understood -- whether it is for purposes of diversion, harassment, provocation or bargaining.

3. Nevertheless it is generally agreed that the United States cannot tolerate the known presence of offensive nuclear weapons in a country 90 miles from our shore, if our courage and our commitments are ever to be believed by either allies or adversaries. Retorts from either our European allies or the Soviets that we can become as accustomed as they to accepting the nearby presence of MRBM's have some logic but little weight in this situation.

4. It is also agreed that certain of our NATO allies would be notified but not consulted immediately prior to any action by the United States; that certain Latin nations would at least be notified; and that, if there is to be military action, the President would hold announcing the existence of the missiles and the justification of our action until after that action had been completed.

generals], and do what they want us to do, none of us will be alive later to tell them that they were wrong."

Thursday, October 18

A faction within Ex Comm argued that a diplomatic approach to the problem—talking with the Soviets and U.S. allies about getting the missiles out—would actually play directly into Soviet hands by giving them the time they needed to complete construction of the launch facilities in Cuba. Secretary of State Rusk told Kennedy he thought the United States should mount an air strike targeted as precisely as possible at the missiles and their support facilities. Rusk said there should be no warning to the Soviets or Cubans prior to the strike.

The Soviet foreign minister, Andrei Gromyko, requested a meeting with Kennedy for that afternoon. Gromyko arrived at the White House at 5 P.M. to see the president, who expected that Gromyko might raise the issue of the missiles in Cuba. But he did not. He talked mostly about Berlin, then he brought up Cuba. It was an open secret that the Soviets had placed defensive surface-to-air missiles in Cuba. The United States accepted that.

"I have been instructed to make it clear that the purpose of any arms is by no means offensive," Gromyko told Kennedy. It was a lie and Kennedy knew it. He had the U-2 photographs. But he did not respond. He did not want the Soviets to know what the United States knew. For if word got out about what Kennedy knew, a showdown might quickly be forced; events could race ahead, beyond the president's control.

Conferring with Secretary of State Rusk (left)

As Kennedy met with Gromyko, other members of Ex Comm were at the State Department continuing their strategy sessions. They were scheduled to return to the White House at 9 P.M. to meet with the president again. The nine men then in the State Department meeting crammed into a single car for the short trip to the White House, fearing that a fleet of limousines pulling in would draw suspicion from the press that there was some sort of crisis or emergency. When the group settled in, it quickly became apparent that there was growing support for the idea of a naval blockade of Cuba.

The president had yet to express an opinion on the matter to the committee, although it was clear to Robert Kennedy that his brother favored the blockade. By not bombing the sites, the United States risked allowing the Soviets to complete the installations and ready the missiles for an attack. But it was Kennedy's belief that a blockade was a reasonable first step: It was the kind of move unlikely to precipitate war. It did not foreclose Khrushchev's options. And if it failed, Kennedy could always move toward the bombing option later. In short, it was a limited response unlikely to result in casualties, and it would not thrust the world to the brink of war. The president was pondering the matter when he got up and walked to the French doors overlooking the Rose Garden. He peered out and mused, "I guess I better earn my salary this week."

Friday, October 19

Secrecy was essential to thoughtful, careful deliberations. The president did not want to be put under the gun. He did not want to have his hand forced in an atmosphere of world crisis. To maintain secrecy, JFK stuck to his planned schedule even as the Ex Comm group met without him. On Friday, October 19, the president headed out to campaign for

Democrats in the midterm congressional elections, but his political outlook was gloomy. He told his brother: "The campaign is over. This blows it—we've lost anyway. [The Republicans] were right about Cuba."

Arguing among the president's advisers intensified. The hawks, those who wanted to bomb the missile sites, were growing impatient. Acheson, Taylor, and Bundy strongly urged Kennedy to commence bombing. McCone; Paul Nitze, assistant secretary of defense; and C. Douglas Dillon, a Republican who had served in Eisenhower's administration and whom Kennedy had chosen as secretary of the treasury, also favored bombing. Time was running out, they argued. Soon the launchpads would be completed and the missiles would be ready for firing. "It comes down to this," Bundy said. "A blockade will not eliminate the bases, an air strike will."

But Robert Kennedy's opposition to air strikes had hardened. He made a moral argument, that a sneak attack would kill thousands of people—Soviets, Cubans, soldiers, technicians, civilians—with no warning. It would be akin to Pearl Harbor, he said, and was unworthy of the United States. Dillon listened to Robert Kennedy's impassioned plea against bombing and decided that he was correct: An unannounced attack was not something the United States could do and still maintain the high moral ground. Dillon switched his position in favor of a blockade.

Saturday, October 20

This was to be decision day. The discussions had gone on long enough. There was beginning to be a repetitive nature to the meetings. Nerves were frayed. It was time. On Saturday morning the president was out on a campaign trip but returned to Washington for a midafternoon meeting with his advisers. Sorensen gave Kennedy a memo that summarized the "two fundamental advantages to a blockade":

1. It is a more prudent and flexible step which enables us to move to an air strike, invasion or any other step at any time it proves necessary, without the "Pearl Harbor" posture.

2. It is the step least likely to precipitate general war while still causing the Soviets—unwilling to engage our Navy in our waters—to back down and abandon Castro.

At the meeting McNamara summarized the case for a blockade and Bundy argued for bombing. The arguments were made by brilliant men devoted to the service of their nation, seeking to give the president the very best advice they could possibly summon. When they were done, the room fell silent. The critical moment had come.

John F. Kennedy wanted the missiles out of Cuba, without bloodshed if possible, certainly without prompting a nuclear exchange between the United States and the USSR. He instinctively felt it was necessary to give Khrushchev some room to maneuver. The blockade was gradual. It was not precipitous. It did not force Khrushchev's hand immediately. It was the least confrontational option short of inaction. This was the course that President Kennedy selected. The group agreed that the blockade—which would be called a quarantine, since under international law a blockade is an act of war—would be declared Monday evening. The president would go on television and announce it to the nation and the world.

Monday, October 22

On Monday all military leaves were canceled, and the armed forces of the United States of America went on alert, prepared for war. Several thousand nuclear missiles and bombs, in silos in the western United States, on submarines, and on U.S. bombers, were at the ready. One hundred thousand troops from the U.S. Army strategic reserve were moved from Texas to Georgia. The president sent emissaries to brief key NATO allies. Starting early Monday morning, U.S. Air Force jets fanned out across the nation to pick up key members of Congress and fly them back to Washington for an urgent meeting with the president. As the House and Senate members were being brought back, Kennedy telephoned Eisenhower, who had been given a background briefing. "Whatever you do you will have my support," Ike told JFK.

There was a different reaction, however, from congressional leaders who later in the day gathered to meet with the president. Senator Richard Russell of Georgia, a Democrat and chairman of the Senate Armed Services Committee, was dismayed by what he considered the weakness of Kennedy's proposed quarantine. There was no guarantee, he said, that it would force the Soviets to remove the missiles. Only bombing could assure that, Russell said.

Kennedy was taken aback. Senator J. William Fulbright, another member of the president's party, had earlier cautioned Kennedy against the Bay of Pigs invasion. Surely Fulbright would come to the president's aide. But Fulbright said he agreed with Russell. An air attack, not a blockade, was the appropriate course. It was not what Kennedy had hoped to hear less than two hours before going on television to speak to an audience of 100 million people.

Before his speech, Kennedy sent a letter to Khrushchev:

> I have not assumed that you or any other sane man would, in this nuclear age, deliberately plunge the world into war which it is crystal clear no country could win and which could only result in catastrophic consequences to the whole world, including the aggressor. . . . I publicly stated that if certain developments in Cuba took place, the United States would do whatever must be done to protect its own security and that of its allies. . . . Despite this, the rapid development of long-range missile bases and other

> offensive weapons in Cuba has proceeded. I must tell you that the United States is determined that this threat to the security of this hemisphere be removed.

On television Kennedy said that there was "unmistakable evidence" of offensive missiles in Cuba:

> The purpose of these bases can be none other than to provide a nuclear strike capability against the Western Hemisphere. . . .
>
> This secret, swift and extraordinary buildup of Communist missiles is a deliberately provocative and unjustified change in the status quo which cannot be accepted by this country, if our courage and our commitments are ever to be trusted again by either friend or foe. The 1930s taught us a clear lesson: aggressive conduct, if allowed to go unchecked and unchallenged, ultimately leads to war.

The president announced the quarantine, then issued the most chilling threat he had ever uttered: "It shall be the policy of this nation to regard any nuclear missile launched from Cuba against any nation in the Western Hemisphere as an attack by the Soviet Union on the United States, requiring a full retaliatory strike upon the Soviet Union." As the president spoke, air force jets were airborne over Florida in case the speech precipitated a missile launch from Cuba.

Addressing the nation at a time of crisis

Historian Michael Beschloss has observed that "the address was probably the most alarming ever delivered by an American president." Throughout the United States and the world, people were shocked and frightened. Never had the world been so close to the brink.

Tuesday, October 23

Kennedy had gained the political advantage he had hoped for: The United States had spoken first and won the ability to frame the world discussion of the issue. A critical piece was added when the Organization of American States (OAS) voted on the matter. Many of the twenty South and Central American nations belonging to the OAS were often prickly about the United States. But on this matter the organization voted 20 to 0 for a resolution calling for "immediate dismantling and removal from Cuba of all missiles." Such an overwhelming vote was a surprise and a major victory for the United States. And a poll showed there was powerful support among the American people, with 84 percent favoring the blockade. At this point the president's control over management of the crisis was such that Robert Kennedy said his brother "supervised everything."

JFK signs the proclamation establishing the Quarantine of Cuba

Wednesday, October 24

So tight was Kennedy's hold on the reins that when Secretary of Defense McNamara and Admiral George Anderson got into a conflict about search procedures for the quarantine, McNamara told the admiral: "This is not a blockade but a means of communication between Kennedy and Khrushchev. No force would be applied without my permission and that would not be given without discussion with the president."

The enormous tension throughout the United States and the world immediately prompted UN secretary general U Thant to try to get the two sides talking. He proposed that both the Soviet arms shipments and the U.S. blockade be suspended for some weeks to allow time for negotiations. Khrushchev accepted the proposal. Kennedy rejected it. He was unwavering: "The existing threat was created by the secret introduction of offensive weapons into Cuba, and the answer lies in the removal of such weapons," the president wrote to the secretary general.

That same day Kennedy received a reply to his letter of Monday night to Khrushchev. "The actions of the USA with regard to Cuba are outright banditry, or, if you like, the folly of degenerate imperialism," Khrushchev wrote, adding that it was "an act of outright aggression pushing mankind toward the abyss of a missile nuclear war."

On Wednesday morning the quarantine went into effect. An antisubmarine aircraft carrier, three cruisers, sixteen destroyers, and 150-plus other ships were dispatched to patrol the quarantine line. The air was thick with apprehension. The president, opening and closing one hand into a fist while covering his mouth with the other hand, stared at his brother. Was war imminent? Would those estimates the president had sought regarding the number of casualties prove to be true? Was it possible that 70 million Americans were about to die in an all-out nuclear exchange?

"It was almost as though no one else was there and he was no longer the President," Robert Kennedy wrote. "I thought of when he was ill and almost died, when he lost his child, when he learned that our oldest brother had been killed."

Suddenly, however, word reached the White House that six Russian ships headed for Cuba either turned back or stopped in the water. Hearing this, Secretary of State Rusk exclaimed: "We're eyeball to eyeball and I think the other fella just blinked."

Thursday, October 25

On Thursday JFK responded sharply to Khrushchev's letter. "I regret very much," the president wrote, "that you still do not appear to understand what it is that has moved us in this matter. This government received the most explicit assurances from your Government and its representatives, both publicly and privately, that no offensive weapons were being sent to Cuba. . . . All those public assurances were false."

When the first Russian ship steamed toward the interdiction line being patrolled by the U.S. Navy, most members of the Ex Comm urged Kennedy to have it stopped and searched. Rather than stop a Russian ship first, Kennedy ordered the stoppage of a ship built in America sailing under Panamanian ownership. "I don't want to put him in a corner," Kennedy said. "We don't want to push him into a precipitous action."

John Scali, a diplomatic correspondent for ABC, was in the pressroom at the State Department when he received a call from an official at the Soviet embassy in Washington, a man named Alexander Fomin. Fomin asked Scali to meet him right away at a restaurant called the Occidental. Scali complied. When he arrived, Fomin asked if Scali could check with his State Department sources on whether the United States was interested in a deal. The deal was simple: The Soviets would remove their missiles from Cuba—and do so under the supervision of UN monitors—if the United States would promise not to invade Cuba. Scali returned immediately to the State Department and was brought in to see the secretary of state. When Scali arrived, Rusk happened to be meeting with Robert Kennedy and McGeorge Bundy. After the three men huddled privately, Rusk told Scali that the United States would indeed be interested in exploring such an arrangement. Scali was then taken to the White House, where he was ushered in to see the president.

~~SECRET~~

45989
T-85/T-94
Russian

[Embossed Seal of the USSR]

Moscow, October 23, 1962

Mr. President:

I have just received your letter, and have also acquainted myself with the text of your speech of October 22 regarding Cuba.

I must say frankly that the measures indicated in your statement constitute a serious threat to peace and to the security of nations. The United States has openly taken the path of grossly violating the United Nations Charter, the path of violating international norms of freedom of navigation on the high seas, the path of aggressive actions both against Cuba and against the Soviet Union.

The statement by the Government of the United States of America can only be regarded as undisguised interference in the internal affairs of the Republic of Cuba, the Soviet Union and other states. The United Nations Charter and international norms give no right to any state to institute in international waters the inspection of vessels bound for the shores of the Republic of Cuba.

And naturally, neither can we recognize the right of the United States to establish control over armaments which are necessary for the Republic of Cuba to strengthen its defense capability.

We reaffirm that the armaments which are in Cuba, regardless of the classification to which they may belong, are intended solely for defensive purposes in order to secure the Republic of Cuba against the attack of an aggressor.

His Excellency
John Kennedy,
President of the United States of America

~~SECRET~~

Orig. Mrs Lincoln 11/14/62

DRAFT

October 23, 1962

Dear Mr. Chairman:

I have received your letter of October twenty-third. I think you will recognize that the steps which started the current chain of events was the action of your Government in secretely furnishing offensive weapons to Cuba. We will be discussing this matter in the Security Council. In the meantime, I am concerned that we both show prudence and do nothing to allow events to make the situation more difficult to control than it already is.

I hope that you will issue immediately the necessary instructions to your ships to observe the terms of the quarantine established by the vote of the Organization of American States this afternoon, ~~We have no desire to seize or fire upon your vessels.~~ which will go into effect 1400 hours Greenwich time October 24, 1962.

Sincerely,

Kennedy instructed Scali to make clear that there was interest in the proposal "at the highest level" of the U.S. government.

That evening Scali and Fomin rendezvoused at the Sheraton Park Hotel at about 7:30. Scali said that he had "reason to believe" that senior officials within the U.S. government saw "real possibilities" in the earlier Fomin proposal. But Scali added that rapid action by the Soviets was required, that the situation had grown "very urgent."

Almost simultaneous with the secret communications between Scali and Fomin, a drama was playing out on the UN diplomatic stage. The U.S. ambassador to the UN, Adlai Stevenson, rose to challenge his Soviet counterpart, Valerian Zorin.

"Do you, Ambassador Zorin, deny that the USSR has placed and is placing medium and intermediate range missiles . . . in Cuba? Yes or no?" Stevenson demanded. "Don't wait for the translation. Yes or no?"

"I am not in an American courtroom, sir," replied Zorin, "and therefore I do not wish to answer. . . . In due course, sir, you will have your reply."

"You are in the courtroom of world opinion right now," replied Stevenson, "and you can answer yes or no."

"You will have your answer in due course," the Russian responded.

"I am prepared to wait for my answer until hell freezes over," Stevenson said.

Then Stevenson displayed a series of large photographs showing the missiles in Cuba.

Friday, October 26

On Friday evening, shortly after 9, John Kennedy received a personal letter from Nikita Khrushchev. It was long and rambling, passionate in its tone, utterly unlike the standard diplomatic correspondence of the day. It quickly became clear that it was a letter from the heart.

> I see, Mr. President, that you too are not devoid of understanding and a proper evaluation of the character of a contemporary war, a sense of anxiety for the fate of the world. What would a war give you? You are threatening us with war. . . . If indeed war should break out, then it would not be in our power to stop it, for such is the logic of war. I have participated in two wars and know that war ends when it has rolled through cities and villages, everywhere sowing death and destruction.
>
> . . . Let us not quarrel now. . . . You can regard us with distrust, but, in any case you can be calm in this regard, that we are of sound mind and understand perfectly well that if we attack you, you will respond the same way. . . . Only lunatics or suicides, who themselves want to perish and to destroy the world before they die, could do this.

Then came a proposal identical to what Fomin had proposed to Scali: The Russians would remove the missiles if the United States pledged not to invade Cuba.

Saturday, October 27

At 10 A.M. Saturday, the Ex Comm members met with the president, hopes high, as they discussed Khrushchev's proposed deal. But barely had their discussion begun when another letter arrived, this one already having been made public by the Kremlin. The hopes of the group plunged upon reading the letter. It was rigid, bureaucratic, lacking in the heart and humanity of the letter from the night before. Worst of all, it offered a different deal. "Do you believe that you have the right to demand security for your country and the removal of such weapons that you qualify as offensive, while not recognizing this right for us?" the letter stated.

I THINK YOU WILL UNDERSTAND ME CORRECTLY IF YOU ARE REALLY CONCERNED ABOUT THE WELFARE OF THE WORLD. EVERYONE NEEDS PEACE: BOTH CAPITALISTS, IF THEY HAVE NOT LOST THEIR REASON, AND, STILL MORE, COMMUNISTS, PEOPLE WHO KNOW HOW TO VALUE NOT ONLY THEIR OWN LIVES BUT, MORE THAN ANYTHING, THE LIVES OF THE PEOPLES. WE, COMMUNISTS, ARE AGAINST ALL WARS BETWEEN STATES IN GENERAL AND HAVE BEEN DEFENDING THE CAUSE OF PEACE SINCE WE CAME INTO THE WORLD. WE HAVE ALWAYS REGARDED WAR AS A CALAMITY, AND NOT AS A GAME NOR AS A MEANS FOR THE ATTAINMENT OF DEFINITE GOALS, NOR, ALL THE MORE, AS A GOAL IN ITSELF. OUR GOALS ARE CLEAR, AND THE MEANS TO ATTAIN THEM IS LABOR. WAR IS OUR ENEMY AND A CALAMITY FOR ALL THE PEOPLES.

IT IS THUS THAT WE, SOVIET PEOPLE, AND, TOGETHER WITH US, OTHER PEOPLES AS WELL, UNDERSTAND THE QUESTIONS OF WAR AND PEACE. I CAN, IN ANY CASE, FIRMLY SAY THIS FOR THE PEOPLES OF THE SOCIALIST COUNTRIES, AS WELL AS FOR ALL PROGRESSIVE PEOPLE WHO WANT PEACE, HAPPINESS, AND FRIENDSHIP AMONG PEOPLES.

I SEE, MR. PRESIDENT, THAT YOU TOO ARE NOT DEVOID OF A SENSE OF ANXIETY FOR THE FATE OF THE WORLD, ~~UEGN *~~ OF UNDERSTANDING, AND OF WHAT WAR ENTAILS. WHAT WOULD A WAR GIVE YOU? YOU ARE THREATENING US WITH WAR. BUT YOU WELL KNOW THAT THE VERY LEAST WHICH YOU WOULD RECEIVE IN REPLY WOULD BE THAT YOU WOULD EXPERIENCE THE SAME CONSEQUENCES AS THOSE WHICH YOU SENT US. AND THAT MUST BE CLEAR TO US, PEOPLE INVESTED WITH AUTHORITY, TRUST, AND RESPONSIBILITY. WE MUST NOT SUCCUMB TO INTOXICATION AND PETTY PASSIONS, REGARDLESS OF WHETHER ELECTIONS ARE IMPENDING IN THIS OR THAT COUNTRY, OR NOT IMPENDING. THESE ARE ALL TRANSIENT THINGS, BUT IF INDEED WAR SHOULD BREAK OUT, THEN IT WOULD NOT BE IN OUR POWER TO STOP IT, FOR SUCH IS THE LOGIC OF WAR. I HAVE PARTICIPATED IN TWO WARS AND KNOW THAT WAR ENDS WHEN IT HAS ROLLED THROUGH CITIES AND VILLAGES, EVERYWHERE SOWING DEATH AND DESTRICTION.

The Soviets would remove their missiles from Cuba, the letter said, if the United States removed its missiles from Turkey.

It was not that the fifteen medium-range ballistic missiles the United States had in Turkey held such great strategic importance. Rather, the missiles were a commitment by the United States to its NATO allies. Kennedy knew it was essential for the United States to be strong and to stand by its allies. At the same time, he was convinced the Soviet proposal would be viewed as quite reasonable—a simple swap. George Ball, a senior State Department official, said it would be very unsettling to Turks for the United States to remove the missiles. Kennedy replied: "Well, this is unsettling now, George, because he's got us in a pretty good spot here, because most people will regard this as not an unreasonable proposal, I'll just tell you that."

The president was very concerned with how the United States would appear before the world if American leaders seemed unwilling to be reasonable. He told Ex Comm members that the U.S. position might well be viewed as "unsupportable" if the United States obstinately refused to withdraw its missiles from Turkey. He characterized the missiles in Turkey as "not militarily useful" and said that "any rational man" would consider removing them in exchange for Soviet removal of the Cuban missiles. That would appear to be "a very fair trade," he said. If the United States remained unwilling to make such a deal, the president said, "I think you're going to find it very difficult to explain why we are going to take hostile military action in Cuba." Besides, Kennedy said, U.S. Polaris subs could substitute for the missiles in Turkey quite easily.

Bundy argued that agreeing to the deal would make it look as if "we were trying to sell our allies for our interests. That would be the view in all of NATO."

But Kennedy insisted, "They've got a—God—they've got a very good proposal, which is the reason they made it publicly not privately." He wondered whether there was a way to get the Turks to propose that the United States agree to the deal. "I'm just trying to cope with what the public problem is about—because everybody's going to think that this is very reasonable."

As the day wore on, there was a sense of gloom, a sense that the nation was close to war. The joint chiefs wanted to commence bombing on Monday. There was discussion within Ex Comm that perhaps there was a power struggle in the Kremlin—that Khrushchev was under pressure from the hard-liners. The situation was in its way not so terribly different in the White House, where the hawks were pushing for action. Since the discovery of the missile sites, the United States had not in any way deterred their construction. U-2 photos showed that work continued, that the launchpads were nearly ready.

Then, suddenly, news came of a casualty: An American U-2 had been shot down over Cuba, the pilot killed—the same pilot who had brought back the original photos of the Soviet installation in progress. The hawks were more determined than ever to attack. There was now no choice.

But the president said no. "We can't very well invade Cuba . . . when we could have gotten [the missiles] out by making a deal on the same missiles in Turkey. If that's part of the record, I don't see how we'll have a good war."

Bundy was one of the most powerful minds in the Kennedy administration and had grown to be one of the president's most trusted advisers. It was Bundy who first proposed an idea that was brilliant in its simplicity: Why not ignore Khrushchev's most recent letter—the tough, formal missive—and instead respond only to the more personal and encouraging one he had sent Friday night? Several members of Ex Comm had had the thought almost simultaneously: Reply to the deal the United States liked; disregard the deal that it did not. Kennedy thought it was certainly worth a try.

Only one man could be entrusted with the mission, and that was the president's brother. Robert Kennedy would go to the Soviet embassy, meet with Ambassador Dobrynin, and propose a deal. John Kennedy told Robert Kennedy that he should tell Dobrynin that "if we don't get a reply by Monday, we'll start a military action against Cuba." Then the president said, in the presence of Rusk, Bundy, Sorensen, and McNamara, that Robert should tell Dobrynin that the missiles in Turkey would not be an obstacle to a settlement.

This was critical, for it showed that Kennedy understood what Khrushchev needed to cement the deal. As Sorensen observed, Kennedy "recognized that for Chairman Khrushchev to withdraw the missiles from Cuba, it would be undoubtedly helpful to him if he could say at the same time to his colleagues in the Presidium, 'And we have been assured that the missiles will be coming out of Turkey.'"

At about 7:30 P.M., Robert Kennedy left the White House on the most important mission of his life. Inside the Soviet embassy, meeting with Dobrynin, the attorney general said that the United States would agree not to invade Cuba if the Russians removed the missiles. In addition, said Robert Kennedy, the president was proposing a part of the deal that could not be made public: The United States would pledge to withdraw its missiles from Turkey, but not immediately. The president's word would have to be trusted. Time was critical, said Robert Kennedy. His brother was under tremendous pressure from the generals to act militarily. He did not know how much longer the president could hold out. If the deal was to work, it had to happen right away.

Dobrynin sent a message to Khrushchev that night. Everyone waited.

SUNDAY, OCTOBER 28

On Sunday morning, 9 A.M. eastern time, Radio Moscow broadcast a new letter from Khrushchev. The announcer

OPPOSITE: *Presidential doodles during crisis*

Scribbled notes during meeting of Security Council Oct 25, 1962

24 hour

missile

missile

missile

missile

veto

veto

veto

veto

veto

Close surveillance

diplomatic

Soviet ship

passenger interest

Barnes

Barnes

Camouflage

Grozny

said that Khrushchev had received Kennedy's message conveyed by his brother Friday night via Dobrynin.

> "I express my satisfaction," Khrushchev said through the announcer, "and thank you for the sense of proportion you have displayed and for recognition of the responsibility you now bear for the preservation of the peace of the world. I very well understand your anxiety and that of the American people about the fact that the weapons you describe as offensive are formidable weapons indeed. . . .
>
> In order to eliminate as rapidly as possible the conflict which endangers the cause of peace . . . the Soviet Government, in addition to previously issued instructions to cease further work on weapons construction sites, has issued a new order to dismantle the weapons which you describe as offensive, and to crate and return them to the Soviet Union."

In one stunning moment, Khrushchev was accepting the deal.

At noon JFK watched television news reporters Marvin Kalb and David Schoenbrun. Kalb said something about the "American victory."

"Tell them to stop that," Kennedy snapped to Pierre Salinger, watching with him. The press secretary picked up the phone and immediately called Schoenbrun. "David, I'm speaking from the Oval Office. The president is right next to me. Please do not let Kalb run on about a Soviet defeat. Do not play this up as a victory for us. There is a danger that Khrushchev will be so humiliated and angered that he will change his mind. Watch what you are saying. Do not mess this up for us." Kennedy told several people that it would be very unwise to boast about any sort of U.S. victory. "Khrushchev has eaten enough crow," the president said. "Let's not rub it in."

As it had been throughout the crisis, foremost in the mind of John Kennedy was the idea of giving Khrushchev room, of making sure he was not cornered. And against the advice of great military and diplomatic minds, Kennedy's instincts had been proven correct.

That afternoon John Kennedy again wrote to Nikita Khrushchev: "I think that you and I, with our heavy responsibilities for the maintenance of peace, were aware that developments were approaching a point where events could have become unmanageable." In the end the essential humanity of the two men triumphed.

Aftermath

It was indeed Kennedy's finest hour. It was a time when the president demonstrated how much he had learned during his early days in office. Michael Beschloss has observed that

> from the moment that the President was told of the missiles he had acted to ensure for himself and Ex Comm six days of quiet in which to scrutinize the problem from every angle. This may have been a legacy of what he had learned during the Berlin Crisis. Another President might have moved more hastily. The time that Kennedy bought for himself proved to be fortuitous: had he been compelled to make a decision within hours, he would probably have opted for an air strike.

Beschloss's view was that,

> without the thirty-nine hours he was given before the quarantine began, Khrushchev might not have reversed himself. This demonstrated the President's wisdom in starting his response not with an irreversible air strike but with milder pressures that gave Khrushchev time to ponder his move. . . . During the three days after his television speech, Kennedy's crisis management had been almost flawless.

Good evening, my fellow Americans:

This afternoon, following a series of threats a

the presence of Alabama National Guardsmen was re

of Alabama campus to carry out the final and unequiv

United State District Court for the Northern District

called for the admission of two clearly-qualified youn

who happened to have been born Negro.

I hope that every American, regardless of

and examine his conscience about these and related e

founded by men of many nations and backgrounds. It

principle that all men are created equal -- and that th

are diminished when the rights of one are threatened.

committed to a world-wide struggle to protect and pr

who wish to be free. And when Americans are sent t

Berlin, to risk their lives for yours and mine, we do

It ought to be possible, therefore, for An

color to attend any public educational institution they

to be backed up by troops. It ought to be possible for

of any color to receive equal service in places of pub

such as hotels, restaurants, theatres and retail store

-2-

to resort to mass demonstrations in the streets. And it ought to be possible for American citizens of any color to register and vote in a free election without interference or fear of reprisal. It ought to be possible, in short for every American to enjoy the rights and privileges of America, regardless of race or color.

But this is not the case. The Negro baby born in America today -- regardless of the section or state in which he is born -- has about one-half as much chance of completing high school as a white baby born in the same place on the same day -- one-third as much chance of completing college -- one-third as much chance of becoming a professional man -- twice as much chance of becoming unemployed -- about one-seventh as much chance of earning $10,000 per year -- a life expectancy which is seven years less -- and the prospects of earning only half as much.

This is not a sectional issue. The ~~cesspools~~ of segregation and discrimination exist in every state of the nation, producing in many cities a rising tide of discontent that threatens the public safety.

"A GREAT CHANGE IS AT HAND"

"I have a dream."

his nation was
ded on the
of every man
we are
rights of all
n or West
or whites only
tudents of any
thout having
in consumers
mmodation --
hout having

In May 1963 Martin Luther King Jr. decided on a daring change in tactics. King had been leading street demonstrations in Birmingham seeking an end to discrimination in that city, but the protests had not had the desired effect. King decided to include children in his demonstrations, thousands of Negro children. When the Birmingham police trained high-intensity fire hoses on the demonstrators, knocking children off their feet like so many bowling pins, Americans were aghast. Kennedy attempted to persuade Alabama governor George C. Wallace to take some action that would show King and his followers that progress was being made in Birmingham. On a trip to Alabama, Kennedy talked to Wallace during a helicopter ride. Pierre Salinger, Kennedy's press secretary, was present for the flight and wrote a memo recounting the conversation. The president began by telling Wallace that things would remain tense in Birmingham as long as no progress was made toward integration. "The president said he could not understand why Negroes could not be hired to work in various downtown stores," Salinger wrote. "He said that the very people who protested this action had Negroes serving their tables at home." Salinger went on:

> The governor said that the big problem in Birmingham was the influence of outside leadership. He particularly singled out Martin Luther King who he described as a faker. He said the vast majority of Negroes in Birmingham did not support King's leadership and "had behaved themselves very well during the recent trouble." (The Governor said that the Reverend Martin Luther King and the Reverend Shuttlesworth vied with each other to see "who could go to bed with the most nigger women, and white and red women too. They ride around town in big Cadillacs smoking expensive cigars.")

Salinger's memo does not note how the president reacted to the savagery of Wallace's racism. But it makes clear that Kennedy persisted in his efforts to get Wallace to take some action to show progress: "The president said that outside leadership would not be needed in a city which was making progress and he again stated that progress was absolutely necessary."

Just weeks later Kennedy and Wallace were again in contact, this time over Wallace's vow to bar the door when two Negro students showed up to enroll at the University of Alabama. In June Wallace complained to the president that the planned enrollments constituted a threat to order. The president replied bluntly in a letter to Wallace that

> the only announced threat to orderly compliance with the law . . . is your plan to bar physically the admission of Negro students in defiance of the order of the Alabama Federal District Court and in violation of accepted standards of public conduct. . . . I therefore urgently ask you to consider the consequences to your state and its fine university if you persist in setting an example of defiant conduct, and urge you instead to leave these matters in the courts of law where they belong.

The students were eventually enrolled, over Wallace's objection and with the intervention of the federal courts and U.S. marshals.

That month Democratic leaders in the Senate met with the president and told him the time had come for a civil rights bill. Kennedy said the administration was working on a bill that would strike a balance of "the minimum we can ask for and the maximum we can stand behind." He remained concerned about overreaching. Kennedy told Martin Luther King that "if we go into a long fight in Congress (over civil rights) it will bottleneck everything else and still get no bill."

The political considerations were crucial. The process of rounding up enough votes to pass the bill was, after all, a political one. Kennedy also anticipated a tough reelection

BIRMINGHAM.

7

THE WHITE HOUSE

WASHINGTON

Following is a memorandum of conversation between President Kennedy and Governor George Wallace of Alabama aboard the helicopter between Muscle Shoals and Huntsville, Alabama, May 18, 1963:

The subject of Birmingham first came up after the helicopter had been up for 15 minutes. The President thanked Governor Wallace for having seen the Attorney General and Governor Wallace said he had been happy to see the Attorney General -- that they had talked for an hour and 22 minutes. He said he felt it was always helpful to have these discussions -- that he was happy the President had come to Alabama today.

The President asked Governor Wallace what the current situation was in Birmingham. Governor Wallace replied that his main interest was in maintaining law and order and that the situation was quiet. The President asked the Governor how many men he had in Birmingham. The Governor replied that counting game wardens, alcohol tax units, investigators and others he had some 600. He said with the city police and sheriffs office, etc., there was a total law enforcement force of some 1,000. He said he was confident that this was enough of a force to maintain law and order. He added that he had moved State troops into Birmingham at the request of city officials -- that he would remove them at any time the city officials asked him to. The President replied that the situation would remain tense in Birmingham as long as no progress was made. He said the same thing was true in a number of other cities throughout the country and that this situation was not peculiar to Birmingham. He said that progress had to be made in Birmingham to avoid future trouble. The Governor replied that he thought he could keep things under control in Birmingham and the President reiterated the fact that things would never be under control in Birmingham until some progress was made.

The President pointed to the City of Washington, D.C. as a city with problems, but at the same time not a city where the Negro

7

had been denied his rights. He said there were a number of things that could be done in Birmingham to achieve some progress. For example, the President said he could not understand why Negroes could not be hired to work in various downtown stores. He said that the very people who protested this action had Negroes serving their tables at home.

The Governor said the big problem in Birmingham was the influence of outside leadership. He particularly singled out Martin Luther King who he described as a faker. He said the vast majority of Negroes in Birmingham did not support King's leadership and "had behaved themselves very well during the recent trouble." (*The Governor said that the Reverend Martin Luther King and the Reverend Shuttlesworth vied with each other to see "who could go to bed with the most nigger women, and white and red women too. They ride around town in big cadillacs smoking expensive cigars.")

The President said that outside leadership would not be needed in a city which was making progress and he again stated that progress was absolutely necessary and that Birmingham was getting an absolutely impossible reputation throughout the country and the world. Birmingham could not afford for this to continue -- its industries would leave and the only way the problem would be solved would be through some progress on rights. The Governor again castigated Martin Luther King and said he thought he could maintain the situation in Birmingham.

The conversation ended with the Governor's assertion of his admiration for the President and his recollection of the fact that he had campaigned for the President in 1960.

# # # # # #

NOTE: This memorandum was shown to Senator Lester Hill and Congressman Robert Jones (with the exception of the sentence *), both of Alabama and both of whom heard the conversation, on the flight from Huntsville, Alabama to Andrews AFB on May 18, 1963 and who both agreed that the memorandum is an accurate representation of the conversation.

Pierre Salinger

PS/smv

campaign in 1964, and he did not want to be perceived as having gone too far and too fast on civil rights. But pressure was building. The images of police with fire hoses and snarling attack dogs squaring off against children—children!—in the streets of Birmingham lingered in the national consciousness.

In early June there came a critical moment. The president asked Vice President Lyndon Johnson, who had been the leader of the Senate for years, whether he had any advice about getting a civil rights bill through Congress. Johnson launched into an impassioned plea for Kennedy to make a major public statement on the issue, to make a dramatic stand. Kennedy listened, then asked Johnson to make the same plea to Sorensen. Johnson did so on June 10. He told Sorensen that "the Negroes are tired of this patient stuff and tired of this piecemeal stuff and what they want more than anything else is not an executive order or legislation, they want a moral commitment that he's behind them." Johnson was fiery about the issue.

"I want to pull out the cannon!" Johnson exclaimed to Sorensen. "The president is the cannon. You let him be on all the TV networks just speaking from his conscience. . . . I know the risks are great and it might cost us the South, but those sorts of states may be lost anyway. . . . He ought to . . . almost make a bigot out of nearly anybody that's against him, a high lofty appeal."

The next day Kennedy met with Sorensen and his brother Robert. It was the day before the two Negro students were to be admitted to the University of Alabama—surrounded by the National Guard and over the vigorous protests of Governor Wallace.

"I wonder whether you want to make a nationwide TV address," Sorensen said.

"I don't think so," Kennedy said.

But Robert Kennedy liked the idea. "I think it would be helpful," said the attorney general. In fact, he added, "I don't think you can get by without it."

The next day, although officials at the University of Alabama had announced they would accept the federal court order requiring that the two Negro students be enrolled, Governor Wallace overruled them. In a dramatic moment aired on television throughout the nation, Nicholas Katzenbach, a deputy attorney general, walked up to the university entrance escorting the two students. Katzenbach asked Wallace to step aside. Wallace refused. Watching a tape of the encounter on TV, Kennedy turned to an aide and said, "I want to go on television tonight."

Gov. Wallace blocks integration at the University of Alabama June 11, 1963

Network airtime was arranged as Kennedy and various aides, including his brother and Sorensen, worked on a speech. But by the scheduled broadcast time of 8 P.M., the speech was not completed. Kennedy went ahead, reading parts of the speech, ad-libbing other parts.

> When Americans are sent to Viet Nam or West Berlin, we do not ask for whites only. . . .
>
> This is not a sectional issue. . . . Nor is this a partisan issue. . . . This is not even a legal or legislative issue alone. . . . We are confronted primarily with a moral issue. It is as old as the Scriptures and as clear as the American Constitution.
>
> If an American, because his skin is dark, cannot eat lunch in a restaurant open to the public, if he cannot send his children to the best public schools available, if he cannot vote for the public officials who represent him . . . then who among us would be content to have the color of his skin changed? Who among us would then be content with the counsels of patience and delay?
>
> We face, therefore, a moral crisis as a country and as a people. It cannot be met with repressive police action. It

> cannot be left to increased demonstrations in the streets. . . . It is time to act in the Congress, in your State and local legislative body, and, above all, in all of our daily lives. A great change is at hand, and our task, our obligation, is to make that revolution, that change, peaceful and constructive for all.
>
> We cannot say to ten percent of the population that your children can't have the chance to develop whatever talents they have; that the only way they are going to get their rights is to go into the streets and demonstrate. I think we owe them and we owe ourselves a better country than that.

It was Kennedy at his best: strong, stirring, visionary. It marked a turning point in the epic struggle for civil rights in America.

On June 11 the president addresses the nation and says civil rights is a moral issue

During his speech, Kennedy had briefly sketched the outlines of a civil rights bill he was about to send to Congress. The bill would ask "Congress to enact legislation giving all Americans the right to be served in facilities which are open to the public—hotels, restaurants, theaters, retail stores and similar establishments. . . . I am also asking Congress to authorize the federal government to participate more fully in lawsuits designed to end segregation in public education."

JFK made sure no Negroes were involved in drafting the legislation. He believed that if there was a perception in Congress that Negro leaders, especially Martin Luther King Jr., were involved the bill would never emerge from committee. Governor Wallace warned that if the bill were enacted Kennedy would have to "bring the troops back from Berlin."

In the wake of the landmark speech, Robert Kennedy suggested to his brother that they set up a series of White House meetings with Negro and white leaders from communities across the country. They would invite sixty to seventy leaders at a time—businesspeople, educators, local elected officials—and hold two to three sessions per week all in an effort to build local support for civil rights legislation and for hiring Negroes.

Two weeks after his speech, Kennedy formally announced his civil rights bill. That day World War II army veteran Medgar Evers, a civil rights leader murdered in Jackson, Mississippi, the night of Kennedy's speech, was buried at Arlington National Cemetery. After the burial the president invited Mrs. Evers and her children to visit him at the White House. Days later A. Philip Randolph and Martin Luther King Jr. announced plans for a "march on Washington for freedom and jobs," scheduled for August 28. Kennedy instinctively disliked the idea. During a White House meeting with Negro leaders including King, Randolph, and Roy Wilkins of the NAACP, the president expressed his opposition to the march. Kennedy was not alone in that view; Wilkins also opposed the idea. Kennedy

TCS - 2nd Draft
6/11/63

Good evening, my fellow Americans:

This afternoon, following a series of threats and defiant statements, the presence of Alabama National Guardsmen was required on the University of Alabama campus to carry out the final and unequivocal order of the United State District Court for the Northern District of Alabama. That order called for the admission of two clearly-qualified young Alabama residents who happened to have been born Negro.

I hope that every American, regardless of where he lives, will stop and examine his conscience about these and related events. This nation was founded by men of many nations and backgrounds. It was founded on the principle that all men are created equal -- and that the rights of every man are diminished when the rights of one are threatened. Today we are committed to a world-wide struggle to protect and promote the rights of all who wish to be free. And when Americans are sent to Vietnam or West Berlin, to risk their lives for yours and mine, we do not ask for whites only.

It ought to be possible, therefore, for American students of any color to attend any public educational institution they select without having to be backed up by troops. It ought to be possible for American consumers of any color to receive equal service in places of public accommodation -- such as hotels, restaurants, theatres and retail stores -- without having feared crowds could get out of hand and create a chaotic street scene that would alienate members of Congress whose votes would be needed for the civil rights bill.

Kennedy said that it seemed to him "a great mistake to announce a march on Washington before the bill was even in committee. . . . We want success in Congress, not just a big show at the Capitol. Some of these people are looking for an excuse to be against us. I don't want to give any of them a chance to say, 'yes, I'm for the bill, but I'm damned if I will vote for it at the point of a gun.' . . . The wrong kind of demonstration at the wrong time will give those fellows a chance to say that they have to prove their courage by voting against us." If there was violence, the movement would be set back decades, Kennedy said, and the civil rights bill would be doomed.

JFK with civil rights leaders after the march on Washington

But the announcement had already been made, and it quickly became clear that the march would go on.

"Okay, we're in this up to our necks," the president told the group.

> The worst trouble of all would be to lose the fight in Congress. . . . A good many programs I care about may go down the drain because of this. I may lose the next election because of this. We may all go down the drain as a result of this—so we are putting a lot on the line.
>
> What is important is that we preserve confidence in the good faith of each other. I have my problems with Congress. You have yours with your groups.

If there was to be a march, then Kennedy wanted as much control over it as possible. He assigned his brother to take a hand in organizing it. Robert Kennedy exerted significant influence over the march. What was to be a protest march on a Saturday evolved into a three-hour rally on a Wednesday. It was located at the Lincoln Memorial—a good distance away from residential and commercial areas and surrounded on three sides by water. The president's favorite advance man was stationed behind the dais with a kill switch for the sound system in the event any speaker grew overly inflammatory. A week before the march, the president was asked at a news conference if he believed in special treatment for Negroes. "I don't think we can undo the past," he said.

> In fact, the past is going to be with us for a good many years in uneducated men and women who lost their chance for a decent education. We have to do the best we can now. That is what we are trying to do. I don't think quotas are a good idea. I think it is a mistake to begin to assign quotas on the basis of religion, or race, or color, or nationality. I think we'd get into a good deal of trouble. . . .

> On the other hand, I do think we ought to make an effort to give a fair chance to everyone who is qualified—not through a quota but just look over our employment rolls, look over our areas where we are hiring people and at least make sure we are giving everyone a fair chance.

Before the march Kennedy was invited to speak. He declined. He was nervous it would somehow get out of control. He was asked whether he would receive the leaders of the march at the White House on the morning of the event. Before deciding on a White House visit, he wanted to see the outcome of the event. The president watched the rally on television from the family quarters of the White House. When Martin Luther King rose and delivered his "I have a dream" speech, Kennedy watched carefully. During the speech Kennedy said of King: "He's damned good. Damned good!"

The event, it turned out, could not have gone better, and Kennedy invited the march leaders to the White House later in the day. When King arrived, Kennedy shook his hand, nodded, and said: "I have a dream," then nodded again. During the meeting Roy Wilkins said to the president: "You made the difference. You gave us your blessings. It was one of the prime factors in turning it into an orderly protest to help our government rather than a protest against our government."

Wilkins raised the subject of education. "Isn't it possible," said Kennedy, "for the Negro community . . . to place the major emphasis on the responsibility of these families, even if they're split and all the rest of the problems they have, on educating their children? . . . With all the influence that all you gentlemen have in the Negro community . . . [you] really have to concentrate on what I think the Jewish community has done on educating their children, on making them study, on making them stay in school, and all the rest."

That September Kennedy said at a news conference that he did not know what would be in store for civil rights in 1964, but he added: "I think a division upon racial lines would be unfortunate—class lines, sectional lines. . . . Over the long run we are going to have a mix. This will be true

GENERAL
HO 2-2

no reply rg'd - Pres. saw personally with group of negro leaders.

The White House Washington

1962 NOV 21 PM 9 02

WA153 PD

FAX ND NEW YORK NY 21 556P EDT

THE PRESIDENT

THE WHITE HOUSE

NATIONAL ASSOCIATION FOR ADVANCEMENT OF COLORED PEOPLE WELCOMES YOUR EXECUTIVE ORDER BARRING RACIAL DISCRIMINATION IN FEDERALLY ASSISTED HOUSING IN THE ANTICIPATION THAT IT WILL REMOVE LONG STANDING BARRIERS TO FREEDOM OF RESIDENCE. IT IS FITTING THAT THE GOVERNMENT OF THE UNITED STATES SHOULD MAKE PLAIN THROUGH ITS EXECUTIVE DEPARTMENT THAT THE NATIONAL POLICY OF NON DISCRIMINATION BETWEEN CITIZENS, WHICH HAS BEEN RECOGNIZED IN OTHER AREAS OF AMERICAN LIFE, APPLIES AS WELL TO HOUSING. NOT ALONE MEMBERS OF MINORITY GROUPS, BUT ALL CITIZENS WHO REVERE OUR CONSTITUTIONAL GUARANTEES OF EQUALITY, MUST HAIL THIS REAFFIRMATION OF OUR NATION'S COMMITMENT TO BASIC DEMOCRATIC IDEALS

ROY WILKINS 20 WEST 40TH ST.

RECEIVED JAN 21 1963 CENTRAL FILES

Telegram from Wilkins

racially, socially, ethnically, geographically, and that is really, finally, the best way."

In a disappointing move, the House Judiciary Committee announced in November that it could not complete its work on the civil rights bill that year and would defer it until 1964. There is no question that the president's support for civil rights legislation hurt him politically. After the Bay of Pigs, when Americans rallied to his side, Kennedy's favorability rating was at 82 percent. But in the fall of 1963 it had slipped to 59 percent. Analysis out of the Gallup polls suggested that Kennedy's civil rights stance was a major reason for the drop. On November 18 Kennedy spoke before the Chamber of Commerce in Tampa and was asked, "Why are you pushing civil rights so vigorously?"

"I know this program has not gotten great support in Florida. . . . I think you gentlemen should recognize the responsibility of the President of the United States. That responsibility is different from what your responsibility may be. In this country I carry out, execute, the laws. . . . This is a matter that is going to be with us long after I have disappeared from the scene. No country has ever faced a more difficult problem than attempting to bring ten percent of the population of a different color, educate them, give them a chance for a fair life. . . . If we are going to have domestic tranquility, if we are going to see that citizens are treated as I would like to be treated, and as you would like to be treated . . . That is my objective and I think that is the objective of the United States."

Remarks at the signing of the Test Ban Treaty October 7, 1963

In its first two decades, the age of nuclear energy has been [illegible] empty of hope. Today the fear is a [illegible] a little greater.

[illegible] we have been able to reach an agreement which can [illegible] dangers of this age. The agreement itself is limited, but [illegible] message of hope has been heard and understood not only by the [illegible] of the three originating nations, but by the peoples and gove[illegible]ents of the hundred other countries that have signed.

This Treaty [illegible] the first fruit of labors in which multitudes [illegible] shared -- [illegible] legislators, statesmen, diplomats -- and soldi[illegible] too. Soberly and unremittingly, [illegible] alone -- has sought the doorw[illegible] [illegible] world whose peace is sure. [illegible] a beginning, and it is right for us to ~~pause in~~ [illegible] acknowledg~~ment to~~ all ~~of~~ those [illegible] work, acro[illegible] has helped to make this beginning [illegible]

What the future will bring[illegible] fruit of hope may or may not be [illegible] harvests. Even this limited Treaty, grea[illegible] survive only if it has from others the d[illegible] spiri[illegible] which I hereby pledge in behalf [illegible]. If this Treaty fails, it will not [illegible] fails, we shall not regret that we hav[illegible] national commitment to the ca[illegible] this Treaty we can and must st[illegible]

But this Treaty need not [illegible] can be followed by others, long[illegible] harder in the taking. ~~Let us today take heart from what has been accomplished here;~~ and with our courage and understanding enlarged by this achievement, let us press onward in man's essential quest for peace.

As President of the United States of America, and with the advice and consent of the Senate, I now ~~ratify this Treaty.~~ sign the instruments of ratification of this treaty.

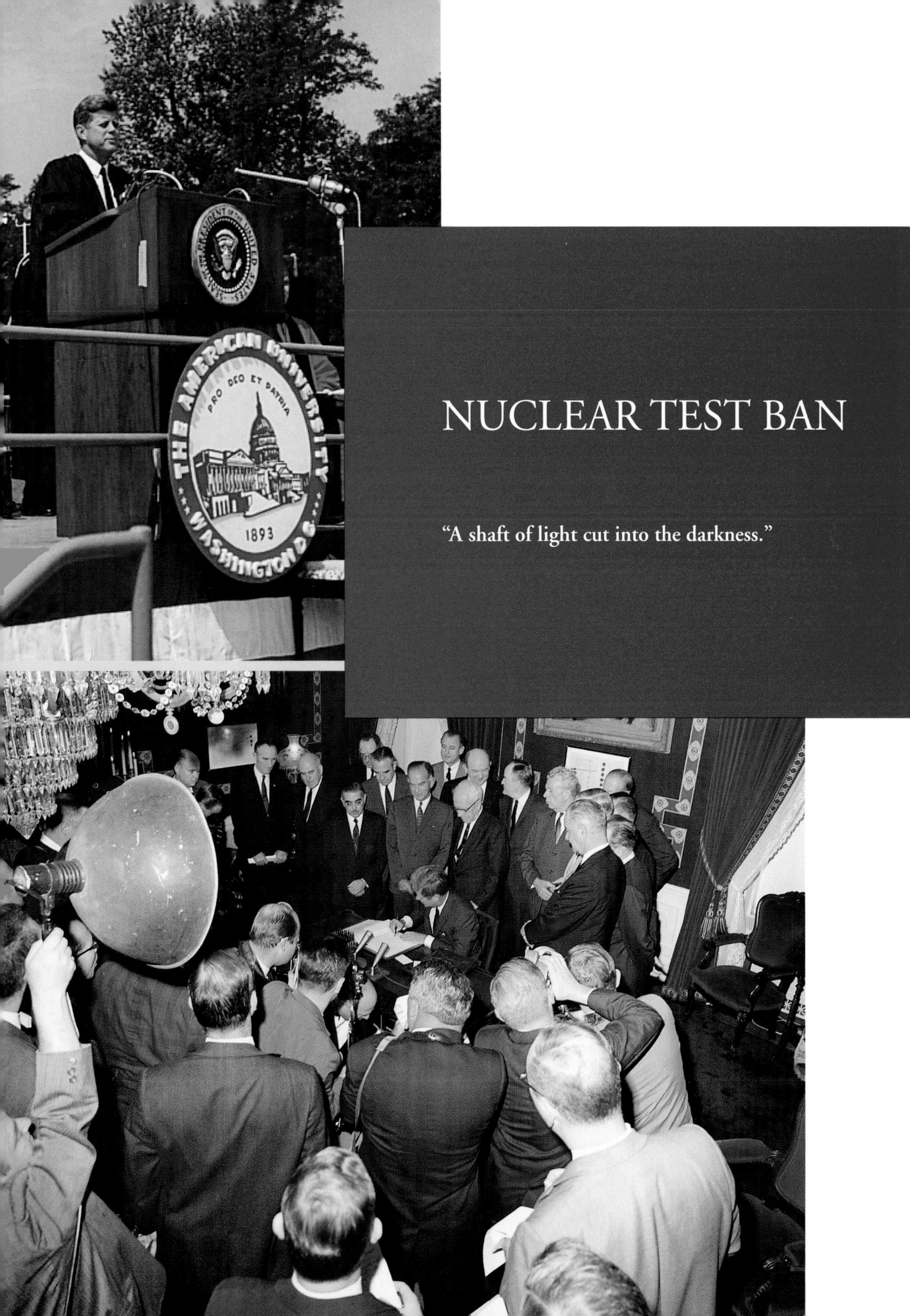

NUCLEAR TEST BAN

"A shaft of light cut into the darkness."

On a rainy day in 1963, President Kennedy met in the Oval Office with his science adviser, Dr. Jerome Wiesner, one of the preeminent scientists of his time. During the president's first two years in office, the megatonnage of nuclear tests by the major powers exceeded all past explosions combined. Radioactive isotopes had begun appearing in milk and other foods. Kennedy asked Wiesner how nuclear fallout returned to earth in the wake of a nuclear test. Wiesner told the president that nuclear fallout settled back down to the earth in the rain. Kennedy gazed out the window, into the Rose Garden. Was it possible, the president wondered aloud, that radioactive fallout was raining down on the earth at that very moment? "Possibly," Wiesner said.

This seemed to stun the president, leaving him visibly saddened. Kenneth O'Donnell, a close Kennedy aide, said he had never seen the president so depressed.

John Fitzgerald Kennedy was a rational man, a cerebral man, but not often a passionate man. Kennedy was suspicious of ideology. He believed that there was no place for emotion in discussing the problems of the cold war and economics, that these were so complex that only rational thinking would lead to solutions. Kennedy feared that emotionalism could lead to a misjudgment, and a mistake in the nuclear age, he knew, could lead to the incineration of the world. Since 1956 John Kennedy had supported a ban on nuclear weapons testing. He believed that if testing were stopped, "America would remain comfortably ahead of the Soviets." He also believed a ban on testing was the most effective way to prevent the spread of nuclear capability to nations throughout the world.

Kennedy had discussed the issue through the years with his old friend David Ormsby-Gore, whom Kennedy had met in London prior to the war. Kennedy saw that Ormsby-Gore, who served as chief British delegate to the Geneva discussions, was knowledgeable on the subject and sought his friend's counsel when he was in the Senate. "Jack was not passionate about nuclear disarmament at first," Ormsby-Gore said. "He was logical and unemotional, just as he was about every other issue, national or international."

Yet for all of his rationalism, in the wake of the Cuban missile crisis Kennedy developed a passion for limiting the proliferation of nuclear weapons. During the second week of the missile crisis, the president had told Ormsby-Gore, "A world in which there are large quantities of nuclear weapons is an impossible world to handle. We really must try to get on with disarmament if we get through this crisis . . . because this is just too much."

When the missile crisis passed, Kennedy was adamant about finding ways to reduce the possibility of a nuclear exchange. He and Khrushchev agreed to install a hot line so that in times of crisis the leaders of the United States and the USSR would be able to communicate instantly. Both nations supported a ban on nuclear weapons in outer space. And as a gesture of peace, President Kennedy approved the sale of 4 million tons of wheat to the Soviet Union.

Kennedy emerged from the Cuban crisis determined as well to seek a treaty banning the testing of nuclear weapons to reduce the number of nations in possession of nuclear weapons, thus reducing the likelihood of nuclear confrontation. In the spring of 1963, the president met with Norman Cousins, the editor of the *Saturday Review* magazine, and made it clear that he recognized the similarity of the situations he and his Soviet counterpart faced:

> One of the ironic things about this entire situation is that Mr. Khrushchev and I occupy approximately the same political positions inside our governments. He would like to prevent a nuclear war but is under severe pressure from his hard-line crowd. . . . I've got similar problems. . . . The hard-liners in the Soviet Union and the United States feed on one another, each using the actions of the other to justify his own position.

Ich Bin Ein Berliner (June 1963)

President Kennedy left for a European trip carrying a memo from George Ball headed "The Mess in Europe and the Meaning of Your Trip." Ball wrote that "never, at any time since the war . . . has Europe been in graver danger of backsliding into the old destructive habits—the old fragmentation and national rivalries that have twice brought the world to disaster in the past."

Ball warned that Germany was a particular danger point. It was essential that the United States and Germany have strong ties, otherwise Germany "can be like a cannon on a shipboard in a high sea. . . . We still have great influence with the Germans. They are closest to the firing line. Berlin is a Soviet hostage, and the German people know that their only defense is the American strength and commitment." It was this strength and commitment that Kennedy would seek to convey to the Germans.

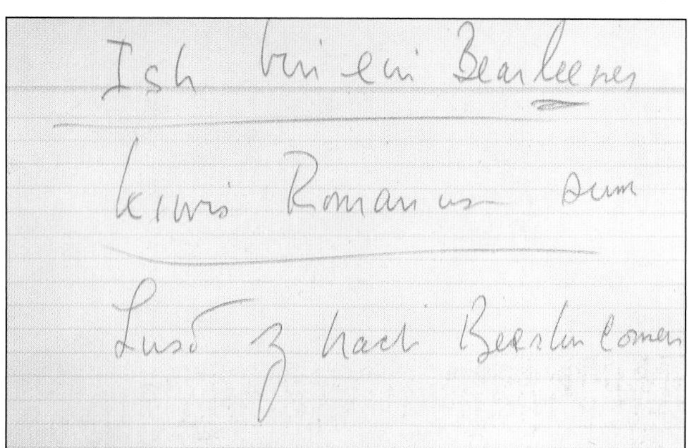
Ish bin ein Bearleener
kiwis Romanus sum
Lust z nach Bearlin comen

As he rode through the streets of one German city after another, the president heard the raucous echos of vast throngs of Germans chanting his name: "Kenn-ah-dee! Kenn-ah-dee!" In Bonn, Kennedy made the U.S. commitment to Germany quite clear: "The United States is here on the continent to stay so long as our presence is desired and required; our forces and commitments will remain, for your safety is our safety. Your liberty is our liberty; and any attack on your soil is an attack upon our own." In Berlin, Kennedy climbed a platform and looked over the wall into East Berlin. At City Hall Plaza, Kennedy stood before 150,000 Germans.

"Two thousand years ago the broadest boast was 'Civis Romanus sum.' Today, in the world of freedom, the proudest boast is 'Ich bin ein Berliner.'"

"All free men, wherever they may live, are citizens of Berlin, and therefore, as a free man, I take pride in the words 'Ich bin ein Berliner.'" I am a Berliner.

The crowd roared, louder and louder, a thunderous response that came in waves, rolling over Kennedy, enveloping him in the affection and gratitude of the German people. That night, as he flew to Ireland on Air Force One, the president told Ted Sorensen: "We'll never have another day like this one, as long as we live."

Having so skillfully led the nation through the crisis, however, Kennedy now had the credibility he needed to try to advance a test ban. The very fact that Kennedy had been to the brink and stood his ground against the Soviets gave the president a political muscle he had never before possessed. Michael Beschloss observed that "in the wake of the near unanimous acclamation, Kennedy felt far more politically self-confident to pursue the kind of Soviet détente that he might have preferred to have started in January 1961."

In a speech at the United Nations earlier in his term, Kennedy said he intended to "challenge the Soviet Union not to an arms race but to a peace race." He said that "every man, woman and child lives under a nuclear sword of Damocles, hanging by the slenderest of threads, capable of being cut at any moment by accident or by miscalculation

Speaking at the United Nations

or by madness. The weapons of war must be abolished before they abolish us."

Khrushchev wrote to Kennedy two months after the conclusion of the missile crisis: "It seems to me, Mr. President, that the time has come now to put an end once and for all to nuclear tests." In his letter Khrushchev stipulated that he would permit two to three weapons inspections a year. This was a major stumbling block. U.S. officials were convinced that the minimum number of inspections necessary was seven. Anything less and it was believed that the Soviets would be able to cheat. As a practical political matter, Kennedy thus set seven as a threshold number. Negotiations stalled for some months. In May an exchange of letters between the two nations set up the possibility for a July meeting of British and U.S. leaders in Moscow for more test-ban talk. In the last week of May, the Dodd-Humphrey resolution was issued proposing that the United States should again offer the Soviet Union a limited test ban rather than a comprehensive ban. A limited ban (with no restrictions on underground testing) would require no inspections to ensure compliance and thus seemed to avoid intractable political problems. The resolution required that if the Russians rejected the offer, then the United States should "pursue it with vigor, seeking the widest possible international support" while pledging no more tests in the atmosphere or underwater as long as the Soviet Union also abstained.

Kennedy was concerned that neither the American people nor the Congress were fully ready for a test ban. Many in Congress (and many average citizens) were reluctant to see the nation engaged in dialogue and negotiations with the Russians. The president feared that even if he were able to negotiate a treaty with Khrushchev, the powerful combination of Republicans and conservative southern Democrats in Congress—the same coalition that had so adamantly opposed the president's civil rights initiatives—would coalesce to defeat the treaty. Blocking a treaty would be relatively easy in the Senate, where a two-thirds majority was required for ratification. The president believed the time had come for him to step forward and frame the issue, to provide the leadership required to persuade the American people and key players in Congress to see the future as he saw it, and to ensure a negotiated arms settlement with the Soviets for the safety of everyone in the world.

The peace speech

He also wanted to demonstrate to Khrushchev and the Russian leadership that he was deadly serious about reaching agreement on a treaty. He would deliver what would come to be known as his "peace speech" at American University in Washington. The date set was June 10, 1963. The day before, Kennedy was in Honolulu. He flew back to Washington throughout the night, landing at Andrews Air Force Base shortly before 9 A.M. He raced to the White House, donned a clean shirt, and went to the campus, where he delivered what may have been the finest speech of his life.

> I have chosen this time and this place to discuss a topic on which too often ignorance abounds and the truth is too rarely perceived—yet it is the most important topic on earth: world peace. . . . I speak of peace because of the new face of war . . . in an age when a single nuclear weapon contains almost ten times the explosive force delivered by all of the allied air forces in the Second World War . . . an age when the deadly poisons produced by a nuclear exchange would be carried by wind and water and soil and seed to the far corners of the globe and to generations yet unborn. . . . I speak of peace, therefore, as the necessary rational end of rational men.
>
> Some say that it is useless to speak of world peace or world law or world disarmament—and that it will be useless until the leaders of the Soviet Union adopt a more

AMERICAN UNIVERSITY

President Anderson, members of the faculty and board of trustees, distinguished guests, my fellow degree recipients -- including my old colleague, Senator Bob Byrd, who has earned his degree through many years of attending night law school, while I am earning mine in the next 30 minutes -- distinguished guests, ladies and gentlemen:

"There are few earthly things more beautiful than a University," wrote John Masefield, in his tribute to the English Universities -- and his words are equally true here. He did not refer to spires and towers, to campus greens and ivied walls. He admired the splendid beauty of the University, he said, because it was "a place where those who hate ignorance may strive to know, where those who perceive truth may strive to make others see."

I have, therefore, chosen this time and this place to discuss a topic on which ignorance too often abounds

> enlightened attitude. I hope they do. But I also believe that we must reexamine our own attitude—as individuals and as a nation—for our attitude is as essential as theirs. . . .
>
> Let us reexamine our attitude toward the Soviet Union. . . . As Americans we find Communism profoundly repugnant as a negation of personal freedom and dignity. But we can still hail the Russian people for their many achievements—in science and space, in economic and industrial growth, in culture and in acts of courage. . . . No nation in the history of battle suffered more than the Soviet Union suffered in the course of the Second World War. At least 20 million lost their lives. . . .
>
> In the final analysis, our most basic common link is that we all inhabit this small planet. We all breathe the same air. We all cherish our children's future. And we are all mortal.

The president then announced that negotiations for a comprehensive test ban treaty were to begin soon in Moscow. Khrushchev later termed it "the greatest speech by any American President since Roosevelt."

Negotiations intensified in mid-July, when President Kennedy sent Averell Harriman, who had been ambassador to the Soviet Union under Roosevelt, as his personal emissary to the discussions. Harriman carried a letter to Khrushchev from JFK stating: "Mr. Harriman comes with my full personal confidence and is in a position to give you my thinking. We continue to believe that it will be best if we can get a comprehensive agreement [but] it is sensible to reach agreement where agreement is now possible, in the area of testing in atmosphere, underwater and in outer space."

In the opening discussion, Khrushchev brought up the question of a comprehensive test ban. Because it would be impossible to monitor for underground testing remotely, inspections would be required, and the Soviets still considered inspections to be espionage. The idea of a comprehensive ban was quickly dismissed, and the discussion shifted to a limited ban. Harriman had brought 3 tons of communications equipment in order to stay in touch with the White House, and he was on the phone to Kennedy three to four hours per day. The president was personally involved in editing the language of the U.S. position.

With Averell Harriman

After intense negotiation the Limited Test Ban Treaty was initialed July 25, 1963. It began, "Each of the Parties to this Treaty undertakes to prohibit, to prevent, and not to carry out any nuclear weapon test explosion, or any other nuclear explosion in the atmosphere, beyond its limits, including outer space, or under water, including territorial waters or high seas."

On July 26 JFK addressed the nation:

> I speak to you tonight in the spirit of hope. Eighteen years ago the advent of nuclear weapons changed the course of the world as well as the war. In an age when both sides have come to possess enough nuclear power to destroy the human race several times over, the world of communism and the world of free choice have been caught up in a vicious circle of conflicting ideology and interest. Each increase of tension has produced an increase of arms; each increase of arms has produced an increase of tension. Yesterday a shaft of light cut into the darkness.

The president said that the treaty would reduce radioactive fallout and block "the spread of nuclear weapons to nations not now possessing them. . . . I ask you to stop and think for a moment what it would mean to have nuclear weapons . . . in the hands of countries . . . stable and unstable, responsible and irresponsible, scattered throughout the world."

July 26, 1963

Good evening, my fellow citizens:

I speak to you tonight in a spirit of hope. Eighteen years ago the advent of nuclear weapons changed the course of the world as well as the War. Since that time, all mankind has been struggling to escape from the darkening prospects of mass destruction on earth. In an age when both sides have come to possess enough nuclear power to destroy the human race several times over, the world of Communism and the world of free choice have been caught up in a vicious circle of conflicting ideology and interests. Each increase of tension has produced an increase in arms; each increase in arms has produced an increase in tension.

Address to the nation urging ratification of the Moscow Treaty.

Opponents of the treaty wanted unlimited nuclear supremacy for the United States, for only in such supremacy, they believed, did true security lie. But members of the Senate overwhelmingly agreed with the president that the treaty was a crucial first step in calming the arms race. The Senate ratified the treaty on September 24, 1963, by a vote of 80 to 19. It was not the full test ban that Kennedy wanted, but it was a start. And for the president personally, it was a shining moment of his presidency.

JFK signs the Limited Test Ban Treaty

RICA
FLY-EAST
OME TO FT WORTH
ERE THE WEST BEGINS

DALLAS

"The president's been shot."

Texas was a tough place. Even though John F. Kennedy had run with Lyndon Johnson, the state's senior senator, as his candidate for vice president, Kennedy had barely eked out a victory in Texas during the presidential campaign. Kennedy's moves on civil rights had weakened his standing in Texas, and now, just six weeks before the dawn of the reelection campaign year, Democrats in Texas were at war. The intraparty animosity was such that it threatened to push the state out of the Democratic column for 1964.

President Kennedy felt he had no choice but to fly down to Texas to sort things out among the warring factions. But what was envisioned as just another humdrum political trip was suddenly transformed into an event of note when the announcement came that Jacqueline Kennedy would be accompanying her husband to Texas. Mrs. Kennedy's travels typically involved promoting various cultural events; this would in fact be Mrs. Kennedy's first domestic political trip. The presidential party flew in to Carswell Air Force Base in Fort Worth on the evening of Thursday, November 21, 1963, and spent the night at the Texas Hotel in Forth Worth. In the morning the president went across the street from the hotel to address a crowd gathered in a parking lot. He then returned to the hotel for a Chamber of Commerce breakfast. It was immediately clear that there was great disappointment that the first lady was not at his side. "Mrs. Kennedy is organizing herself," the president said. "It takes longer, but, of course, she looks better than we do when she does it." During the breakfast she entered the room and was greeted with applause as she took a seat at the head table.

Forth Worth, the morning of Nov. 22, 1963

The motorcade in Dallas would be simple enough: The president and his wife along with Governor and Mrs. John Connally would ride together in an open car followed by Vice President Johnson and his wife in a second car. The motorcade would wind through a portion of the city to the Trade Mart, where the president was scheduled to deliver a luncheon speech.

"There were such big crowds of such waving, nice, happy people," Mrs. Kennedy recalled. "I certainly did have a feeling it was going well. . . ."

"The crowds were so enthusiastic and so loving, we didn't get to do much chatting because of the noise,"

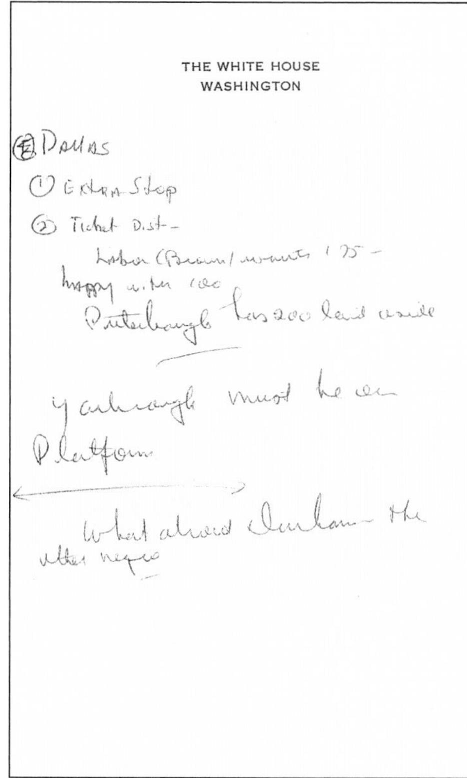

THE WHITE HOUSE
WASHINGTON

(E) Dallas
(1) Extra Stop
(2) Ticket Dist —
Labor (Brown) wants 175 — happy with 100
Puterbaugh has 200 laid aside
if Puterbaugh must be on Platform
What about Durham — the other negroes

Meeting
Hasn't been an incumbent Pres. except Truman in Dallas
Across street from school —
Citizens Council to give blessing to ticket
Council gave 4 members to the member
Conservatives & Republicans
1000 members of assembly getting 4 ea
500 divided among 214 precinct workers
50 to County Dems
50 to "other" Dems
10 to negroes
10 to Labor
10 to Dem Men's Club
Young Dems getting 6
Sanders doesn't have any tickets
Puterbaugh given to Betty Harris
Two alternatives —
• Spontaneous rally — across street
• Expand ticket list

JFK's notes during the trip to Texas

recalled Nellie Connally, wife of the governor. "But I was so pleased with our reception, I turned around in my seat and said, 'Mr. President, you can't say Dallas doesn't love you.' And just then the first shot rang out."

Arriving at Love Field, Dallas

While the president was riding in an open car through Dealey Plaza, his parents were at Hyannis Port. His father was an invalid by then, having been impaired by a severe stroke. His mother, however, was as vital as ever.

"I remember Friday, November 22, began as one of those perfect late autumn days on the Cape," recalled Rose Kennedy.

> At that time of year the air is crisp but not cold, just cool enough to make some warmth from fireplaces most welcome even if not entirely needed, and it has such freshness from the sea that one's spirits are lifted up. There is a special quality to the light then, too: it is golden, pure, making everything stand out in clear relief and with a peculiar and lovely luminosity—every white clapboard house and every tree and autumn-colored leaf or bare branch, every bayberry and sumac and wild beach rose. . . .
>
> And so, on that beautiful morning . . . a news bulletin [came on] that along the route in Dallas someone had taken some shots . . . and he had been wounded. . . .
>
> . . . He had been through so much, from the time he was in danger of death from scarlet fever as a little child to the time he nearly died from his back operation, and so many things in between, so that almost automatically I had in the back of my mind the thought "Jack is having some more hard luck . . . but he'll surmount it. . . ."

Initially, there were those in the motorcade, including some agents of the Secret Service, who thought the rifle shots were a car backfiring or a firecracker or a cherry bomb or even a motorcycle.

When the president lurched forward in his right rear seat in the Lincoln and was grabbed by his wife, it was clear something was horribly wrong. The first bullet entered the back of his neck; the second struck the back of his head.

Suddenly, the motorcade roared forward, Secret Service agents hovering over the president and first lady. The car raced through the city to Parkland Hospital. Mrs. Kennedy cradled her husband's head in her arms, and even after arriving at the hospital she was reluctant to let him be taken away from her. She saw the massive wounds, and she knew that he was dead. She wept over him.

"I'm not going to let him go," she said to Secret Service agent Clint Hill.

"We've got to take him in, Mrs. Kennedy," agent Hill replied.

"No, Mr. Hill," she said. "You know he's dead. Let me alone."

Hill gave her his jacket, and she wrapped the president's head in the jacket.

She suddenly cried out: "He's dead—they've killed him—Oh Jack, oh Jack, I love you."

It was 1:38 P.M. when Parkland Hospital admitted case number 24740, a "white male" with a "gunshot wound."

Two minutes later Walter Cronkite came on the air, interrupting the soap opera *As the World Turns,* and said: "In Dallas, Texas, three shots were fired at President Kennedy's motorcade. The first reports say that the President was 'seriously wounded.'"

Two priests were summoned to the hospital and the last rites of the Catholic faith were administered. One of the priests dipped his hand in holy water and blessed the president's body. "Through this anointing, may God forgive you whatever sins you have committed. Amen." The priest said the Lord's Prayer and was joined by a doctor and Mrs. Kennedy. They then said the Hail Mary.

Robert Kennedy was home for lunch at his Hickory Hill estate in Virginia, sitting by the pool. Fifteen minutes after the president had been hit, J. Edgar Hoover called the attorney general. Hoover was unemotional.

"I have news for you," said the FBI director. "The President's been shot."

There was a moment of stunned silence from Robert Kennedy. Then he asked whether it was serious.

"I think it's serious," Hoover replied. "I am endeavoring to get details. I'll call you back when I find out more."

Robert Kennedy got off the phone and turned to his wife and others present and said, "Jack's been shot!"

It was only minutes later when the president's brother received another call from a White House military aide informing him that the president had died.

"Oh, he's dead!" cried out the beloved brother to his wife. She cried.

"He had the most wonderful life," Robert Kennedy said.

President Kennedy was pronounced dead at 2:00 P.M. eastern time by Dr. Kemp Clark. Thirty-six minutes later, assistant White House press secretary Malcolm Kilduff made the official announcement to the press corps: "President John F. Kennedy died at approximately one o'clock Central Standard Time today here in Dallas."

A furious battle erupted at the hospital over whether an autopsy would be conducted at Parkland. Local officials said Texas law demanded it. The president's aides insisted they were taking his body back to Washington. The two sides nearly came to blows. The presidential aides prevailed, and Kennedy's body was placed in a coffin and removed from the hospital for the flight back to Washington aboard Air Force One.

Charles Roberts recalled the scene when the president's body was being taken from the hospital to begin the trip home:

> The casket was one of these little rubber-tired dollies and Mrs. Kennedy was walking on the right side of it. . . . She was walking with her left hand on the casket and a completely glazed look on her face, obviously in shock. It was deathly still in that corridor as this casket was wheeled out. . . .
>
> I saw the priest on the loading platform. In fact, Mrs. Kennedy stopped and talked to him for what seemed to me like minutes. . . . They put the bronze casket in the back door of the hearse. The curtains of it were drawn, and Mrs. Kennedy insisted on riding in the back of the hearse rather than in the front seat. [A doctor] tried to talk her into getting into the front seat . . . but she wouldn't. Jackie Kennedy, still wearing the raspberry-colored wool suit and matching pillbox hat in which she had started the day's campaigning—and still looking beautiful—walked slowly beside the casket, her . . . hand resting gently on it.

Fifteen minutes after the president was pronounced dead, the joint chiefs of staff placed U.S. armed forces throughout the world on alert.

In the wake of the president's death, the intelligence community feared an organized plot against the U.S. government. "We all went to battle stations over the possibility that this might be a plot," recalled Richard Helms, deputy director of the CIA. The agency had its people throughout the world work to determine whether there was evidence to "indicate that a conspiracy had been formed to kill the President." According to historian Michael Beschloss,

CIA men were staggered to learn that they could not locate Nikita Khrushchev. They agonized over every imaginable conspiracy. Could there be a plot, perhaps by the Chinese, to murder the leaders of both superpowers? Was the Soviet leader staying away from Moscow in anticipation of an American nuclear strike in revenge for a Soviet plot against the President?

LBJ taking the Oath of Office aboard Air Force One on the ground at Love Field

Six cabinet members along with presidential press secretary Pierre Salinger were in an Air Force jet over the Pacific en route to Japan when they heard the news. The plane was turned around immediately, but they were still hours from reaching Washington.

The Washington, D.C., phone system was so overwhelmed so abruptly that it all but broke down. Word circulated that this was an act of sabotage.

Vice President Lyndon Johnson was at Parkland Hospital when the president died. Johnson wanted to get to Air Force One as quickly as possible. He said to an aide: "We don't know whether it's a Communist conspiracy or not. I'd better get out of here and back to the plane." Secret Service officials, fearful that there would be an attempt on Johnson's life, raced through the streets with the vice president, reaching Air Force One in just seven minutes. On board, the vice president huddled with aides to determine the best course of action. He determined that he would be sworn in on the plane before it left the ground. An official at the Justice Depart-

President Johnson

ment dictated the oath of office to a Johnson aide over the phone.

With Mrs. Kennedy at his side, Johnson became the thirty-sixth president of the United States at 3:38 P.M., ninety-eight minutes after the death of President Kennedy. Nine minutes later Air Force One had climbed to 40,000 feet above a dark and angry storm.

John Kennedy's body arrives at Andrews Air Force Base

After the plane landed at Andrews Air Force Base, John Kennedy's body, accompanied by his widow and his brother Robert, was taken to Bethesda Naval Hospital. An autopsy was performed, and then his body was prepared for burial. This work took much of the night. At 4:30 A.M. Kennedy's body was returned to the White House East Room. Mrs. Kennedy, Robert Kennedy, and other family members gathered around the coffin.

David Pearson, an aide to Sargent Shriver, recorded the scene in his diary:

> She takes the five steps to the casket and quickly kneels down, almost falling. . . . Her hands hang loosely at her sides. She lays her forehead against the side of the casket. She picks up the edge of the flag and kisses it. Slowly she starts to rise. Then, without any warning, Mrs. Kennedy begins crying, her slender frame is rocked by sobs, and she slumps back down. Her knees give way. Bobby Kennedy moves up quickly, puts one arm around her waist. He stands there with her a moment and just lets her cry.

All of America, it seemed, had come to an abrupt halt. The entire nation huddled around television screens, silently watching, shocked by the horror of his death.

Rosemary, Jack's younger, handicapped sister, whom he

President's body lies in state at East Room of the White House, Nov. 23

had taken to Saturday night dances at the club, making sure his friends cut in so she would feel popular—Rosemary was watching television when the news of President Kennedy's death was announced. When her mother, Rose Kennedy, received the news, she left her home in Hyannis Port and walked across the broad expanse of lawn leading down to the sea. She walked back and forth, back and forth, for the longest time, alone. She and her husband had lost yet another child. First it had been young Joe in the war. And then Kathleen. And now Jack. Wonderful, precious, devil-

The Rotunda of the United States Capitol, Nov. 24

World leaders mourn the president's death

ish Jack. He had been so sick so often, had triumphed over so much physical hardship. And now this.

Senator Edward M. Kennedy flew from Washington to Hyannis Port to break the news to his father. Joseph P. Kennedy Sr. was rocked by the news, and he sat and cried. He fought to compose himself and insisted the television be turned on. When it was, he saw the coffin containing his son in the East Room of the White House, and he sobbed.

Leaders of nations throughout the world were deeply saddened by the death. "I am stunned," said Charles de Gaulle. "They are crying all over France. It is as though he were a Frenchman, a member of their own family." But perhaps the most telling reaction came from the man with

Robert, Jacqueline, and Edward Kennedy lead the procession

whom Kennedy had dueled over the fate of the earth: Nikita Khrushchev. When the leader of the USSR heard the news, he burst into tears. Khrushchev went to the residence of the U.S. ambassador to the Soviet Union to pay his respects and sign a condolence book.

The funeral brought together world leaders and the most prominent Americans. But it also drew countless average citizens who were shattered by grief. The funeral was held on Monday, November 25. The president was buried on a hill in Arlington National Cemetery. An eternal flame was lit.

John Fitzgerald Kennedy was forty-six years old when he died. He had served as president for 1,036 days.

OPPOSITE: *Notes from Theodore H. White's conversation with Jacqueline Kennedy*

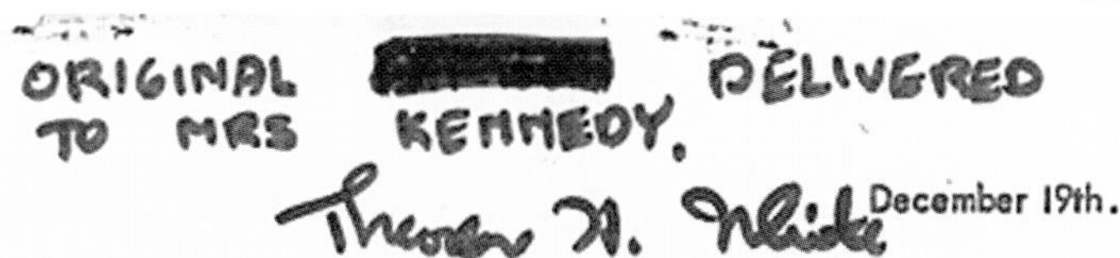

December 19th.

No quiet moment uhtil now to write up the Jacqueline Kennedy notes. Of conversation on Friday, 29th, November. She was absolutely composed when I arrived (at about 8:30 in driving rain; and stayed and worked until 2 AM; and then drove back all in a Corey Limousine).

There present were: Chuck Spaulding; Franklin D Jr.; and Dave Powers; and Pat Lawford; and perhaps one or two others, plus service personnell. But left it that way.

The chief memory I have is of her composure; of her beauty (dressed in black trim slacks, beige pullover sweater, her eyes wider than pools): and of her calm voice and total recall.

We began by sitting down on the sofa and she leaned forward and asked (I paraphrase because it is too long ago to recall quotes) what whall I say? What can I do for you? It was more as if she were asking me for help than anything else. I listened and offered the thought that she continue from the fragment of conversation we had had on the telephone in which she'd said that now Arthur Krock and Merriman Smith and all those people were going to write about him as history, and that was not the way she wanted him remembered.

How did she want him remembered--- I suggested. But she had a series of thoughts of her own and whether she took off from the springboard I offered I don't know. This, however, is what my notes recall:

I'm not going to bethe Widder Kennedy and make speeches like some people who talk about their family). When this is over I'm going to crawl into the deepest retirement there is. I'm going to live in the place I lived with Jack; I'm going to live in Georgetown, I'm going to live on the Cape, I'm going to be with the Kennedys; Bobby is going to to teach Johnny. He's a little boy without a father, he's a boyish little boy, he'll need a man. That first night Bob McNamara he said he'd buy back our ~~[illegible]~~ old house in Georgetown. That was the first thing I thought that night-- where will I go? I wanted my old house back. Actually Jack had said(when he was elected) why sell it? maybe one day we'll go back there. But then(she's referring to the night at Bethesda) I thought-- how can I go back there to that bedroom. I said to myself-- you must never forget Jack, but you mustnt be morbid.

There'd been the biggest motorcade from the airport; hot; wild-- like Mexico and Vienna; the sun was so strong in our face; I couldnt put on sunglasses and then we saw this tunnel ahead.. I thought it would be cool in the tunnel; and I thought if you were on the left the sun wouldt get into your eyes.

They were gunning the motorcycles; there were these little backfires ; there was one noise like that; I thought it was a backfire. Then next I saw Connolly grabbing his arms and saying no no no nonono, with his fist beating--- then Jack turned and I turned --- all I remember was a blue gray building up ahead; then Jack turned back, so neatly; his last expression was soneat; he had his hand out, I could see a piece of his skull coming off; it was flesch colored not white--- he was holding out his hand-- and I can see this perfectly clean piece detaching itself from his head; then he slumped in my lap; his blood and his brains were in my lap... Then Clint Hill, he loved us, he made my life so easy, he was the first man in the car... we all lay down in the car and I kept saying Jack, Jack, Jack and someone was yelling hes dead hes dead. All the ride to the hospital I kept bending over him saying Jack, Jack can yourhear me, I love you Jack. I kept holding the top of his head down trying to keep the

THE JOHN F. KENNEDY LIBRARY AND MUSEUM

The John F. Kennedy Library was dedicated on October 20, 1979. Bright autumn sunshine, a brisk onshore breeze, and fanfare from the Boston Symphony Orchestra greeted an audience of 10,000 invited guests and many more spectators in boats crowding the waters of nearby Dorchester Bay. President Kennedy's wife, Jacqueline, and children, Caroline and John, Jr., watched as Senator Edward M. Kennedy, representing the Kennedy family and the John F. Kennedy Library Corporation, builders of the facility, presented the Library to the people and government of the United States, represented by President Jimmy Carter. Thirty million people had contributed to the Library's construction fund, a measure of the sense of loss experienced around the world following President Kennedy's death. The sixth presidential library operated by the National Archives thus was permanently established at Columbia Point in Boston.

The intersecting geometric forms of the building, designed by I.M. Pei, and its smooth surfaces of concrete and glass compose one of Boston's most dramatic architectural statements. Located in the Dorchester section of the city, where the president's mother lived as a child, the Library commands sweeping views of Boston's skyline, its broad harbor, the offshore islands, and the Atlantic Ocean. The 135,000-square-foot complex includes a nine-story, white precast-concrete tower, 125 feet high, which is contiguous to a glass-enclosed pavilion. The upper floors of the tower contain office, research, and document storage facilities. The lower floors house two elliptical-shaped 230-seat theaters and an 18,000-square-foot exhibition area. An addition, the Stephen E. Smith Center, also designed by I.M. Pei, was dedicated in 1991 and contains spaces for lectures, conferences, and meetings as well as more archival storage.

The facility is on 9.5 acres of the 280-acre Columbia Point peninsula, adjacent to the University of Massachusetts and Massachusetts State Archives, four miles southeast of downtown Boston. The John T. Fallon State Pier adjoining the Library's property renders the complex accessible by boat.

The Library's grounds comprise lawns along the water's edge, beds of wild roses, slopes of dune grass, and groves of pine trees, all reflecting the landscape of Cape Cod, where John Kennedy spent his summers. In summer, his 26-foot sloop, *Victura*, is displayed on one of these lawns, facing the entrance to Boston Harbor, a waterway coincidentally known as President Roads. From this channel on immigrant ships from Ireland, JFK's greatgrandparents first glimpsed the city in which the Kennedy family's political tradition would flourish.

In this setting, the Library seeks to promote appreciation of the values and themes about which John Kennedy cared most deeply, and which best illuminate his life. These include the importance of historical scholarship in framing choices for the nation; the encouragement of service to community and country; and the potential for each individual to advance the public interest through participation in our democratic political process.

The Kennedy Library is noted for the large number of researchers it serves, its museum, and its educational programs which encourage thoughtful citizen participation in the democratic process. The Library preserves and makes available important collections related to the life of John Kennedy and mid–20th-century American politics and government. The Library is administered by the National Archives and Records Administration. A public-private partnership with the John F. Kennedy Library Foundation provides private funds to support many programs.

Library Collections

The Library's research facilities are among the busiest of presidential libraries, accommodating 700 researchers each year with 1,600 additional users served by mail. Library staff answer annually nearly 10,000 inquiries and provide 150,000 pages of photocopies of documents to researchers.

To promote a better understanding of the study of history and the formation of public policy, the Library encourages students from the region's colleges and high schools to work with the Library's primary sources. This openness is part of the Library's commitment to serve all interested citizens and not just scholars, reflecting President Kennedy's conviction that history should be a living presence in the life of community and nation.

Papers

The papers of John F. Kennedy comprise one-third of the 32 million pages of documents in the Library's collections. They are divided into personal papers, pre-presidential papers and presidential papers.

The Personal Papers of John F. Kennedy (1917–1963) include academic records donated by Harvard University, correspondence, Kennedy's World War II U.S. Navy service records, and manuscripts for Kennedy's books, *Why England Slept* and *Profiles in Courage*.

The Pre-Presidential Papers (1947–1960) are the office

files of John F. Kennedy's fourteen-year career as congressman and senator, reflecting his major interests and activities during that period. They contain correspondence, speech, subject, legislative and campaign files as well as material from the 1960 presidential transition period.

The Presidential Papers (1960–1963) contain several subcollections. The President's Office Files are the working files of President Kennedy kept by his personal secretary, including correspondence, speech, press-conference, legislative, staff memoranda, subject and country files as well as presidential recordings. The National Security Files are a critical resource for understanding U.S. foreign relations during the 1960s. The Presidential Papers also include the files of members of the president's staff.

The personal papers of Kennedy administration cabinet members and other Kennedy associates are also found in the Library's archives. Of special interest are the papers of Robert F. Kennedy, (U.S. attorney general, and U.S. senator from New York,) and the Library's collection of more than 1,100 oral history interviews of individuals associated with John F. Kennedy and Robert F. Kennedy. Additionally, the Library houses 35,000 printed volumes.

Audiovisual Collections

Important collections of non-textual materials also document the life and career of President Kennedy and include coverage of campaign appearances, meetings, speeches, press conferences, official travels and events, and leisure-time activities.

The still photograph collections comprise more than 180,000 images, mostly taken by White House staff, while other collections include photographs of Robert F. Kennedy (1925–1976), and Rose Kennedy's collection of Kennedy and Fitzgerald family photographs (1878–1978). Gifts from individuals, government agencies, and private organizations have expanded the collections and include Burton Berinsky's photographs of JFK, 1960, RFK, 1964 and 1968; and selected photos from *Look* Magazine, *The New York Times*, and the U.S. Army.

The motion picture collections measure 7,000,000 feet of film. Major donations were made to the Library after President Kennedy's death by U.S. government agencies, CBS-TV, and NBC-TV.

Researchers may listen to over 5,000 hours of sound recordings including President Kennedy's. In addition to public speeches and press conferences, they include recordings of meetings made secretly by the president in 1962 and 1963. The recent release of recorded deliberations of the Executive Committee of the National Security Council during the Cuban Missile Crisis indicates the significance of these materials for the study of presidential leadership. Many recordings of President Kennedy, some as early as 1940, predate his administration.

Three Dimensional Objects

The Library's museum collection comprises some 20,000 artifacts, including personal and political memorabilia, gifts received from world leaders and ordinary citizens from every continent, and objects associated with important events in President Kennedy's career, the work of Jacqueline Kennedy as first lady, and the life and career of Robert F. Kennedy.

Educational Programs

The John F. Kennedy Library has always aspired to be a lively educational center and resource. The Library's programs in American history and contemporary politics promote responsible, thoughtful citizenship.

Since 1979, the scope and number of its educational programs have been hallmarks of the Kennedy Library: some speak to elementary, high school, or college students; some are challenging to scholars; and most are appropriate for general audiences of curious, well-informed men and women. Whereas the museum and most archival research focus on the life and presidency of John Kennedy, topics for educational programs are often more diverse, covering historical and contemporary public affairs on the local, regional, national, and world scenes.

John F. Kennedy Library Foundation

The John F. Kennedy Library Foundation is a nonprofit organization established in 1984 to support and advance the mission of the Library itself. Through its Board of Directors, committees, and staff, the Foundation assists the Library in the planning and establishment of its long-term strategic goals and objectives and provides the Library with financial and creative resources to enrich its educational programs, expand its research and archival capacity, undertake public information projects and volunteer programs, and enhance its museum and exhibits.

By sponsoring programs such as the Profile in Courage Award, the Distinguished Foreign Visitors Series, History in the First Person, and the JFK Library Corps, the Foundation is united with the Library in a common mission to perpetuate President Kennedy's own ideal—that political and public service be conducted as an honorable profession. The relationship between Library and Foundation illustrates the benefits to society and the American taxpayer that accrue from such public/private partnerships.

The Foundation created the Profile in Courage Award to recognize and promote the quality of political courage that President Kennedy valued. The award is presented annually on or around May 29th, the anniversary of President Kennedy's birthday, to a current or former elected official whose actions best demonstrate the political courage President Kennedy described in his Pulitzer Prize-winning book *Profiles in Courage*. The award consists of a $25,000 monetary prize and a silver lantern modeled after lanterns found on 19th-century sailing vessels.

The Museum At The Kennedy Library

On October 29, 1993, the Kennedy Library opened its new museum, replacing the original 18,000-square-foot exhibit installed in 1979. President Clinton joined members of the Kennedy family, Library staff, and invited guests in the dedication ceremony. The new museum is designed to convey John Kennedy's enthusiasm for the American system of politics and government and to help visitors better understand our nation's recent history. Aware of the growing number of visitors with no recollection of the Kennedy administration and aiming to engage their interest in history, the Library has embarked on a new approach to presidential library museum design that is less dependent on visitor memories. Visitors to the museum now learn about the career of John F. Kennedy, the challenges he faced, the decisions he made, and his commitment to public life as he *speaks for himself* on film, video, and sound recordings from the Library's audiovisual collections. Visitors encounter a first-hand, "you are there" experience of President Kennedy's life, leadership, and legacy and are exposed directly to the Library's historical resources. Following a chronological path, 21 exhibits, including 21 video presentations, detail the sights and sounds of President Kennedy's lifetime and presidency.

ACKNOWLEDGMENTS AND SOURCE NOTES

The John F. Kennedy Library and Museum collection and the archivists who oversee that collection are a remarkable resource for an author seeking to write about JFK. The research collection contains some 34 million pages of documents and manuscripts, 147,000 photographs, 66,000 reels of film, more than 10,000 reels of audio tape and 25,000 books.

Archivists within the library have culled their vast holdings to create exhibits that are educational and insightful. These exhibits, presenting carefully selected materials of the highest quality and relevance, are of immense value. A visitor to the museum begins the experience by seeing a twenty-minute film on the life of JFK and then moving into the museum galleries where one is thrust back in time to the Democratic National Convention of 1960. There are the Kennedy-Nixon debates in a recreation of the studio in which the first debate took place. Farther along the inaugural speech is shown in color. Exhibits illuminate the Peace Corps, the president's televised press conferences, the Cuban Missile Crisis, civil rights, the space race and foreign policy. There are sections, as well, on both Jacqueline Bouvier Kennedy and Robert Kennedy. All of these exhibits proved invaluable in the creation of this book. In a number of cases text panels from the exhibits have been used verbatim in the book (and are so indicated in notes below).

This book is based on documents and artifacts contained within the John F. Kennedy Library and Museum as well as from a number of superb books about Kennedy and his times. This book is in many respects derived from the library and museum. While the exhibits were central to the creation of the book, so, too, were the library experts who know their specialties; who know what is contained within the library and where it is; who know what is worth spending time reviewing and what can safely be passed over. Library experts provided information, facts, analysis, and direction. Invariably, the best material from the library collection was contained in the documents, photographs, artifacts, and video tapes identified by library staffers intimately familiar with the library's contents. Important information and assistance came from experts at the library including: John Stewart, former director of education; Sam Rubin, education specialist; William Johnson, former chief archivist; Megan Desnoyers, archivist; Frank Rigg, museum curator; Jim Wagner, museum specialist; and Brad Gerratt, former director. Allan Goodrich, archivist in charge of audio-visual archives, possesses an encyclopedic knowledge of the library's photographic holdings. His efforts helped make this the richly illustrated work that it is. Sheldon Stern, who formerly served as historian at the library, carefully reviewed the manuscript and provided important guidance. His comments and suggestions improved and strengthened the book.

While this work draws upon the library and its contents, it also relies substantially on a number of important books. Hundreds of authors through the years have told one aspect or another of JFK's story. But there are a few authors whose work has proved invaluable for the purposes of this book. *The Making of the President, 1960* by Theodore H. White (New York: Atheneum, 1962), was a groundbreaking work that revealed the workings of the modern political campaign in a manner that was both insightful and dramatic. *Kennedy* by Theodore C. Sorensen (New York: Harper and Row, 1965), is an important work by a man who authored some of the great political rhetoric of the Kennedy era and who worked closely with Kennedy. *The Presidency of John F. Kennedy* (American Presidency Series) by James N. Giglio (Lawrence, Kansas: University Press of Kansas, 1991) is a careful, intelligent work of scholarship. Rose Kennedy was neither journalist nor scholar, but her book, *Times to Remember*, (Garden City, New York: Doubleday, 1974) provides rich details and anecdotes that offer unique insight into her son. *A Thousand Days: John F. Kennedy in the White House* by Arthur M. Schlesinger, Jr. (Boston: Houghton Mifflin, 1965) is a comprehensive work by the esteemed historian. *President*

Kennedy: Profile of Power by Richard Reeves (New York: Simon & Schuster, 1993) is a powerful, eminently readable work. Reeves's book is an intelligent examination of Kennedy that is both impressive in its scope and unflinching in its nature. This book relies heavily on Reeves, particularly for his excellent recounting of the dramatic moments during the Cuban Missile Crisis.

A great debt is owed to Michael Beschloss, the general editor of the PublicAffairs Presidential Library series and author of the definitive work, *The Crisis Years: Kennedy and Khrushchev, 1960–1963* (New York: Edward Burlingame Books, 1991). Michael Beschloss's remarkable knowledge of John F. Kennedy and his era helped set the tone for the book and provided important guidance for its direction. Thanks are owed to Kristin Kimball who provided important research and editorial suggestions. The idea for the PublicAffairs Presidential Library series originated with Edwin Schlossberg. The talented staff at ESI, especially John Branigan, created the initial design for the book. At PublicAffairs, Peter Osnos and Robert Kimzey had the vision to see what the book might become and the diligence to make it happen. They were supported by their formidable design and production team that included Jenny Dossin, Evan Gaffney, Joan Greenfield, and Della Mancuso.

"Carry on"

Of great value, not only to this chapter, but to the entire book, were the contents of the Library's "JFK Personal Papers (1917–1963)." These papers cover Kennedy's life and include useful information on his childhood and student days at Choate, Princeton, Harvard, and Stanford. This collection also includes information about his time in the Navy, as a member of the United States House and the Senate. As described by the library: "This is an artificial subcollection of the Papers of John F. Kennedy created by the library staff for the convenience of researchers . . . It brings together items originated by or associated with John F. Kennedy, particularly from the years prior to his presidency. The collection is diverse and fragmentary. It includes childhood letters, diaries, correspondence, academic records (copies donated by Harvard University), and notebooks, financial papers, Navy records including medical files, records relating to the sinking of the S.S. *Athenia* (copies donated by the State Department), manuscripts of *Why England Slept* (1940) and *Profiles in Courage,* (1956), some Boston office House of Representatives files, presidential doodles and scrap books." Also valuable for this chapter are the Kennedy Library's "Pre-Presidential Papers (1946–1961)," which cover roughly the period from Kennedy's first run for Congress to the Inauguration. These files are described by the library as "a rich source of information on the major issues, events, themes, and legislation of the 1950s and on the 1960 Presidential campaign and transition." John F. Kennedy Library video tapes where the president reflected back upon his youth were especially helpful. In addition, this chapter derived information from various books, including *Times to Remember* by Rose Kennedy, *The Presidency of John F. Kennedy* by Giglio, *The Crisis Years* by Beschloss, *Kennedy* by Sorensen and *JFK: Reckless Youth* by Nigel Hamilton (New York: Random House, 1992). The sidebar about the Kennedy-Bouvier wedding draws directly from the library's text panel.

The Closest Election in U.S. History

This chapter relies upon the "Pre-Presidential Papers (1946–1961)," which contain extensive files pertaining to the 1960 campaign. (Particularly noteworthy are the extensive files indicating just how virulent the anti-Catholic bias of the day was.) It relies heavily upon Theodore H. White's *The Making of the President, 1960* and Theodore C. Sorensen's *The Kennedy Legacy: A Peaceful Revolution for the Seventies* (New York: Macmillan, 1969). The chapter makes use of the text panels from the Kennedy Library and Museum exhibits concerning the election, including those concerning: polling information indicating Americans' belief that the Soviets led the U.S in development of long-range missiles; information about the presidential debates and their significance as well as subjects covered in the debates; the size of the debate audience and the difference in the appearances of the two candidates; and the final election results. The chapter draws from Kennedy Library videos and from the papers of Evelyn Lincoln, Kennedy's personal secretary. It also draws from Giglio and Beschloss as well as *John Fitzgerald Kennedy: As We Remember Him* (New York: Macmillan, 1965), a book including recollections about Kennedy from a variety of his friends and colleagues.

Perilous World

This chapter relies heavily upon Beschloss's *The Crisis Years.* It also draws from the "President's Office Files (1961–1963)" at the Kennedy Library. These are, according to the library's definition, "working files of President Kennedy as maintained by his personal secretary, Mrs. Evelyn Lincoln, in the Oval Office of the White House." The chapter also draws from Giglio and from *Kennedy: Profile of Power* by Richard Reeves. It draws, as well, from *As We Remember Him* and from *A Thousand Days* by Schlesinger; from *RN: The Memoirs of Richard Nixon* (New York: Grosset & Dunlap, 1978); from *JFK Wants to Know: Memos from the President's Office 1961–1963,* selected and edited by Edward B. Claflin (New York: William Morrow and Co., 1991); from *Conversations with Kennedy* by Benjamin C. Bradlee (New York: W.W. Norton, 1975); from *American Epoch: A History of the United States Since the 1890s,* Arthur S. Link with the collaboration of William B. Catton, Third Edition (New York: Knopf, 1967); and from *Kennedy and Latin America* by Edwin McCammon Martin, (Lanham, MD.: University Press of America, 1994).

Civil Rights

This chapter relies upon exhibits in the Kennedy Library and Museum and from the "JFK Personal Papers." It draws from *The Unfinished Journey: America Since World War II* by William H. Chafe (New York: Oxford University Press, 1991)—particularly chapter seven "John F. Kennedy: The Reality and the Myth,"—Reeves's *President Kennedy: Profile of Power,* which carefully examines much of President Kennedy's work on civil rights, and Giglio and Beschloss. It also draws from Link's *American Epoch: A History of the United States Since the 1890s, The Burden and the Glory: President John F. Kennedy* edited by Allan Nevis, foreword by Lyndon B. Johnson (New York: Harper and Row, 1964), and from Herbert S. Parmet, *JFK: The Presidency of John F. Kennedy* (New York: Dial Press, 1983).

The Power of Symbols

This chapter draws heavily from the Kennedy Library exhibits on the Peace Corps and the space race. It relies upon exhibit text panels concerning the Peace Corps and the first wave of volunteers as well as the growth in the number of Peace Corps volunteers and their achievements. The chapter relies upon a report from *U.S. News and World Report* entitled "The Kennedy Image: How It's Built," published April 9, 1962. The chapter draws from Reeves and Beschloss and from *A Thousand Days* by Schlesinger. It also relies upon *With Kennedy* by Kennedy's press secretary Pierre Salinger (New York: Doubleday, 1966).

Jacqueline Bouvier Kennedy

This chapter relies upon the Kennedy Library exhibit on Jacqueline Kennedy. It draws from the exhibit's text panels including: information about Jacqueline Kennedy's upbringing and her mother's remarriage to Hugh D. Auchincloss; characterizing Jackie as a girl as "lively and full of mischief"; describing the importance of her study at the Sorbonne; describing her work as the Inquiring Camera Girl; concerning the courtship and marriage of Jackie and Jack Kennedy as well as their wedding and reception; the dedication of *Profiles in Courage* to Jacqueline Kennedy; description of the tour of the White House given by the First Lady after the renovation was complete; describing a painting done by Mrs. Kennedy which she gave to her husband; concerning her possible collaboration on a children's book; describing the plans for renovating Lafayette Square; and characterizing the President and First Lady's trip to Paris. The chapter relies upon *Jacqueline Kennedy, The White House Years* by Mary Van Rensselaer Thayer (Boston: Little, Brown, 1971). The chapter draws from *As We Remember Her: Jacqueline Kennedy Onassis in the Words of Her Family and Friends* by Carl Sferrazza Anthony (New York: HarperCollins, 1997). It also draws from *A Woman Named Jackie* by C. David Heymann (New York: Carol Communications, 1989), and from *My Life with Jacqueline Kennedy* by Mary Barelli Gallagher (New York: McKay, 1969).

Robert F. Kennedy

This chapter relies upon the Kennedy Library exhibit on Robert F. Kennedy. It draws from text panels concerning Robert Kennedy's work on organized crime and his book, *The Enemy Within,* as well as on his work as attorney general and his travels overseas in 1962. It draws from *Robert Kennedy and His Times* by Arthur M. Schlesinger, Jr. (Houghton Mifflin, Boston, 1978), as well as from Schlesinger's *A Thousand Days.* It also draws from Reeves and Beschloss, as well as from Sorensen's *The Kennedy Legacy,* Bradlee's *Conversations with Kennedy;* and from *The Kennedys: An American Drama* by Peter Collier and David Horowitz (New York: Summit Books, 1984).

The Cuban Missile Crisis

This chapter relies on the Kennedy Library exhibit on the Cuban Missile Crisis. It also depends heavily upon Beschloss's *The Crisis Years* and Reeves' *President Kennedy.* It benefits enormously from the research, study and analysis of the missile crisis conducted by Beschloss and from the recounting of those events by Reeves. This chapter draws as well from Giglio and from *The Kennedy Tapes: Inside the White House During the Cuban Missile Crisis* by editors Ernest R. May and Philip D. Zelikow (Cambridge: Harvard University press, 1998).

"A great change is at hand"

This chapter draws from the Kennedy Library exhibits and from the JFK Personal Papers. It also relies upon William H. Chafe's *The Unfinished Journey: America Since World War II, The Burden and the Glory: President John F. Kennedy* edited by Allan Nevis, *Bearing the Cross: Martin Luther King Jr. and the Southern Christian Leadership Conference* by David J. Garrow (New York: Random House, 1988); and from *Parting the Waters* by Taylor Branch (New York: Simon and Schuster, 1988); as well as from Reeves, Giglio, and Beschloss.

Nuclear Test Ban

This chapter draws from the Kennedy Library exhibit. It also relies heavily upon Beschloss. And it draws from Giglio and from Nevis's *The Burden and the Glory.*

Dallas

This chapter relies upon the Kennedy Library exhibit. It draws, as well, from Rose Kennedy's *Times to Remember* and it relies upon Beschloss as well as William Manchester's *The Death of a President* (New York: Arbor House, 1985).

PHOTO CREDITS

All photographs in this book are courtesy of the John F. Kennedy Library, with the exception of the following:

page 12 *Kennedy family,* © Bachrach
14 *The Kennedys in England,* © Marcus Adams
29 *Wedding photo* (bottom right), © Lisa Larsen/TimePix
34 *Joseph Kennedy,* © Price Studio
36 *Kennedy waving from car to policeman* (top left), © Burton Berinsky
36 *Kennedy political cartoon* (bottom right), Bill Mauldin, © St. Louis Post Dispatch
36 *Jackie, Caroline, and John Kennedy* (bottom left), © Jacques Lowe
36 *Kennedy speaking to large crowd* (background), © Burton Berinsky
37 *Kennedy waving from car to crowd* (bottom), © Burton Berinsky
38 *The Roman Octopus* (left), unknown, and *The White House* (right), © V.E. Howard
40 *Campaigning in West Virginia,* © Hank Walker/TimePix
41 *Face the Nation appearance,* © CBS
43 *Thriving in the spotlight,* © Walter Sanders/TimePix
45 *Campaigning in Pennsylvania,* © Burton Berinsky
48 *Fired up on the campaign trail in New York,* © Burton Berinsky
52 *Television debates,* © Burton Berinsky
56 *Covers of Time and Newsweek,* © TimePix and © Newsweek
60 *Embassy building,* © Life Magazine
60 *Khrushchev* (top left), © Al Fenn/TimePix
61 *Tanks rolling down main street* (top right), © Will McBride/Black Star
62 *Fidel Castro,* © AP Wire Wide World Photos
64 *Communist threat,* © Life Magazine
65 *Khrushchev* (left), and *an issue of Life* (right) © Al Fenn/TimePix and © Life Magazine
86 *Early manifestation of the Berlin Wall* © Flip Schulke/Black Star
90 *Freedom riders' bus burns* (bottom left), © Flip Schulke/Black Star
93 *Rev. Martin Luther King and Coretta Scott King* © AP Wire Wide World Photos
94 *American Justice on Trial,* unknown
96 *Roy Wilkins,* © Fred Ward/Black Star
105 *James Meredith,* © Flip Schulke/Black Star
108 *Kennedy at NASA* (bottom left), © U.P.I.
108 *Kennedy speaking from podium* (bottom right), © New York Times
122 *Jackie, age 2,* © Morgan Studio
123 *Jackie, age 3* (top), and *age 12* (bottom), © Morgan Studio
124 *Jackie in the late 1950s,* © Jacques Lowe
125 *Vogue's Prix de Paris,* © Vogue
128 *Jackie and Caroline,* © Jacques Lowe
129 *Eve of the inauguration* (top), © Paul Schutzer/TimePix
130 *The First Lady with Chris Collingwood,* © CBS News
144 *Robert, Jack, and Ted Kennedy* (bottom right), photographer unknown
144 *Robert Kennedy* (bottom left), photographer unknown
144–45 *Robert and Jack Kennedy* (top), photographer unknown
145 *Robert Kennedy and family* (bottom), photographer unknown
148 *RFK,* courtesy of the John F. Kennedy Library Foundation
152 *Robert Kennedy and Jimmy Hoffa* (bottom), © U.P.I.
157 *The brothers confer,* © U.P.I.
170 *JFK conferring with Secretary of State Rusk,* © Jacques Lowe
191 *Overhead Shot of March on Washington* (top), © AP Wire Wide World Photos
191 *Police dogs in Birmingham, Alabama* (bottom), © Charles Moore/Black Star
197 *Gov. Wallace blocks integration,* © Black Star
211 *JFK speaking at the United Nations,* courtesy of the United Nations
219 *John F. Kennedy, Jr., saluting his father, © U.P.I.*

INDEX

Abernathy, Ralph David, 93–94
Academy of Television Arts and Sciences, 131
Acheson, Dean, 67, 172
Alliance for Progress, 67
Alsop, Joe, 81
American University, 213
Anderson, George, 176
Arlington National Cemetery, 199, 230
Army, U.S., 84–85
Assassination of JFK, 220–225
  Johnson swearing in, 226–227
  response to death, 224–226, 227–230
Athenia, 17
Auchincloss, Hugh D. Jr., 122

Bail Reform Act, 153
Balanchine, George, 131
Baldridge, Tish, 143
Ball, George, 184, 210
Barnett, Ross, 104–107, 157
Bay of Pigs
  invasion, 62–68
  JFK, impact on, 70–72
  Khrushchev reactions, 70–71, 73, 76–77
  Robert Kennedy, 71, 146, 158–159
Belafonte, Harry, 101
Bellow, Saul, 131
Bemelmans, Ludwig, 134
Bennett, James V., 153
Berlin, 96, 158, 170, 210
  as danger spot, 66–67
  Khrushchev's demands, 73–75, 77–80
  JFK's response, 81–85, 89
  Berlin Wall, 85–89
Bernstein, Leonard, 132
Beschloss, Michael, 146, 175, 189, 211, 225–226
Bethesda Naval Hospital, 227
Billings, Lem, 6, 8, 11, 24–25
Birmingham, Ala., 192–196
Bissell, Richard M., 63–64, 66, 71
Boston Globe, 17
Braun, Wernher von, 116
Bundy, McGeorge, 83
  and Cuba, 65, 165, 172–173, 178, 184–186
Bureau of Prisons, 153

Canterbury School, 5
Cape Canaveral, Fla., 118
Capehart, Homer, 163
Carswell Air Force Base, 220
Carter, Marshall, 166, 167, 168
Casals, Pablo, 132
Cassini, Igor, 123
Castro, Fidel, 62–63, 66, 72, 159, 162
Catholicism
  campaign issue, 38–42, 45, 49–50, 54, 92–94
  Kennedy family, 5, 30, 34
CBS news, 188
Central Intelligence Agency (CIA), 146, 225
  Bay of Pigs, 62–66, 67, 68, 71
  Cuban missile crisis, 162, 166, 167
  Operation Mongoose, 71–72, 159
Chamberlain, Neville, 17, 18, 80
Chayefsky, Paddy, 131–132
Choate School, 2, 4, 6–8, 9–11, 146
Churchill, Sir Winston, 18, 43
CIA. *See* Central Intelligence Agency
Civil rights, 41, 49–50, 115
  in education, 104–107, 155, 157–158, 193, 196
  in housing, 102–104, 107, 204
  JFK address on, 196–199, 200
  JFK campaign and, 46, 50, 92–94
  JFK timetable for, 95–96, 103–104, 155
  legislation, 193, 196, 199, 201–203
  march on Washington, 199, 201–203
  Robert Kennedy and, 150, 153–158
  See also Birmingham, Ala.; Freedom Riders; King, Martin Luther, Jr.
Civil Rights Commission, 97, 104
Clark, Kemp, 224
Clay, Lucius D., 89
Coast Guard Academy, 95
Collingwood, Charles, 130
Congress of Racial Equality (CORE), 98
Connally, John, 221
Connally, Nellie, 221–222
"Conversation with the President, A ," 115
Cooper, John Sherman, 129
Copeland, Aaron, 132
Cousins, Norman, 209
"Crisis," 115
Cronkite, Walter, 223
Cuba, 62, 71–72, 96
  See also Bay of Pigs
Cuban missile crisis
  Soviet missile buildup, 162–164
  U.S. options, 166–170, 171–173
  U.S. response, 170–171, 174–177
  public opinion, 163, 168, 176
  negotiations, 177–186
  agreement, 186–189
Curley, James Michael, 27
Curtis, Charlotte, 133, 139
Cushing, Richard James, 140, 142

Dallas. *See* Assassination of JFK
De Gaulle, Charles, 139, 229
Democratic National Convention 1956, 31
Dillon, C. Douglas, 172
Dobrynin, Anatoly, 162–163, 164, 186, 188
Dodd-Humphrey resolution, 212
Dulles, Allen, 63–64, 66, 71

Eisenhower, Dwight David, 30, 31, 46, 174
  and Cuba, 62–64, 71
  on Nixon, 113–114
Elizabeth, Princess (of England), 15
Enemy Within, The (R. Kennedy), 148, 152
Evening News (London), 17
Evers, Medgar, 199

Farmer, James, 98–100
Federal Bureau of Investigation (FBI), 146, 152–153
Fitzgerald, John "Honey Fitz," 3–4, 27, 28, 34
Fomin, Alexander, 178, 181
Freedom Riders, 98–101, 154–155

Friendship 7, 118
Fulbright, J. William, 67, 72, 174
Future (magazine), 28

Gagarin, Yuri, 72, 115–116, 117
George Washington University, 124
Germany, 85
  Soviet treaty threats, 78–79, 81, 89
  World War II, 16, 17, 18
  See also Berlin
Gilpatrick, Roswell, 167
"Gimme That Old-Time Religion," 40
Glenn, John, 118–119, 133
Goodwin, Richard N., 51
Great Britain, 14–16, 17–18, 21, 34
Greater Houston Ministerial Association, 49
Gromyko, Andrei, 170–171

Harriman, Averell, 215–216
Hartington, Lord, 23
Harvard University, 11–13, 16, 17–18, 34, 148
Hatcher, Andy, 104
Helms, Richard, 225
Hersey, John, 28
Hesburgh, Father Theodore, 97
Hill, Clint, 223
Hitler, Adolf, 18
Hoffa, James Riddle, 63, 152, 153
Hoover, J. Edgar, 152, 153, 224
Horton, Ralph, 8
House of Commons, 17
House of Representatives, U.S., 25, 205
Hull, Cordell, 15
Humphrey, Hubert Horatio, 39–40, 42, 110
Hyannis Port, 34, 45, 53, 85

"Ich Bin Ein Berliner," 210
"I have a dream" speech, 203
International News Service, 25
Interstate Commerce Commission, 155

Johnson, Lady Bird, 117
Johnson, Lyndon Baines, 89, 155, 165, 221
  civil rights, 155, 196
  on JFK and Robert, 146, 151
  on space program, 116, 117
  as running mate, 45, 63, 220
  swearing in, 226–227
Junior Chamber of Commerce, U.S., 28
Justice Department, 148, 152–153, 155

Kalb, Marvin, 188
Katzenbach, Nicholas, 197
Kefauver, Estes, 31
Kennedy, Caroline, 128, 142
Kennedy, Edward M., 9, 229
Kennedy, Ethel, 158
Kennedy, Eunice, 9
Kennedy, Jacqueline Bouvier, 117, 143
  and the arts, 126, 130–134
  Bay of Pigs, 70
  courtship and marriage, 29, 126–127, 140
  early life, 122–126
  election night, 54
  as equestrienne, 122, 123, 126
  health, 128
  historical preservation, 137–138
  at JFK's death, 220–221, 223–224, 225, 227, 231
  journalism and writing, 31, 126–127, 131, 134–135
  and Khrushchev, 77, 139–140
  language skills, 122, 130, 139
  love of books, 124, 126, 127, 133–134
  motherhood and children, 126–127, 137, 140, 142
  popularity of, 126, 129, 138–140
  White House restoration, 128, 129–131, 134–135, 137
Kennedy, John Fitzgerald
  age, 29, 54, 77
  background, 27, 34
  Congressional career, 25–28, 28, 30–31
  education, childhood, 2, 5–8, 9, 10–11, 146
  education, college, 11–13, 17–18
  in Europe, 13–17
  fatalism, 24–25
  health, Addison's disease, 24, 28, 31
  health, back problems, 12, 21–22, 30–31, 73, 127
  health, general, 3–4, 5–6, 11, 22–25, 222
  humor, 4, 8, 115, 220
  image building, 112–115
  Inauguration Day, 128
  independence, 6–8, 10
  Khrushchev correspondence, 174–175, 178, 189, 215
  love of books, 4, 127
  marriage and family, 9, 23, 29, 126–127, 140, 142
  military service, 21–22, 23, 28, 41–42
  "miscalculation" issue, 76–77, 78–79, 165, 167, 178
  personality, 4, 8–9, 17, 49, 147
  political potential, 10–11, 28, 31, 35
  popularity, 49, 72, 205
  rationality, 208–209
  reliance on Robert, 146–147, 149–151, 158–159, 165
  sports and fitness, 12–13, 133
  style, 27, 45, 53
  and women, 25, 28, 30
  world affairs, as youth, 15–18, 20–21, 25
  writings, 4, 17–19, 25
  Profiles in Courage, 31, 33, 127
  Why England Slept, 17–19
  See also under specific topics and events
Kennedy, John Fitzpatrick, Jr., 128, 142
Kennedy, Joseph Patrick, 23, 222, 228
  as ambassador, 14–15, 17–18, 21, 34
  background, 11, 12, 34, 39
  on JFK, 10
  on Robert, 147, 149–150
  wealth, 27, 34, 39, 42
Kennedy, Joseph Patrick, Jr., 25
  death, 23, 228
  education, 4, 6, 11–13
  military service, 21, 41–42
Kennedy, Kathleen, 8, 23, 228
Kennedy, Patrick Bouvier, 23, 140
Kennedy, Patrick "P.J.", 27, 34
Kennedy, Robert Francis, 34, 147

RFK (cont.)
  Attorney General appointment, 149–151
  as campaign manager, 28, 53–55, 93, 149
  civil rights, 100–101, 105–107, 153–158, 196–197, 199, 202
  Cuba, 71–72, 158–159
  Cuban missile crisis, 162, 167–168, 171–172, 178, 185–186
  early career, 147–148
  influence on JFK, 146–147, 149–151, 158–159, 165
  at JFK's death, 224, 227
  on JFK, 11, 23, 70, 176, 177
  organized crime work, 148–149
  Enemy Within, The, 148, 152
Kennedy, Rose, 8, 17, 28, 30, 34
  at JFK's death, 222, 228–229
  on Jacqueline, 128
  on JFK's health, 3–4, 5–6, 11, 23, 25
  on JFK's schooling, 6
Kennedy, Rosemary, 9, 227–228
Kennedy Library, 3, 22, 73, 96, 107
  election of 1960, 38, 46, 52
  JFK schooling, 10, 13
Kennedy-Nixon debates, 51–53, 56, 59
Khrushchev, Nikita, 96
  as campaign issue, 48, 56
  and Jacqueline 77, 139–140
  at JFK death, 227, 230
  on JFK's "peace speech," 215
  Kennedy correspondence, 88, 177, 179, 181–183, 186, 188, 212
  and Nixon, 48, 77
  on *U-2* flights, 42, 77
  Vienna conference, 72–80, 102
  See also Bay of Pigs; Berlin; Cuban Missile Crisis; Nuclear weapons; Soviet Union (USSR)
Kilduff, Malcolm, 224
King, Coretta Scott, 92–94
King, Martin Luther, Jr., 92–94, 103, 192–193, 199, 203
King, Martin Luther, Sr., 92–94
Krock, Arthur, 18

Lafayette Square, 138
Latin America, 65, 67–68, 176
Lee, Janet Norton, 122
LeMay, Curtis, 168, 170
Life (magazine), 115
Limited Test Ban Treaty, 216–217
  See also Nuclear weapons
Lincoln, Evelyn, 140, 150
Lodge, Henry Cabot, 28, 30, 35

McCarthy, Joseph, 148
McCone, John, 165, 167, 172
MacLeish, Archibald, 131
Macmillan, Harold, 80, 140
McNamara, Robert, 146, 165–167, 173, 176, 186
"Man Who's Old Enough to Know But Young Enough to Do, A ," 48
Martin, Louis, 104
Meredith, James, 104–107, 155, 157
Miller, Arthur, 131
Milton Academy, 147
Milwaukee Journal, 39
Muckers Club, 7–8, 10

Nation, 103
National Association for the Advancement of Colored People (NAACP), 96–97, 199
National Conference on Bail and Criminal Justice, 153
National Security Council Executive Committee, 165–173, 178, 182, 184–185
NATO. *See* North Atlantic Treaty Organization
Navy, U.S., 21
New Frontier, 103, 111
New Yorker (magazine), 28
New York Times, 53, 123, 133, 139
Nitze, Paul, 172
Nixon, Richard M., 31, 71, 77, 127
  election issues, 46, 48, 114
  election results, 54, 59
  health, 51–52
Nixon-Kennedy debates, 51–53, 56, 59
North Atlantic Treaty Organization (NATO), 82, 174, 184
Nuclear weapons crises, 89, 208, 209
  test ban negotiations, 209, 211–216
  JFK speech to UN, 211–212
  JFK "peace" speech, 213–215
  Limited Test Ban Treaty, 216–217
  See also Berlin; Cuban missile crisis

OAS. *See* Organization of American States
O'Donnell, Kenneth, 208
Office of Naval Intelligence, 21
Operation Mongoose, 71–72
Organization of American States (OAS), 67, 176
Ormsby-Gore, David, 208–209

Palestine, 15–16
Parkland Hospital, 223, 224–225, 226
Peace Corps, 101, 110–112, 113, 115
Peale, Norman Vincent, 49
Pearson, David, 227
Pius XII, Pope, 15
Potsdam conference, 25
Powers, Dave, 27
Presidential election of 1956, 31
Presidential election of 1960
  JFK plans to run, 31
  Democratic primary race, 38–42
  Democratic Convention, speech to, 42–45
  general election campaign, 45–51, 92–93, 149
  Kennedy-Nixon debates, 51–53, 56, 59
  results, 53–54, 56, 59
Princeton University, 11
Profiles in Courage (J.F. Kennedy), 31, 33, 127
PT-109, 21–23, 28, 48
Pulitzer Prize, 31, 33

Randolph, A. Philip, 199
"Report on Civil Rights: Fumbling on the New Frontier," 103
Reston, James, 53, 80
Riverdale Country Day School, 4
Roberts, Charles, 225
Robinson, Jackie, 96
Roosevelt, Franklin Delano, 14, 18, 34
Roosevelt, Franklin Delano, Jr., 41
Rostow, Eugene, 101–102, 154

Rothko, Mark, 132
Rusk, Dean, 79, 86, 165–166, 170, 177–178, 186
Russell, Richard, 151, 174

Salinger, Pierre, 73, 115, 188, 192, 226
Scali, John, 178, 181
Schlesinger, Arthur Jr., 157
Schoenbrun, David, 188
Schriber, Butch, 8
Seigenthaler, John, 100
Selassie, Haile, 139
Senate Committee on Foreign Relations, 67
Senate Permanent Subcommittee on Investigations, 148
Shepard, Alan, 117, 118
Shriver, Sargent, 92, 110–111
Smith, Al, 40
Sorbonne, 124, 139
Sorensen, Theodore, 31, 51, 70, 96
  civil rights, 196–197
  missile crisis, 165, 168, 173, 186
Soviet Union (USSR), 46, 63, 70
  space program, 72, 115–117
  strength of, 80
  U-2 flights over, 42, 77
  See also Berlin; Cuban missile crisis; Khrushchev, Nikita; Nuclear weapons
Space Council, U.S., 116
Space program, 115–119
Spalding, Charles, 71
Sputnik, 115, 117
St. John, George, 7–8, 10
Stanford University, 18
State Department, 65, 82
Steeger, Henry, 102
Stevenson, Adlai, 31, 148, 167, 181
Stravinsky, Igor, 132
Supreme Court, 98

Taylor, Maxwell, 165, 168, 172
Television, 130–131, 139
  JFK press conferences, 113–115
  role in election, 52, 56, 59
  space coverage, 115, 116–117, 118–119
Thant, U, 177
Time (magazine), 116
"Tour of the White House with Mrs. John F. Kennedy, A ," 131
Tretick, Stanley, 142
Truman, Harry S., 69
Turkey, 162, 166, 184–185

U-2 flights
  over Cuba, 164–166, 170, 181, 185
  over Soviet Union, 42, 77
United Nations, 25, 177, 181, 211
University of Alabama, 157–158, 193, 196
University of Michigan, 110
University of Mississippi, 104–107, 155, 157
University of Notre Dame, 97
University of Virginia Law School, 148
Urban League, 102
U.S. News and World Report, 112–113

Vassar College, 123, 126
Vienna conference, 72–80, 102, 139–140
Vogue Prix de Paris, 122, 124–126

Wallace, George C., 157–158, 192–194, 196–197, 199
Warsaw Pact countries, 83
Washington Post, 168
Washington Times-Herald, 126
While England Slept (Churchill), 18
White, Theodore H., 53
White House Fine Arts Association, 130
White House Long Ago, The (painting), 131
Why England Slept (J.F. Kennedy), 17–19
Wiesner, Jerome, 208
Wilder, Thornton, 131
Wilkins, Roy, 96–98, 102, 199, 203
Williams, Tennessee, 131
Wofford, Harris, 97, 100, 102
World War II, 16, 17
Wyeth, Andrew, 132

Yale Law School, 101, 154
Young, Whitney, 102

Zorin, Valerian, 181

PublicAffairs is a new nonfiction publishing house and a tribute to the standards, values, and flair of three persons who have served as mentors to countless reporters, writers, editors, and book people of all kinds, including me.

I.F. STONE, proprietor of *I. F. Stone's Weekly*, combined a commitment to the First Amendment with entrepreneurial zeal and reporting skill and became one of the great independent journalists in American history. At the age of eighty, Izzy published *The Trial of Socrates,* which was a national bestseller. He wrote the book after he taught himself ancient Greek.

BENJAMIN C. BRADLEE was for nearly thirty years the charismatic editorial leader of *The Washington Post.* It was Ben who gave the *Post* the range and courage to pursue such historic issues as Watergate. He supported his reporters with a tenacity that made them fearless and it is no accident that so many became authors of influential, best-selling books.

ROBERT L. BERNSTEIN, the chief executive of Random House for more than a quarter century, guided one of the nation's premier publishing houses. Bob was personally responsible for many books of political dissent and argument that challenged tyranny around the globe. He is also the founder and longtime chair of Human Rights Watch, one of the most respected human rights organizations in the world.

For fifty years, the banner of Public Affairs Press was carried by its owner Morris B. Schnapper, who published Gandhi, Nasser, Toynbee, Truman and about 1,500 other authors. In 1983, Schnapper was described by *The Washington Post* as "a redoubtable gadfly." His legacy will endure in the books to come.

Peter Osnos, *Publisher*